Morton Leborey Wachles, Ph.D. May, 1956

W. deB. Wachles, Ph.D.

Your Marriage and the Law

Your Marriage

and the LAW

HARRIET F. PILPEL &
THEODORA ZAVIN

RINEHART & COMPANY, INC.
NEW YORK   TORONTO

PUBLISHED SIMULTANEOUSLY IN CANADA BY
CLARKE, IRWIN & COMPANY, LTD., TORONTO

To
our husbands and children
to whom we owe our
appreciation of marriage
and to
Morris L. Ernst
for whose professional guidance
we are profoundly grateful

ACKNOWLEDGMENTS

We are grateful to John Selby, Editor-in-Chief of Rinehart & Co., who first suggested that we write this book and to the many friends and colleagues who helped us with it. We particularly want to thank Morris L. Ernst, Natalie Flatow and Robert C. Pilpel for their suggestions on the entire manuscript and the following people for assistance on the particular subject matter indicated: Judge Paul Alexander (family courts); Morris Goldman (Pennsylvania divorce law); Alexander Lindey (separation and divorce law); Robert V. Sherwin (sex laws); Manuel Siegel (adoption); Dr. Abraham Stone (all medical aspects); William F. Wolff, Jr. (property aspects of marriage) and Amram Scheinfeld (genetics).

We wish to express gratitude also to Ida K. Null who put at our disposal the library of her late husband, Judge Samuel Null, and to Rosemary V. Tauroney for her ever-ready assistance in the typing and preparation of the manuscript.

Harriet F. Pilpel
Theodora Zavin

New York, N. Y.
May, 1952.

CONTENTS

Part IV Termination of Marriages

Foreword

*T*HE ESSENCE OF the law is simple. In the words of Justinian, it is "to live honorably, to injure no other man, to render every man his due." In other words, it is the golden rule of life—to do unto others as you would have them do unto you. Yet, few people can abide by these simple precepts. In one way or another, they transgress against the rights of others with resulting hurt and damage, and to avoid or remedy these, society has surrounded most of our activities with specific rules, regulations and laws.

Because sex, marriage and reproduction always involve other people, many laws have been enacted to control marital and sex behavior and to protect individual rights. Some of these laws are expressive in nature, expressive of the desires and the needs of the people, while others are merely repressive in character, the result not of social needs but of the attitude of certain groups and factions within society. In the human body, there are many organs that originally had served a useful purpose, but during the course of evolution have become obsolete. Now they are "vestigial structures," which, because they no longer have any useful function, are often a source of trouble. Similarly, in the body politic, many of the laws relating to sex and marriage are "vestigial" in nature and a source of social difficulty.

For the educator, the marriage counselor, as well as for anyone interested in the social problems of the day, a literate awareness of the laws on marriage and family life is desirable and helpful. Such information will be found in the present volume. Written by two highly competent experts in family law, the present legal situation is set forth with knowledge, good sense and good humor. The authors discuss the legal situation of marriage and family life in our culture, and point out some of the confusion which results from multiplicity and diversity of the existing laws.

"A pennyweight of love," says a Scotch proverb, "is worth a pound of law," but there are times when there is not love enough left, and then those involved may turn to the law. For information about the nature of the law, they may well turn to this volume.

Abraham Stone, M.D.

Introduction

$\mathscr{M}$ANY YEARS AGO Charles Dickens said, in exasperation, "The Law is a ass." Being an Englishman, he had only one law to contend with. But the United States federal system is such, that on any given subject matter there are apt to be forty-nine laws—one for each state and one promulgated by the federal government. Most of the law governing marriage and family relationships in this country is *state* law since, under the Federal Constitution, the states retained the right to make their own laws in this field. However, that same Constitution delegated to the federal government the power to regulate interstate and foreign commerce and the mails. Such regulation, as in the case of contraceptives, for example, inevitably impinges on what goes on within the states.

Since the forty-eight states are widely different in their historical backgrounds, their economics and their mores, it is hardly surprising that there is considerable variation in their attitudes toward marriage and the family. Puritan Massachusetts and pioneer Wyoming could not be expected to develop the same set of rules on the subject. There are some who decry this lack of uniformity on the ground that it introduces confusion and uncertainty into the law. Others believe that the admitted disadvantages do not begin to outweigh the benefits flowing from having so many experimental laboratories to test the efficacy of various different ways of handling the same legal problems.

Although, therefore, we refer throughout to "the law," it must be noted at the outset that there are many laws. Furthermore, the law in any given American state originates from two distinct sources. Many of our legal rules derive from the common law, which means that they are judge-made in particular cases and thereafter given general application. On the other hand, many of such rules are the result of legislation—statutes of general application officially passed by lawmaking bodies. In the pages that follow, we have given state-by-state breakdowns primarily in those areas which are covered by statute. In many jurisdictions, the greater part of marriage and family law continues to be judge-made; where this is the case, it becomes extremely difficult to assert with finality what the law of a particular jurisdiction is with reference to any specific subject matter.

In some states, there may be no law on a particular question in the sense that there is no statute that applies and the courts of that state have not been presented with that specific problem. Thus, there are three or four states where no one can tell with certainty whether a husband must pay damages if his wife strikes and injures a neighbor. The courts in these states have not recently been presented with this kind of problem and have not yet had a chance to interpret in this context certain changes in the statutes concerning married women. In other states there may be too much law on a point. A court in New York City and one in Buffalo may rule quite differently on the same question. If one of the cases is appealed to the New York Court of Appeals, the highest court in the state, that court will settle the question one way or the other. If neither case is appealed, there are, for the time being, *two* laws on the point in a single state—possibly more since there is nothing to prevent a Schenectady court from taking a third position.

Moreover, the law in every jurisdiction is in a constant state of flux. New concepts creep in; new statutes are passed; some new set of circumstances results in a court holding not foreshadowed by the earlier decisions. What appeared to be the law on a particular subject in a given state when this book

was written may well, by the time it is published, be super-
seded by some more recent development.

For these reasons, except where statutes make possible
a state-by-state breakdown, we have confined ourselves to
indicating in general terms the varying viewpoints of the states
(and the federal government where it has one) on each subject
matter discussed. Thus the book is written neither for lawyers
who need a far more comprehensive and detailed presentation,
nor is it intended for laymen as a substitute for legal advice.
No book can or should take the place of consultation with an
attorney who is trained to apply legal principles to the particular facts of his client's case.

We do hope, however, that the book will give to husbands
and wives, parents and children, some idea of their rights and
duties as such, and, where necessary, direct them to the lawyers' offices. Most people know when to consult a doctor because nature has provided such warning signals as fever and
pain when something is wrong. We have begun sufficiently
to understand the nature of our bodies to appreciate the value
of preventive medicine. We vaccinate our babies before there
is a sign of smallpox. But most people do not know enough
about their legal rights and obligations in family matters even
to know when they need a lawyer. Just as proper medical precautions can avert disease, so can adequate legal counsel given
in time avoid chaos and tragedy. It is time we thought in terms
of preventive law, too, and a first step in that direction calls
for an ability to recognize the legal danger spots.

In addition, husbands and wives, parents and children,
are also citizens. As such, whether they know it or not, they
make the laws that govern their marriages and families. Unless
they know in general what those laws are, they cannot intelligently decide whether they approve the laws as they stand or
whether they wish to support or oppose proposed changes.
For a long time, reforms in the field of marriage and family law
have lagged behind reforms in other fields. This is, in large

part, because pressure groups operate elsewhere. Bankers watch the banking law; merchants the Sales Act; real estate interests follow the law of vendor and purchaser, landlord and tenant, and so forth. But no one has bothered much with the field of law which effects everyone—marriage and family law. The law schools slight it in their curricula; law firms which pride themselves on their skill in corporate reorganization often refuse entirely to take a case involving family reorganization. If the members of families and the parties to marriages come to know that the laws as to marriage and the family have an impact on almost everything they do as human beings, perhaps they too will constitute a pressure group which will force through some badly needed changes in our marriage and family law structure.

Finally, there are the experts—that rapidly growing group of nonlegal professionals who are engaged in marriage and family counselling and who are probably best equipped to suggest what the laws affecting marriage and the family should be. In order to do this, however, they must be acquainted with the existing laws. Their specialized education—in medicine, theology, social work, and the like—gives them very little idea, if any, of the legal framework in which they must operate. Such a lack of knowledge may seriously affect their functioning in their own field. There is no point in a family-counselling agency recommending that a wife, who is unable to care for her present children, seek contraceptive advice, if, in that jurisdiction, such advice may not be given legally. Marriage counselors who are not lawyers should not try to solve legal problems, but they should know the areas and contours of the legal problems that exist in connection with the marriage and family relationships with which they are dealing.

To the extent that the experts become more familiar with the laws which so largely condition their functioning, they will not only function better but they will also be in a better position to do something to bring the law more into harmony both with what is and with what ought to be. As husbands and wives and parents and children we may and should be aware of what is wrong. We have a right to look to the nonlawyer experts for help in devising a way out of the many situations where the law of marriage and the family continues to be "a ass."

PART I

Husbands and Wives

CHAPTER 1

The Engagement

A CYNIC ONCE defined an engagement as a period during which a girl looks around to see if this is really the best she can do. Actually, the function of the engagement period has shifted substantially in the past hundred years. The interval between betrothal and marriage was not, until fairly recently, considered as a grace period during which a couple were free to change their minds about the wisdom of marrying. When a young lady accepted a proposal of marriage, the time between the engagement and the marriage was intended primarily for practical purposes—the accumulation of a trousseau, the preparation of a home for the newlyweds, and the acquisition of skills suitable to the married state. As one eminent etiquette authority put it, this was the time for the prospective bride to learn to cook and for the groom to learn to carve.

On a more personal level, the time of engagement served as a period of transition from the extreme formality imposed on young people to what must often have been the terrifying intimacy of marriage. A certain amount of permissible hand-holding and somewhat less strict chaperonage during the engagement period helped to increase the acquaintanceship between the couple. They were not, however, supposed to change their minds about marrying. If they did, the additional freedom which they had enjoyed during their betrothal was apt to make the young lady considered thereafter not quite so pure as she should be.

Customs have changed. The engagement period has lost

many of its old functions. Since a trousseau is no longer made
by hand, a week's concentrated shopping can provide the
bride-to-be with enough to keep her father dizzy paying the
bills long past the couple's first wedding anniversary. Cooking
and carving are usually learned after marriage, if at all. Perhaps the only practical purpose of an engagement in these days
of housing shortages is to give the couple several months to
find an apartment. For most young people today, a prime function of an engagement is to enable both to be sure that they
want to marry. Broken engagements are no longer a scandalous
exception to the rule but a fairly frequent phenomenon which
usually involves no loss of face for either party.

As the mores have shifted, the law regarding engagements
has shifted somewhat too in many states, although in many it
fails sufficiently to reflect the changed customs and attitudes.
Unfortunately, this is frequently true of the law affecting marriage and the family. Rules which served well a hundred or
five hundred years ago are still being applied to situations un-
dreamed of by the legislators and judges who formulated them.

Breach-of-promise suits may at one time have served a
valuable social function. It is still true that in the eyes of the
law, when a couple becomes engaged they do so by mutual
promises to marry which constitute as binding a contract as a
commercial lease agreement. If either breaches the contract,
that is, refuses to go through with the marriage, the other, until
recently in virtually every state, could sue for and collect
damages. Within the past few decades, however, a number of
states have outlawed such suits, among them: Alabama, California, Colorado, Florida, Maryland, Indiana, Maine, Michigan, Massachusetts, Nevada, New Hampshire, New Jersey,
New York, Pennsylvania and Wyoming. Illinois also passed
such a statute outlawing breach-of-promise suits, but the Illinois courts declared it invalid under that provision of the state
Constitution which says that citizens may not be deprived of a
remedy for their wrongs.

There are a number of policy reasons behind the recent

tendency of legislatures to abolish suits for breach of promise to marry. Generally, the lawmakers are less concerned with the breach-of-promise suits which do get into court than with those which do not. The threat of such a suit has been a means of blackmailing many a man who has been guilty of no wrong-doing but who is unwilling to face the kind of publicity involved in a breach-of-promise trial even if he wins. A hypothetical but not untypical case may serve to illustrate why men frequently pay off their ex-fiancées rather than face trial.

Andrew, a doctor who has succeeded in building up a good practice in a small town, becomes engaged to Lucy. After a few weeks of their engagement, he finds that Lucy is less interested in him than she is in the money and position which she will have as his wife. She is pathologically jealous and accuses him of improper relations with his female patients. Her fury at his being called away on professional business when they have planned to spend an evening together convinces him that she is not temperamentally suited to be a doctor's wife. He breaks off the engagement and Lucy threatens to sue him for breach of promise. In a situation like this it is quite probable that Andrew would pay any amount he could raise to induce Lucy not to sue. For one thing, a trial would involve Lucy's bringing into court all the letters he ever wrote her and few men can bear with equanimity the prospect of hearing a sarcastic attorney read to a jury love letters written at the height of passion. Moreover, if Lucy repeated in court her unfounded accusations of his immorality with women patients, some tar would always stick to Andrew, even if he won the case. No matter how impeccable his conduct or how futile Lucy's attempts to prove any wrong-doing, there would always be people who believe that "where there's smoke there's fire." Rather than risk ruining his practice, Andrew is likely to pay Lucy whatever she demands as the price of not bringing suit.

Our hypothetical case also suggests another good reason behind the abolition of breach-of-promise suits. Many states

recognize as valid only a few grounds for breaking an engagement—fraud, unchastity and disease are the most commonly
accepted. In some situations, facts which would not legally
excuse a person for breaking an engagement are considered
serious enough to warrant a divorce. Lucy's behavior might
well be viewed in many states as sufficient evidence of cruelty
to warrant Andrew's getting a divorce once they were married.
Yet the same behavior might not be considered sufficient legal
justification for his refusing to go through with the marriage if
Lucy brought a breach-of-promise suit.

Breach-of-promise suits have also fallen into disrepute
because of the exorbitant verdicts handed down by juries in
many such cases. Apparently juries have often been motivated
not so much by a desire to repair damage suffered as by a
wish to impose punishment for what they conceived to be
reprehensible conduct. It is not rare to find cases where a
man has had to pay a quarter of his capital for the dubious
privilege of having been engaged for a few months. Still another objection to the breach-of-promise suit is that it is not a
remedy that in usual circumstances is available to both parties.
While theoretically a man can sue a woman who jilts him, it is
practically impossible to find a breach-of-promise suit brought
by a man. The chances are that the courts would have little
sympathy for any man who attempted to collect damages from
a woman, no matter how wealthy, for *his* wounded feelings or
loss of opportunity to marry. The remedy is, as a practical matter, one-sided.

Perhaps, however, the most cogent argument against permitting breach-of-promise suits to be brought is that they defeat what we have come increasingly to believe is one of the
chief functions of an engagement period, namely to give people
an opportunity to appraise their chances of a happy marriage
with each other and to call off their plans to marry if it becomes
evident that they are not suited to each other. Society has an
interest in the quality of marriages, not just their quantity. The
frightening increase in our divorces has led clergymen, law-

yers, sociologists, marriage counselors, and others concerned with the stability of the family to put increased emphasis on the intelligent choice of a marriage partner and on the appreciation of the emotional, psychological, and sexual implications of marriage. It is better for a couple who are ill suited to break their engagement than to be coerced into a marriage that leads eventually to divorce by which time there may be children to complicate matters. Many people feel that the possibility of being sued for breach-of-promise to marry prevents a full and intelligent utilization of the engagement period by giving to betrothal the kind of finality which should be reserved for the marriage itself.

The fact remains, however, that in the majority of states a suit for breach of promise to marry can still be maintained. If both parties agree to call off the engagement, neither can sue the other; like any contract (other than the marriage contract itself) the agreement to marry can be broken by mutual consent. There may be sometimes, however, difficulty in proving whether an engagement was broken by the agreement of both or by the unilateral action of one.

In a Wisconsin case, Mildred sued Charles for breach of promise. Charles produced in court a letter he had received from Mildred which seemed on any intelligent reading to say that Mildred had decided to break the engagement. Among other things, she suggested that they meet to decide how to handle future invitations which their friends might extend to them jointly. At the trial of the case, Mildred offered rather tortured explanations for this and the other parts of the letter which seemed clearly to indicate her willingness to break the engagement. Her explanations were given weight primarily by the fact that she had retained the engagement ring which Charles had given her. This the court took to be evidence that she had not consented to the breaking of the engagement.

Reference has already been made to the fact that there are some circumstances which in the eyes of the law justify a fiancé in breaking an engagement without subjecting himself to a breach-of-promise suit. Promises to marry exchanged by people whom the law prohibits from marrying will not be enforced by the courts. For example, if James promises to marry Beth as soon as she gets a divorce from her current husband, Beth cannot sue him for breach of promise if he has changed his mind by the time she gets back from Reno. The law views a man or woman who is already married as incapable of entering into a valid contract to marry. Similarly, no breach-of-promise suit will be entertained where the parties involved are disqualified by state law from marrying each other, where, for example, they are blood relations, or members of racial groups forbidden to intermarry or where one of them is syphilitic or epileptic or a member of any of the other groups discussed in Chapter 2.

Our hypothetical case of Andrew, the young doctor, and Lucy, his shrewish fiancée, presents a situation which would not constitute a defense to a breach-of-promise suit in most jurisdictions. The fact that one finds character flaws or comes to the conclusion that he and his affianced are incompatible is not legal justification for calling off the marriage. The law, however, has a higher regard for chastity than for character. If during an engagement, the man finds that his prospective wife has been unchaste either before or after they became engaged, he is entitled to call off the marriage without becoming legally liable for breach of promise. In many states this right to break the engagement because of his fiancée's unchastity does not exist if he himself had intercourse with her or if he knew before they became engaged that she had had intercourse with other men. Apparently the law considers that a man is not entitled to expect such a "promiscuous" woman to be capable of fidelity after they are engaged and, having "condoned" her conduct he has, in many states, no right to break the engagement no matter what her subsequent behavior.

If a man discovers that his fiancée has a disease which renders her unfit to marry he is legally justified in breaking the engagement. There are several kinds of disabilities which may constitute such a justification. The first is the presence of a contagious disease such as syphilis where normal marital contact would be likely to infect the other party. The second is a malady which makes the sufferer incapable of engaging in sexual intercourse, thereby depriving the other party of what the law considers one of the fundamental rights of married people. If a woman contracts a disease which is apt to prove fatal in a short time or which makes her an invalid, some states permit the man to break the engagement on the ground that she will be incapable of performing her part of the marriage contract. A third type of physical disability which excuses a breach of promise to marry, if it is discovered after the promise is made, is the existence of an undesirable hereditary strain which might result in the birth of defective children. Thus, if Fred learns that Jean's father and her uncle are both in insane asylums, he is, in many states, entitled to call off the marriage even though Jean herself is perfectly normal.

A somewhat more difficult problem arises in considering whether a man has a right to break off an engagement because of the state of his own health. He is not entitled to refuse to go through with the marriage simply because he does not feel in the pink of condition. In one Michigan case, Bessie and George had been engaged for six years. George broke the engagement on the ground that he was suffering from a lip cancer. The court held that this was not sufficient justification in view of medical testimony that the cancer was curable, not contagious and not hereditary. In the opinion of the court, George's health might have been sufficient reason for postponing the marriage, but not for calling it off altogether.

An Iowa case, on the other hand, illustrates the kind of situation in which some states permit a man to break an engagement without being liable for damages. Edward was engaged to Nancy, his housekeeper. Before their marriage, Edward became ill and was informed by the doctor that he was suffering from pernicious anaemia and would probably die within a few months. The doctor also told him that his brief life span might be shortened even further if he married. He, not unnaturally, broke his engagement to Nancy and died a few months later. Nancy brought suit against his estate to recover damages for his breach of promise to marry her. The court refused to award her damages, holding that when two people agreed to marry there was an implied condition in their agreement that it would be carried out only if both continued in good health. Either party, said the court, was entitled to revoke if one of them became afflicted with a fatal disease or one which might be communicated to spouse or children or which would be aggravated by marriage.

A few courts have taken a contrary position and have held that such circumstances do not entitle a man to break the engagement if the woman is willing to enter into a "marriage in name only" with him, thereby enabling him to marry without injury to his health.

In some states, a man is entitled to break an engagement if he finds that his fiancée has fraudulently misrepresented some important fact about her circumstances or background. This is merely an extension of the general rule that a contract will be declared legally void if one party used fraudulent misrepresentations to get the other party to enter into it. In one case the woman had told her husband-to-be, prior to becoming engaged, that she had divorced her previous husband because of his cruelty to her. During the engagement, the fiancé learned that actually her first husband had divorced her for gross cruelty including an assault on him with a knife. The court implied that if the lady had said nothing to her fiancé about the cause of her previous divorce, he would not have been free to break the engagement merely because he found out that she was not sweet tempered. But since she had misrepresented the facts, he could call the whole thing off on the ground that he had been fraudulently induced to enter into the engagement in the first place. Not every slight exaggeration, of course, is fraud sufficient to warrant the other party in breaking an engagement.

But falsification of a major fact regarding one's family, social or economic background has been held to be enough.

If a breach-of-promise suit is brought and the defendant has no legally acceptable defense, the amount of damages awarded to the woman will depend on a variety of factors. Perhaps the principal one is how successful the woman has been in vilifying her erstwhile fiancé and arousing the jury's indignation on her behalf as a poor, wronged little girl. It is not at all unusual for a judge to step in and reduce the amount of the verdict where the jury, in his opinion, has awarded a verdict far beyond any reasonable assessment of the actual damage suffered. Damages in this kind of suit cannot, in any event, be assessed objectively because the jury is permitted to award an amount sufficient not only to reimburse the woman for her actual pecuniary loss but also for the injury to her feelings and other intangibles. If the amount which could be recovered in breach-of-promise suits had been limited to actual financial loss, it is unlikely that the action would have fallen into such disrepute.

The types of financial loss which a woman may actually suffer as a result of a broken engagement are illustrated in a Rhode Island case. Florence, a saleslady, gave up her job when she and Oscar became engaged. She spent $825 of her own money for a trousseau. Oscar subsequently broke the engagement and Florence sued him for breach of promise. The court held that she was entitled to recover for her lost earnings and for so much of the expenditure on the trousseau as was a total loss, that is, things which she could not use as a single woman. In another case a young Southern schoolteacher lost her job as a result of the scandal centering around her broken engagement. She was held entitled to recover for this loss. Permitting a woman to recover her actual damages in situations like these does not seem unreasonable, but in neither case was the award limited to recompensing the plaintiff for her tangible loss. Another factor for which both young ladies were awarded substantial sums of money was the loss of the financial benefits which they would have derived from the marriage. The theory of the law seems to be that if a girl is clever or lucky enough to become engaged to a man of means, he must, if he refuses to marry her, pay her sufficient damages to put her in as comfortable circumstances as if the marriage had taken place. On this theory the jury is justified in making a wealthy man pay greater damages than a poor one since his prospective wife has lost more in the way of potential financial benefit.

This and several other elements which a jury may take into account in assessing damages in a breach-of-promise suit are illustrated in a rather curious rags-to-riches story. Bertha owned a little real property which gave her some income. She met and became smitten with John, who was at that time working on an assembly line earning five dollars a day. They carried on an affair for seven years with an intermission when John was drafted to serve in the army during World War I. Bertha claimed that during this period she had several times become pregnant by John and had undergone abortions at his request. After his discharge from the army John decided to go into the real-estate business. Bertha loaned him $1800 for his enterprise which he later returned to her. John's rise in the business world thereafter was phenomenal. Within a few years, he was worth over two million dollars. Nevertheless, Bertha claimed, he kept postponing their marriage on one pretext or another. He then proceeded to marry a second young lady whom he had also impregnated; the real-estate business apparently did not absorb *all* of his time. Bertha sued for breach of promise and a sympathetic jury promptly awarded her the neat sum of $450,-000 which was later reduced by the judge to $150,000. The superior court which reviewed the case justified the size of the reduced verdict by a number of factors. To begin with, seduction always increases the amount of damages which can be collected, on the theory that a non-virgin is "damaged goods" on the marriage market and may not be able to find another man who is willing to marry her once she has become "unchaste."

The length of the engagement also played a part; a woman who has been engaged for three months is generally believed to suffer less damage than one who has been engaged for several years and who may during this period have lost her best opportunities to marry. Finally, damages are also awarded for the humiliation, damaged reputation and generally injured feelings of a jilted woman. The theory of the law where breach-of-promise suits are allowed is that such feelings can be alleviated in part by sufficient coin of the realm acquired from the jiltor. Thus, the damages awarded in such actions are supposed to compensate the woman, not to punish the man. Punitive damages are supposed to be recoverable only in cases where in an effort to defend his own conduct the man has falsely or maliciously accused his ex-fiancée of lewd or unchaste conduct and has not been able to offer convincing proof at the trial that she was guilty of such conduct or that he honestly believed her to be guilty of it. As a practical matter, however, juries often award sizable damages by way of punishment rather than because they honestly believe that the woman has been so seriously hurt.

There is no other explanation for cases such as a Wisconsin one, for example, in which the jury awarded the woman a very large verdict on the following set of facts. Gus and Edith had been engaged for five months. Gus broke the engagement because he came to the conclusion that they were not compatible. Edith retained the engagement ring and sold it for almost $300. She brought suit for breach of promise but before the case came to trial she met and married another man. At the trial she said that she was very happily married and that her husband was a far better man than Gus in every way. There was, incidentally, no question of seduction here and Edith admitted that Gus had behaved "like a perfect gentleman" all during their engagement. In the circumstances it is difficult to see what damage Edith suffered. Nevertheless, the jury ruled that Gus had to pay her $4000, a large portion of his total worldly goods.

Not only is the person who breaks the engagement contract liable for damages, but anyone who induces him to break it may have to pay as well. One leading case involved a suit by Edith against Mary. Edith alleged that Mary had maliciously induced Joseph to break his engagement to her. She contended specifically that Mary had taken Joseph into her house, had supported him in luxurious style and had made every effort to win his love for herself. As a result of all these wrongful actions on Mary's part, said Edith, Joseph had broken their engagement. The court held that if Mary was motivated by ill will toward Edith, Mary was liable for the damage which she caused Edith by inducing Joseph to cancel the engagement. It is, of course, always a question in such a situation whether the second young lady is motivated by a desire to harm the original fiancée or whether she tries to win the man simply because she wants him for herself. The latter is probably closer to the truth in most cases, but malice or ill will toward the complaining fiancée may be imputed from any determined campaign waged by a woman for the affections of an engaged man. It must not be assumed, however, that everyone who tries to convince another not to marry a girl to whom he is engaged is liable for damages. A parent, for example, is privileged to advise his child as he sees fit without having to pay damages to a girl whom he counsels his son not to marry. A friend, particularly a friend of the same sex, who gives similar advice does not have quite the immunity of a parent but it is ordinarily not easy for a jilted fiancée to prove that a friend was motivated by malice toward her when the friend is of long standing and in no way personally involved.

An engaged couple frequently exchange gifts, receive gifts from others and generally start accumulating property which they expect to use after their marriage. If the engagement is broken in a friendly manner, most couples manage to make

their own arrangements about the disposition of such possessions. If there is strong antagonism between them, gifts and
property may become the subject of a lawsuit. Where the engagement is broken by mutual agreement each party is ordinarily entitled to the return of gifts he gave, the purpose being
to restore each of them as far as possible to the position he was
in before the engagement. A person who unilaterally terminates
an engagement, on the other hand, cannot legally insist on the
return of his gifts. Where the person breaking the engagement
is the one who received and now holds the property or gifts,
the question of whether he is entitled to keep them depends on
whether the gifts were "conditional" or "absolute."

To illustrate: May and Walter became engaged in September. Walter gave May a diamond engagement ring and a
pearl necklace which belonged to his mother. Every week
thereafter, he gave her fifty dollars to deposit in a special bank
account which they expected to use to furnish their home. At
Christmas he presented May with a fur jacket. Once, after a
quarrel, he brought her an expensive compact as a reconciliation present. While window-shopping one night, May admired
a satin bedspread in a display. Walter surprised her by buying
it for her the following day. The couple planned to be married
in June, but May met another man with whom she fell in love
and proceeded to break her engagement to Walter. She refused to return any of the gifts he had given her or the money
in the special account. Walter brought suit for the return of
everything on the ground that May broke the engagement and
was not entitled to retain any of its proceeds.

In most states he may recover whatever he gave her in
contemplation of their intended marriage which he would not
have given to her had they not intended to get married. The
engagement ring is an obvious example of this kind of conditional gift; a ring is given in exchange for the promise made
by the girl that she will marry the man who gives it to her.
If she refuses to marry him, she has no right to the ring. The
money for furniture, the bedspread and any other household

furnishings which Walter gave to May are likewise considered to be hers only if she fulfills the implied condition that she will marry him. On the other hand, the fur jacket which he gave her for Christmas, the compact and other gifts of a personal nature may be considered absolute gifts which were not given only on the implied condition that May would go through with the marriage. Not every gift during an engagement period is conditional on the marriage taking place even though the donor might not have given such generous gifts to a girl whom he did not expect to marry. Walter's gift to May of his mother's necklace may raise an intricate question of fact. If he could show that the necklace had been in the family for generations or that his mother had left it to him by Will with the request that it be presented to his wife, the court would probably decide that Walter gave it to May in reliance on her promise to marry him and would not have given it otherwise. This distinction between absolute and conditional gifts is also relevant where the engagement has been broken by mutual consent. In such a case, while the courts try to restore to each his own property, they will not insist on the return of every small gift given during the enagement. Christmas presents or birthday gifts are not ordinarily regarded as conditional even if the parties were engaged when they were given and subsequently terminate the engagement.

A peculiar situation with regard to the return of gifts exchanged by an engaged couple has arisen in those states which have outlawed breach-of-promise suits. In New York a suit for return of gifts or property given during the engagement has been declared by the courts to be a kind of breach-of-promise suit and therefore illegal. In practical operation this doctrine leads to rather dubious results. Take the case of Ralph and Hortense, an engaged couple. Ralph gave Hortense money to deposit in a special account to be used for furnishing a home. He also gave her an engagement ring and other jewelry. Hortense broke the engagement and refused to return the ring, the jewelry or the money. Ralph sued for their return. The case was thrown out of court on the theory that Ralph was really bringing an action based on Hortense's breach of her promise to marry him and that such a suit was outlawed in New York.

In another case, a New York court refused to allow Abraham to sue Lucretia for the return of $600 in cash and jewelry worth over $400, all of which Lucretia declined to return after she broke the engagement. Abraham claimed that his ex-fiancée had never intended to marry him at all but had become engaged to him for the sole purpose of getting and keeping whatever gifts or property he could be induced to give her. Whether or not this was true in the particular case cited, we have, of course, no way of knowing. But Abraham's claim raises the question of whether applying the law prohibiting breach-of-promise suits to actions for the return of gifts may not give rise to a new racket as undesirable in its way as the one which the legislature hoped to destroy when it abolished actions for breach of promise. Apparently, under the present interpretation of the New York law, an unscrupulous woman can become engaged to a succession of men, get money and expensive gifts from each of them in turn and then break the engagement when she feels she has reached the limit of what she can get out of it. It is doubtful whether the legislature when it outlawed breach-of-promise suits had any intention of prohibiting the recovery of gifts and property by a discarded fiancé. The chances are that the legislature did not even consider what should be done in such a situation. They were primarily concerned with the exorbitant damages paid for injured feelings and not with the recovery of specific property given in contemplation of marriage. As a matter of fact, a bill to allow suits for the restoration of such property was passed by both houses of the New York State Legislature in 1950 but was vetoed without explanation by Governor Dewey.

New Jersey, with the same type of statute as New York, permits suit to be brought for the return of gifts and property given in contemplation of marriage. The equities in the first case brought after the passage of the statute prohibiting breach-of-promise suits helped to bring about this result. Sylvia, a stenographer, had worked for Martin, a lawyer, for several years. They became engaged and for five years Martin put five dollars of Sylvia's salary aside each week, their purpose being to accumulate a fund she could use to furnish a home after their marriage. After the engagement was broken, Sylvia sued for the return of the several hundred dollars which had been put aside for her. The court decided that the statute prohibiting breach-of-promise suits did not prevent Sylvia from suing for the return of her property.

California, which also outlawed breach-of-promise suits, has settled the whole problem of the return of gifts by a special statute which provides that, where a return seems just, gifts or property given on the assumption that a marriage would take place may be recovered by the donor if the engagement is broken either by mutual consent or by the one who received the gifts.

Gifts given to the engaged couple by friends or relatives as engagement or wedding presents are practically always conditional and if the marriage does not take place, the donor is usually entitled to the return of the gift regardless of who broke the engagement.

As we shall see, when a man and woman marry, they automatically acquire certain rights in each other's property. In many states a wife is vested by marriage with an interest in her husband's real property which he cannot after the marriage wipe out by selling or giving the property away without her consent. In almost every state a surviving spouse is entitled to receive not less than a stated portion of the other's estate when he dies. In New York, for instance, a wife has an absolute right to one third of her husband's property at his death. He cannot deprive her of this right by making a Will leaving all of his property to other people. (Realistically he may be able to take away her share in whole or in part by giving away everything he owns *before* he dies. These and the other property rights of husband and wife vis-à-vis each other are more fully discussed in later chapters.)

Within certain limits, however, a man and woman contemplating marriage can make an agreement before they marry which alters what would normally be their rights in each other's property after the marriage. Such an ante-nuptial agreement or marriage settlement is usually made to cover some special situation. For example: Harold and Paula become engaged. Harold feels obligated to care for an orphan niece and nephew. He has been contributing to their support and wishes, in the event of his death, that his estate be used for their continued maintenance and education. Paula has property of her own and is not likely to need Harold's should he die, but, according to state law, she would as his wife have a right to a large portion of his estate. Paula and Harold enter into an agreement before their marriage whereby Harold transfers to Paula a certain valuable tract of land in return for which Paula waives all of her future rights to any part of Harold's estate.

Ante-nuptial agreements are often made to protect the wife's property too, since in many states the husband has somewhat similar rights in his wife's estate. Caroline is an heiress who has always been afraid that a man might be tempted to marry her for her money rather than for her personal attributes. When she and Dick become engaged, they may for psychological reasons enter into an agreement whereby Dick agrees to waive all of his rights in her property and to claim no interest in her estate if she predeceases him. Occasionally ante-nuptial agreements are made to assure a spouse of more rather than less of a share of the other's estate than that specified by law and such agreements are equally enforceable.

Sometimes a premarriage settlement may be made with one spouse by a third party such as a parent. Agreements of this kind are not as common as they once were when it was customary for a father to give his daughter a dowry; this might

be given by an agreement to transfer property at some future
time. Even today, however, parents or other relatives of an
engaged couple sometimes enter into a contract whereby they
agree to give a certain amount of money to the couple when
the marriage takes place or at some time thereafter. Such promises are frequently motivated by the desire of the relative to
see his young kinsman married or to make it easier for him to
marry if he so desires. This type of contract is enforceable.
In an Iowa case some years ago Mrs. W. sued her father-in-law
on an ante-nuptial contract. Mrs. W. had given birth to Ed W.'s
child out of wedlock. The grandfather of the child promised
Mrs. W. that if she would marry Ed, he, the grandfather, would
support her and the child if at any time within five years of
their marriage Ed failed to provide properly for them. About a
year after the marriage, Ed left his wife and child. She sued her
father-in-law and was awarded a sum of money sufficient to
support her and the child for the remainder of the five-year
period.

An ante-nuptial settlement by a third party need not mention a specific person whom the donee must marry. If Mr. X.
promises to give his nephew $5000 when he marries, the
nephew is entitled to the money upon his marriage unless the
offer has been withdrawn or canceled by mutual consent before any marriage takes place.

While an ante-nuptial settlement can alter some of the
property rights and obligations of marriage, there are others
which as a matter of public policy cannot be affected by agreement. The courts, for example, will not enforce any agreement
which attempts to free the husband from the duty of supporting his wife and children or which tries to shift the duty of
support to the wife. Nor will the courts enforce any agreement
which tends to encourage or facilitate divorce. A farsighted but
cynical couple cannot sit down on the eve of their marriage
and work out what alimony the wife is to get in the event they
are divorced and expect the courts to pay the slightest attention to their agreement if in fact their marriage works out badly

and they separate. While a married couple who have already separated may make such an agreement which will be enforced by the courts (see Chapter 16 on Separation Agreements) a like arrangement made in advance of marriage is regarded as invalid on the ground that it facilitates marital break-ups. Nor will the courts uphold any agreement which attempts to limit or eliminate the personal or conjugal rights of marriage as distinguished from property rights. An agreement that the parties will not live together after marriage is void. So is an agreement not to engage in sexual intercourse or not to have children. One court has even held that it is against public policy for an engaged couple to agree that they will live in whatever place the wife chooses. Under the law, said the court, that is the husband's prerogative and he cannot relinquish it.

Of course, a married couple is free to abide by any of these types of agreements so long as they both want to, but if one spouse has a change of heart and is no longer willing to live up to an ante-nuptial contract, whether or not the courts will force him to do so depends on whether in their opinion the agreement strikes at any essential element of the marriage relationship. If it does, the court will totally ignore the agreement. If it does not, the court will respect its provisions unless there has been fraud or undue influence.

An engaged couple are considered entitled to rely on each other for absolute honesty in the making of ante-nuptial agreements. Neither is obligated to deal at arm's length with the other. If Eugene tells Helen that he owns real estate worth $5000 and offers to give her $2000 in cash if she will waive her rights to it so he can leave it to his mother, the courts will not consider Helen bound by the agreement if it later turns out that Eugene's property was to his knowledge worth $50,000. Even in the absence of direct evidence that there has been fraud, the courts tend to assume fraud or undue advantage if the agreement attacked by the wife is grossly inadequate for her needs and would probably not have been made by any sensible person in possession of all the facts. Since women are, by and large, less versed in financial matters than men, the courts tend to scrutinize more critically the conditions under which women waive their rights than those where men do.

For the most part, ante-nuptial agreements are the province of the well-to-do. They are, however, worthy of consideration by people of moderate means in any situation where one of the parties has financial or moral obligations to a person other than the intended spouse, such as children by a previous wife, a dependent mother or other person for whom he wishes to make provisions which will take precedence over the rights the law would otherwise confer on the spouse.

CHAPTER 2

Whom You May Marry

OEDIPUS was destroyed by the gods because he violated the taboo against incest. Eugene O'Neill's *Strange Interlude* revolved in part about his heroine's desire not to perpetuate the insanity in her husband's family by having his child. Lillian Smith's *Strange Fruit* and a host of contemporary motion pictures such as *Lost Boundaries* and *Pinky* are concerned with the problem of marriage between members of the so-called white and colored races. The plight of Enoch Arden with its implications of unintentional bigamy has become a classic. Who knows what would have happened had Romeo and Juliet been over twenty-one? All of these find their reflection in the laws of the forty-eight states governing who may marry whom.

It is generally assumed that the members of a democratic society may marry whom they please. But this is true only within limits. The fact is that there are whole categories of persons whom one may not marry. In the first place, every state has some law designed to prevent people from marrying close relatives. Nowhere in this country can a parent marry his own child or a grandparent marry his grandchild or a brother marry his sister or a man his niece or a woman her nephew. The marriage of first cousins is prohibited in Arizona, Arkansas, Delaware, Idaho, Illinois, Indiana, Iowa, Kansas, Kentucky, Louisiana, Michigan, Minnesota, Mississippi, Missouri, Montana, Nevada, New Hampshire, North Dakota, Ohio, Oklahoma,

23

Oregon, Pennsylvania, South Dakota, Utah, Washington, West Virginia, Wisconsin, and Wyoming. A few states prohibit the marriage of second cousins or the marriage of a man to his grand-aunt or a woman to her grand-uncle.

These prohibitions have their origin in the ancient taboo against incest which arose long before any scientific knowledge of genes and chromosomes, or of recessive and dominant hereditary characteristics, was available to demonstrate the dangers of in-breeding. Perhaps our remote ancestors who formulated the rules were concerned less with the quality of the offspring of incestuous unions than about the possibility of intra-familial warfare which might result if permissible sexual relationships were not strictly defined. There is some evidence for this theory in the fact that marriages of step-parents and step-children and other unions of people related to each other, not by blood but by marriage, were likewise prohibited. Chapter 18 of Leviticus, for example, prohibits the marriage of a man with his daughter-in-law, his mother-in-law, the daughter or granddaughter of his wife or his aunt by marriage. Some of these restrictions are still reflected in the laws of various states. Roughly half the states prohibit the marriage of step-child and step-parent. The prohibition against marrying one's parent-in-law exists in the District of Columbia, Georgia, Iowa, Kentucky, Maine, Maryland, Massachusetts, Michigan, New Hampshire, Rhode Island, South Carolina, Vermont, and West Virginia. Curiously enough, the Texas statute prohibits a man from marrying his "son's widow," or a woman from marrying her "daughter's husband." Perhaps the legislature was trying to make some distinction here between situations where the prior marriage is terminated by divorce on the one hand and by death on the other. Some other states which do not generally prohibit marriage with parents-in-law do prohibit the marriage of a man with his son's widow.

It is quite likely that if the standards for marriages of relatives were being laid down today for the first time, they might be quite different from those presently on the statute books.

Eugenically, for example, it would be hard to defend the fact that Maryland prohibits marriage of a man with the wife of his grandfather (not his grandmother) but permits him freely to marry his first cousin. Perhaps the fact that several generations of one family no longer live under the same roof, as was common in Biblical times, today makes unnecessary many of the statutes restricting unions of people who are related to each other only by marriage. Be that as it may, the fact that comparatively few people are affected by the laws makes it improbable that the state legislatures will feel impelled to reconsider the wisdom of their statutes on the subject.

When it comes to the marriage of minors there are two distinct types of age restrictions. Each state sets a so-called "age of consent" below which youngsters are considered incapable of entering into marriage. In most states, this age has been set as eighteen years for a boy and sixteen years for a girl, though in a few states it is as low as fourteen for a boy and twelve for a girl. In addition each state has fixed a somewhat higher age bracket in which young people under age are permitted to marry provided they have the consent of their parents. Customarily such consent is needed where the boy is under twenty-one or the girl under eighteen.

In some states a couple is permitted to marry even though one spouse is under the age of consent or, in the higher bracket, even without parental consent, where exceptional circumstances exist. A judge or sometimes the official authorized to issue licenses can waive the age requirements if the girl is pregnant or has borne a child by the prospective husband or if they have been living together as man and wife. In other states the consent of both the parents and a judge is required in order for people within certain age brackets to marry. Here, too, the court's consent will usually be given only where there is a child in the offing.

For the most part, the states attempt to enforce their laws concerning the age at which people may marry by aiming at the prevention of the marriage. Officials are prohibited from issuing licenses without proof of age and can be penalized for their dereliction of duty; in some states the responsibility and the threat of penalty is extended also to the person who performs the ceremony. But if youngsters do succeed in having the knot tied by misrepresenting their ages, the marriage is not necessarily void. The question of when a marriage can be annulled for non-age will be discussed in some detail in the chapter on annulment. Generally, however, it can be said that a marriage of people below the legal age of consent is subject to annulment. If the husband and wife are over the age of consent but still in the age bracket where the consent of parents or judge should be obtained and is not, most states nonetheless recognize the validity of the marriage.

Today, 1952, more than half of the states have laws prohibiting miscegenation: the fancy name given to the unfancy idea that there is something wrong about so-called "white" people marrying members of other—and by inference—"inferior" races. Far from being scientifically sound, such laws usually reflect nothing but sheer unadulterated local prejudice.

The most common prohibition is, as might be expected, against the marriage of whites and Negroes. Such unions are prohibited in Alabama, Arizona, Arkansas, Colorado, Delaware, Florida, Georgia, Idaho, Indiana, Kentucky, Louisiana, Maryland, Mississippi, Missouri, Montana, Nebraska, North Carolina, North Dakota, Oklahoma, Oregon, South Carolina, South Dakota, Tennessee, Texas, Utah, Virginia, West Virginia, and Wyoming. These laws have been justified on a variety of grounds ranging from reference to a "divine law" requiring keeping the races separate to the claim that only the "scum" of both races ever want to intermarry anyway so they might just as well be prevented from doing so. The practical success of the miscegenation statutes in achieving the ends of "racial purity" may be questioned in view of the fact that between one third and three quarters of the entire Negro population is estimated to be partly white. The mulatto population of the United States increased 500 per cent between 1850 and 1910, the period when almost all of the states had anti-miscegenation statutes. The chances are, of course, that marriage accounted for only a small portion of the mulatto children born during this period.

The mixture of white and Negro strains makes it extremely difficult to determine who is a Negro for the purposes of the miscegenation laws. Some states have attempted to meet the problem by fixing a definition in their statutes. Indiana, Mississippi, Missouri, Nebraska, North Dakota, and Utah define a Negro as a person having one eighth or more of Negro blood. Maryland, North Carolina, and Tennessee say a Negro is a person of Negro descent to the third generation. In Oregon you are a Negro if you have one quarter or more Negro blood. Some states prohibit the marriage of whites and mulattoes, without bothering to specify what constitutes a mulatto. Strictly speaking, a mulatto is a person one of whose parents was Negro and one white, but the courts in interpreting the term have generally not restricted the designation of mulatto to people having 50 per cent Negro blood. Virginia, which insists that white people marry only other whites or people with a strain of American Indian, defines a "white person" as one who has no trace of any blood other than Caucasian except a strain of no more than one sixteenth American Indian.

Negroes are not the only people with whom marriage of whites is prohibited. Marriages between whites and Indians are prohibited in North Carolina and South Carolina. Mongolians, Chinese or Japanese may not marry whites in Arizona, Idaho, Mississippi, Missouri, Montana, Nebraska, Nevada, Oregon, South Dakota, Utah, and Wyoming. A white may not marry a Malayan in Arizona, Maryland, South Dakota, Utah, and Wyoming. Arizona, apparently concerned with the possibility of having the ranges overrun by turbaned riders, prohibits the marriage of whites with Hindus. Georgia, Louisiana, and Virginia have all-embracing statutes prohibiting whites from marrying anyone but whites. Louisiana's statute prohibits the marriage of whites with "people of color."

In all but a few of the states having miscegenation statutes, the effort is not merely, as in the case of minors, for example, to try to prevent the marriage. The marriage is considered void and, for the most part, the children of such marriages are considered illegitimate. In addition to this sanction, entering a miscegenetic marriage is a crime in most such states. In some it is considered so grave an offense against society that it is not merely a misdemeanor but a felony.

Interestingly enough, a California statute prohibiting the marriage of whites with Negroes, Mongolians, Malayans or mulattoes was recently declared unconstitutional by the highest court of California. Our federal Constitution guarantees everyone the right to "equal protection of the laws." This means that no legislature can pass a law which does not have the same impact on all people unless there is a really valid reason why the law should be different for different people. It is constitutional, for example, for a town to permit doctors to park their cars on streets which are generally closed to parking. If, however, parking were permitted only for people having an income of $10,000 a year or more, the discrimination could not be justified by a valid reason as it could in the case of the doctors. Such discrimination would be unconstitutional.

Using this test of whether there was a "reasonable classification," the California court held the miscegenation statute unconstitutional on the ground that there was no evidence of Negro inferiority to justify the statute. "The right to marry is the right of individuals, not of racial groups," said the court flatly. This decision is in direct contrast to one of the Supreme Court of Missouri which upheld that state's miscegenation statute on the ground that the right to marry as one pleased was no part of the rights granted by the Constitution. The California court did not, of course, say or mean that the state had no right to make any laws prohibiting certain marriages. The ground for its decision against the miscegenation statute was that there was no *valid* reason for the limitations on marriage which it imposed. A statute prohibiting the marriage of people suffering from venereal diseases can be justified because it can be shown that there is a real affirmative evil which the state is trying to prevent. But no scientific proof of the potential evils of mixed marriages could be offered; hence it was an unreasonable classification.

The logic of the California decision may in years to come appeal to the courts of other states confronted with the question of the validity of their own miscegenation statutes. Of course, it cannot be denied that in our present society the marriage of a white and a Negro is a difficult undertaking for the people involved and is not too easy for the children of the marriage. Often the parties to a mixed marriage find that they are not fully accepted by either whites or Negroes. It takes great patience, devotion and courage to live in the No Man's Land of a society which practices segregation. The California court has taken the position that it is the right of the individual in a democracy to undertake this most difficult of all marriages if he wishes to do so.

In contrast to the many states which consider racially mixed marriages undesirable, only a few consider habitual criminals, drug addicts and chronic alcoholics unsuited for marriage and reproduction. Delaware, North Dakota, Ohio, Oregon, and Washington prohibit the marriage of chronic alcoholics. Drug addicts come under the ban in Delaware and Oregon. The marriage of "a habitual criminal" is prohibited in North Dakota, Virginia, and Washington. Epileptics are forbidden to marry in Connecticut, Delaware, Indiana, Missouri, Nebraska, North Carolina, North Dakota, Ohio, Oregon, Pennsylvania, Virginia, and Washington. Four states prohibit the marriage of people with advanced or infectious tuberculosis— North Carolina, North Dakota, Rhode Island, and Washington.

Pennsylvania requires the applicants for a license to swear that they have no transmissable disease. In North Dakota, Virginia, and Washington, people in some of the categories forbidden to marry are permitted to marry if the prospective wife is over forty-five, that is, past the age where it is probable that she can bear children.

The marriage of insane and other mentally defective people is specifically prohibited in a dozen states, and in all states is voidable if the defective party lacked the power to understand what he was doing at the time of entering into the marriage. In Nebraska and South Dakota certain classes of mental defectives may marry only if the defective person has been sterilized. However, as the later discussion of premarital tests will indicate, very few of the states really have any effective way of discovering mental incapacity and preventing such marriages.

A few states try to prohibit the marriage of people incapable of supporting a family. New Jersey prohibits the marriage of anyone who is an inmate of an institution for the indigent. Indiana and Pennsylvania will not permit the marriage of a man who, in the five years prior to the application for a marriage license, was an inmate of any asylum or any home for the indigent unless he can prove that the cause of his stay has been removed and that he is capable of supporting a family. Delaware and Maine prohibit the marriage of paupers.

Indiana has an interesting requirement for men who are entering a second marriage. Where such a man has minor children who are dependent on him, he must prove that he will be capable of continuing to support them despite his remarriage.

For the most part, these prohibitions against the marriage of people whom the state considers physically, mentally or financially unfit to marry are enforced by trying to prevent the marriage in the first place. If the marriage does take place despite the fiat against it, in most cases it will be accorded full recognition as a valid marriage except where one party is mentally defective and unable to understand the nature of the marriage contract.

All states prohibit bigamous marriages, but the question of whether one of the parties is already bound by a prior existing marriage is not always quite as clear cut as it may seem at first glance.

A marriage is, of course, terminated by the death of one of the parties. Where a spouse is considerate enough to die in his own bed so that the family doctor can fill out and file a death certificate no question as to bigamy can arise. But the husband who walks out of the house one morning and is not seen or heard of for the next ten years may be dead or may have obtained a divorce. Yet his wife may have a hard time proving that she is free to marry again. Some states provide that where a spouse is not heard of for a fixed period of years, the husband or wife, as the case may be, can bring an action to declare the marriage terminated. In those states where desertion is a ground for divorce, the spouse left behind can, of course, end the marriage even if he or she knows that the marital partner is alive. In other states, no fixed rules are laid down by statute but the courts adopt a presumption of death where a person has not been heard from for a period of years. The length of time and the circumstances required to presume death vary from state to state.

More recently, the courts have also begun to talk in terms of a presumption that a divorce has been obtained. In one California case, for example, wife #1 claimed a share in her deceased husband's estate despite the fact that the parties had not lived together and that she had remarried twice after her husband's disappearance. Wife #2 proved that she had married the deceased in a ceremonial marriage, that they had lived together continuously up to the time of his death and had raised a family of ten children. She therefore claimed that she, not wife #1, was the legal wife of deceased although she could not present any evidence of the legal termination of his marriage with wife #1. The court ruled in favor of wife #2 on the theory that in the light of the circumstances there was a presumption that the deceased husband had at some time obtained a divorce from his first wife.

Sometimes even being able to prove that a divorce was obtained does not eliminate the barriers to remarriage. Many states, in granting divorces, place restrictions on the right of one or both parties to remarry (see Chapter 20), which may prevent them from getting a license to marry again in their home state. In those states the official who grants marriage licenses usually demands to see a copy of the decree where one of the applicants admits to a prior marriage and divorce. The license will not be issued if the decree indicates that the divorced person is not entitled to remarry.

The most common solution for people whose divorce decree in their home state commands them not to remarry is to journey to a neighboring state which has no such restrictions and to get married there. The question whether or not an out-of-state marriage will be accepted by the home state arises, not only in this situation, but also in connection with all the prohibited marriages which have been discussed—marriage of relatives, non-age, miscegenetic unions, and marriage of people who, by the standards of their own states, are physically, mentally or financially unfit to marry.

For example: John and Mary are first cousins. They live in New Hampshire. In applying for a marriage license, they are told by the clerk that a marriage between them is prohibited by the laws of the state. They thereupon proceed to get in John's car and drive to New York where they fulfill New York's requirements for marriage by having blood tests, securing a license and being married after the required three-day waiting period. This marriage is perfectly good in New York, and if the couple stayed in that state, no question about its validity would arise. However, in the usual case of this kind, the couple stay in the state in which the marriage was performed only long enough for the ceremony and then promptly return to their home state. The problem then becomes whether New

Hampshire will recognize the validity of an out-of-state marriage between its residents which is prohibited within its borders. In the supposititious case, the marriage would probably be upheld in New Hampshire, which follows the common-law rule that if a marriage is valid in the state where it is performed, its validity will be recognized everywhere. States which follow this rule are primarily concerned with the uncertainty of status which would result if each state or country which a married couple entered were to judge the validity of the marriage afresh by its own standards. Children would be legitimate in some places and bastardized in others by the simple process of crossing an invisible state border.

Other states, however, have taken the position that each state should have the right to enforce its laws at least vis-à-vis its own residents. This is their position toward both their own inhabitants and people from other states who try to get married within their borders. If John and Mary had journeyed to Massachusetts, which does not prohibit the marriage of first cousins, they would nonetheless have been denied a license. Massachusetts has adopted the Uniform Marriage Evasion Law designed to prevent just this type of evasion of the home-state law. No license will be issued there to nonresidents whose marriage would be prohibited in the state in which they live. This policy has been adopted also by Illinois, Louisiana, Vermont, Wisconsin, and Wyoming. Most states, however, will marry out-of-state residents without bothering to investigate whether the marriage would be legal in the home state.

In order to prevent their own residents from evading their marriage laws, many states have passed laws to the effect that if residents leave the state for the purpose of being married and return to their home state after the ceremony, the marriage will not be recognized there if it would have been prohibited by the laws of that state. This is the law in Arizona, the District of Columbia, Georgia, Illinois, Indiana, Louisiana, Maine, Massachusetts, Tennessee, Vermont, West Virginia, and Wisconsin. Thus, if James, a Negro, and Alice, a white woman, living in

Georgia where miscegenetic marriages are prohibited, go to the District of Columbia to be married and promptly return to Georgia, that state will not recognize the validity of their marriage even though it was perfectly good where contracted. If, however, James gets a job in New York and the couple live there for a substantial length of time, they no longer come under the provisions of the statute, which is in its terms applicable only to people who do not establish a residence outside of the state after their marriage.

Most of the states which do not have this kind of statute have adopted the rule that a marriage good where contracted shall be recognized as valid within their borders. But there are limitations even here, insofar as marriages of residents outside their home state is concerned. The Colorado statute recognizes out-of-state marriages with the proviso that the law shall not be so construed as to allow bigamy or polygamy in the state. Mississippi will recognize the validity of out-of-state marriages unless the marriage is in violation of Mississippi's statutes against miscegenation or incest. A few other states likewise exempt by statute bigamous, miscegenetic or incestuous marriages from the class of out-of-state marriages which they will recognize. Even where the state's statute makes no exceptions, some courts have held that the obligation of one state to recognize the validity of a marriage performed in another is limited to the acceptance of the "form" of the marriage. But they do not feel obliged to recognize an out-of-state marriage if the other state's laws as to the "essentials of the marriage contract" do not coincide with what they themselves have laid down as the requirements for the marriage of their residents. Some courts have said that a state is not required to recognize marriages which are "against the public policy" of the state, or marriages which would be absolutely void if performed within the state. The marriages most commonly attacked on this theory are miscegenetic, incestuous and bigamous ones—and the latter class has in some cases been held to include the situation where one party was prohibited by the divorce decree from remarrying.

Ordinarily miscegenetic, incestuous and bigamous marriages are the only out-of-state marriages which will not be recognized because they do not accord with the home-state law. Utah has refused to recognize the validity of a common-law marriage which was legal where contracted but most states which do not themselves recognize common-law marriages will do so if common-law marriage was legal in the state in which it took place. Leaving the state to avoid the law requiring pre-marital blood tests or to avoid the home state's age requirements ordinarily does not invalidate the marriage.

It should be remembered that all these questions as to the validity of a marriage apply only when residents of one state marry in another but continue their residence in their home state where the marriage would have been forbidden. A marriage between two residents of a state in accordance with the laws of that state will be accepted as valid anywhere. Here, as elsewhere, the fact that we have forty-eight states has advantages to counterbalance the inevitable confusions that result. Within limits, prospective spouses (as well as prospective divorcés) can shop about until they find a jurisdiction tailored to their needs. Were it not for our federal system, it would not be possible, in this day and age, for whites to marry Indians, Orientals or Negroes in substantial parts of this nation which prides itself on being the champion of democracy throughout the world. A uniform law as to whom one may marry would be apt to reflect, as would a uniform divorce law, the least common denominator of the states, that is, the most regressive state laws. In the circumstances, the crazy-quilt pattern described in this chapter is probably the lesser of two evils.

CHAPTER 3

Getting Married

*T*HE LAWS defining who may marry whom are deeply rooted in the past. By contrast, the laws providing for licenses, waiting periods and premarital tests of fitness are comparative newcomers. They reflect a general awareness of the fact that stiff divorce law as a method of protecting the state's interest in the family unit is a clear-cut case of locking the stable door long after the horse has departed for other pastures. An ever-increasing number of authorities feel that we should make it harder for people to get married and easier to get divorced. In some states, it is possible if you're so inclined to marry a person whom you had never seen an hour earlier. The statutes of the same states which call for a judicial examination into questions of guilt and responsibility for the termination of a marriage concern themselves but little with insuring the fitness of a couple to marry in the first place.

To a certain extent, marriage must remain a gamble. The romantic tradition is so deeply imbedded in our culture that there would probably be rioting in the streets if any state attempted to prevent young people in love from marrying on the ground that the prognosis for success was poor. To an increasing extent, however, the states are exercising their power to prevent hasty and ill-considered marriages and to forestall the marriage of people suffering from serious physical or mental illness.

The most common premarital test is, of course, the test for venereal disease which has been adopted in one form or another by almost three quarters of the states. Usually the law provides that in order to obtain a marriage license, each party must present a medical certificate stating that he or she has had a physical examination and/or a standard laboratory test for syphilis within the thirty days prior to the application for the license and has been found either free from syphilis entirely, or not to have the disease in a communicable state. This is the law in Alabama, California, Connecticut (40 days), Delaware, Florida, Georgia, Idaho, Indiana, Iowa, Kansas, Kentucky (15 days), Massachusetts, Missouri (15 days), Montana (20 days), Nebraska, New Hampshire, New York, Ohio, Oklahoma, Rhode Island (40 days), and West Virginia.

Eleven states require the certificate also to state that the applicant is not infected with any other venereal disease such as gonorrhea or chancroid. This is the law in Colorado, Illinois, Michigan, New Jersey, North Carolina, North Dakota, Oregon, Tennessee, Texas, Utah, and Wyoming. Wisconsin requires both to be tested for syphilis and the man for other venereal diseases as well. The state of Louisiana, with an admirable display of shortsighted gallantry, requires the male only to be tested for venereal diseases. Washington does not even require the man to have a test but simply provides that the male applicant for a marriage license must make an affidavit swearing among other things that he has no contagious venereal diseases. If he swears falsely, the wife whom he has succeeded in infecting has the dubious comfort of having him indicted for perjury, and possibly too, the right to sue for the annulment of the marriage on the grounds of fraud. Pennsylvania likewise requires both applicants for a license to swear that they have no transmissible disease but requires no medical certificate.

Virginia has its own variation. There the medical certificate must simply state that a test for syphilis has been made and that the results of the test have been communicated to both parties and that, if one is infected, the doctor has fully informed the other of the presence of the disease and the possibility of infection. However, the existence of the disease does not prevent the couple from marrying. If they do marry, the one infected must promptly undertake treatment of the disease and failure to do so constitutes a misdemeanor. Similarly, in Montana, infected people are not prohibited from marrying, but a certificate must be presented stating that the test for syphilis has been made and that each party has been told the results of the other's test.

In Illinois, Oregon, Michigan, and Wisconsin, if syphilis is discovered, the parties can only marry if the state Board of Health certifies that the disease is not in a transmissible state. Other states permit the doctor making the examination to decide the question of whether the disease is communicable.

The requirements of the premarital test statutes can be waived—usually by a judge—under special conditions in all states except Louisiana, New Jersey, Oregon, and Wyoming. Some of the states specifically provide that the test can be waived if the prospective wife is pregnant or has borne a child by the prospective husband. Others permit the test to be waived if one of the parties is near death. Still others provide that the test can be waived in an "emergency." The test was commonly waived during wartime for soldiers on leave where time was short. Many of the states wisely provide that where special permission to marry is granted in a case where one or both of the parties is infected, the health authorities must be notified and the infected person must submit to treatment for the disease. This also enables the authorities to keep watch on whether the marital partner becomes infected.

Most states do not require that the test be made by a doctor licensed to practice in that state. However, the medical certificate often must be on a form provided by the state issuing the license. The certificates of medical officers of the armed forces will usually be accepted for army or navy personnel applying for a license.

The blood-test requirements are enforced mainly by refusing to grant a license unless the appropriate medical certificates are presented. If the marriage does take place without the tests having been made, its validity is not at all affected.

The requirements can be evaded by going to another state which does not require any test and the validity of the marriage will be recognized in the home state. Fortunately, more and more states are requiring such tests so that it will probably only be a matter of a few years before evasion by crossing state lines will be impossible. A few attempts have been made to prevent evasion. Georgia requires that residents who marry outside of the state and return to Georgia must, within sixty days of the marriage, file evidence that they have had an examination and serological test for syphilis. Rhode Island requires that the couple take a blood test as soon as feasible after their return to Rhode Island. A number of states catch up with people who have evaded the premarital test by requiring that every pregnant woman have a blood test for syphilis. Detecting the presence of venereal disease during pregnancy is hardly as salutory as finding it before marriage but it is certainly better than finding it only after a defective child has been born.

In those states which prohibit the marriage of certain types of mental defectives or others whom the state considers mentally unfit to marry, the authorities who issue the license are for the most part given the responsibility of enforcing the prohibitions. This makes sense in states having relatively small population concentrations and is apt to be fairly effective in a rural area or small town where the clerk of the court has known Joe, the village idiot, all his life and can determine instantly that no license should be granted. In more populated regions, enforcement is more difficult. A busy clerk in a large city cannot be expected to spot feeble-mindedness, much less epilepsy or chronic alcoholism. In Iowa and South Dakota the court clerks who issue licenses are kept supplied by the state with a list of all persons known to be feeble-minded or otherwise disqualified by their mental state from entering into a marriage contract. A few other states, recognizing the futility of relying on licensing officials have made it mandatory for an applicant to present a medical certificate attesting to the fact that he has been examined by a physician and that the physician has found no signs of feeble-mindedness, epilepsy, drug addiction, chronic alcoholism or advanced tuberculosis. Kansas, North Carolina, and Oregon all require a medical certificate as to some or all of these factors as a prerequisite for the marriage license.

All of these attempts to supervise to some extent the fitness of people to marry are almost completely negated in those states which recognize common-law marriage, that is, a marriage which takes place without the procurement of a license or a formal ceremony. This type of marriage flourished and was to some extent justifiable when people lived far from licensing officials or clergymen qualified to perform a ceremony and when the cost of a ceremonial marriage was high. The validity of the common-law marriage was recognized in order to regularize unions which the parties were otherwise free to abandon at will and to prevent the bastardization of children.

Today common-law marriages are recognized in only eighteen states: Alabama, Colorado, the District of Columbia, Florida, Georgia, Idaho, Indiana, Iowa, Kansas, Michigan, Mississippi, Montana, Ohio, Oklahoma, Rhode Island, South Carolina, South Dakota, and Texas.

Traditionally the courts have recognized two distinct kinds of common-law marriages. One of the two is practically obsolete today. It was deduced from a promise to wed some time in the future plus a copulation. Given these two factors, it was presumed that at the time of their first intercourse, the parties had given each other their consent to marry. Most courts at the present time agree with the New York court which said, ". . . whatever indiscretions the parties may commit after making such promises (to marry in the future), they do not become husband and wife until they have actually given themselves in such relation."

The second type of common-law marriage is more generally recognized today in the eighteen states which allow common-law marriages at all. It comes into being by words of present consent. In effect, Bill says to Mary, "I take you for my wife as of this moment," and she similarly agrees to consider herself married to him from that point on. This is sufficient to constitute a valid and binding marriage in some states. Other states require an additional element—namely, subsequent cohabitation between the parties. Cohabitation means more than merely having intercourse; it means openly living together and having the status of married people in the eyes of the community. In a Michigan case, a woman brought suit under the Workmen's Compensation Act for the death of her alleged husband who was killed in the course of his employment. She claimed that she was entitled to a widow's benefits because she and the deceased had entered into a common-law marriage. She was able to prove consummation of the alleged marriage (the couple had had a child) but she could not prove that they had ever lived openly together as man and wife. She claimed that economic circumstances had prevented their doing so. The court refused to recognize the validity of the common-law marriage without proof of cohabitation as a married couple.

This case suggests why an increasing number of states insist on proof of cohabitation as husband and wife before according legal status as a marriage to a common-law union. Social security laws, workmen's compensation laws and the like have greatly increased the number of cases where the attempt to prove the common-law marriage is made after the death of one party. If the man and woman have not been living openly together it is often difficult for the court to determine whether the deceased person regarded their union as a marriage or as an extramarital affair. Often there is no proof (except the testimony of the party who has a financial interest in so proving) that there was any relationship between the parties at all. Cohabitation as man and wife, therefore, becomes an important element in proving the marriage. Not all courts insist on it, however; in some states, it is considered merely one form of evidence that the marriage actually took place.

Some authorities object to the doctrine requiring cohabitation as an essential prerequisite to the recognition of marriage by consent. They point out that where it is required, there is theoretically a period when the parties are in limbo, half married and half not, that is, until they have had a chance to live together long enough to establish themselves as married people in the community.

There are many objections to common-law marriages generally. Because many such a marriage is not recorded, questions as to legitimacy, title to property and so forth may arise at a time when proof of the marriage may be difficult to obtain. Failure to procure a license prevents the state from having any control over the physical or mental fitness of the people who marry. Furthermore, acceptance of common-law marriages leaves the door open to spurious claims of marriage. For all of these reasons, the common-law marriage has been losing favor rapidly. While the majority of states prohibit such unions, if a common-law marriage is recognized as valid in the state in which the parties consented to the marriage contract, and lived together, its validity will be recognized in other states in which the couple may later reside.

Every state, including those which still recognize common-law marriage, has laws governing the conditions under which people may enter into a ceremonial marriage. Ordinarily, a license must be obtained from an official authorized to issue it (usually a county clerk or judge), the ceremony must be performed by an authorized official (ministers, judges, justices of the peace, etc.), and the fact that the marriage has taken place must be reported to the state department in charge of keeping records. Errors in following the formula laid down do not usually invalidate the marriage if an honest attempt has been made by the parties to enter into a legal marriage. The responsibility for issuing a license only in situations where a license is authorized is usually that of the issuing officer. The obligation to report the marriage is upon the person who performs the ceremony. Mistakes or omissions on these levels do not affect the marriage unless it is one which the state considers void anyway as, for example, where the state laws prohibits the issuance of a license for a bigamous, incestuous or miscegenetic union and declares that such a marriage, if performed, is absolutely void. A somewhat more difficult question is presented where the person who performs the marriage ceremony was not legally authorized to do so. Most states hold that marriages performed by such a person are valid if at least one of the parties honestly believed that the solemnizing officer had authority.

Largely to curb the kind of hasty elopement which was at one time widely considered a suitable climax for a gay party, most states have now imposed a waiting period between the time the parties decide to marry and the time when the ceremony can be performed. This is, of course, entirely apart from whatever delay may be occasioned by the requirement of serological tests. The waiting period, usually ranging between one and five days, is sometimes imposed between the issuance of the license and the ceremony. Even Maryland, which used to be a Mecca for hasty marriages, now imposes a two-day waiting period. A recent magazine article reported that every night and every day young couples still arrive in Elkton, the border town once famous as the American Gretna Green, expecting to be married within the hour only to find that they could probably have been married just as quickly in their home state.

At present, the waiting period is two days in Maryland and three days in Arkansas, District of Columbia, Florida, Kansas, Kentucky, Louisiana, Missouri, New Jersey, New York, Oregon, Pennsylvania, Washington, and West Virginia. There is a five-day wait in Connecticut, Maine, Massachusetts, Michigan, Minnesota, Mississippi, New Hampshire, Ohio, Vermont, and Wisconsin. Three states have different requirements for residents and nonresidents: North Carolina has a two-day waiting period for nonresidents, but none for residents; Rhode Island requires a six-day wait for nonresidents, and Delaware requires residents to wait one day and nonresidents for four. Georgia and Tennessee have a five-day waiting period only where there is a question of the bride's being under age. Almost all of the states have provisions for getting a waiver of the waiting period in case of emergency.

Some states require that the license be obtained in the county where the woman resides; others require that it be obtained in the county where the marriage is to take place. In most states, however, the license may be obtained anywhere in the state.

Three states permit the marriage to take place without the prior obtaining of a license if banns are published a suitable time before the wedding. In Ohio, the banns must be posted on two days of worship at a church in the county where the prospective bride resides. Georgia and Maryland have somewhat similar laws.

Only Maryland and West Virginia require that the marriage ceremony must be performed by a minister or some other cleric. Delaware has a similar requirement with the one exception that the Mayor of Wilmington is authorized to perform marriages. In all other states, a marriage can be performed either by a clergyman or by a designated state official. No particular form of ceremony is required. Some states have specific statutes validating the Quaker form of marriage in which the parties consent to the marriage in the presence of the congregation without having any third party act as the solemnizing authority. Almost all states provide that any form of ceremony practiced by any *bona fide* religious sect is acceptable. A minority of the states require clergymen to register or to be specially licensed in order to perform ceremonies. This type of regulation is usually accompanied by a requirement that all persons performing marriages duly report them and is in essence an effort on the part of the state to keep its marriage records straight.

During World War II, questions arose as to the validity of proxy marriages, marriage by telephone, and even marriage by mail. All of these have in common the fact that the marriage takes place when the man, the woman, and the person officiating are not all in the same place. Sometimes such marriages meet a real need.

Consider, for example, the case of Joe, a soldier serving overseas, who receives a letter from his girl, Nancy, telling him that as a result of their having had intercourse during his last leave in the United States, she is pregnant. Joe wishes to marry her, both to legitimize the child and to make Nancy and the baby eligible for a dependants' allowance and other benefits which the government extends to the families of servicemen. Since he cannot return home to marry her, he appoints his brother John to act as his agent or proxy and to go through the marriage ceremony in his place. Such a proxy marriage is valid in a number of states. Then there are cases where marriages are sought to be solemnized over the telephone with the minister on one wire, the bride on another and the groom on a third.

Proxy, telephone, and radio marriages (the question appears not yet to have arisen in connection with television) are barred in many states by the fact that the laws require both parties personally to appear in applying for the license or to have blood tests made by a doctor licensed in the state or to be married in the presence of an authorized official. On the other hand, a Nebraska court held a proxy marriage valid on the ground that it was recognized by "the rites and customs" of a religious society of which the parties were members. It is interesting to note that the Roman Catholic Church is the only large denomination which specifically authorizes proxy marriages.

Some states which do not recognize the validity of common-law marriages occasionally recognize a proxy marriage as a defective ceremonial marriage. For the most part, however, proxy marriage is most likely to be upheld in states which recognize common-law marriage by the exchange of consents without any requirement of cohabitation. Moreover, even where the state of domicile does not recognize common-law or proxy marriages, the fact that such a marriage took place in a state or country where it was legally binding will sometimes validate it for all purposes. Where a soldier and his girl each had a proxy go through the marriage ceremony for them in Mexico where proxy marriages are legal, they were deemed married by the state where they resided even though a proxy marriage performed within that state would have had no legal effect.

In the rare case of a marriage by mail, the relevant law is the law of the state in which the offer of marriage is accepted since marriage is, among other things, a contract and a contract is deemed to be made at the place of acceptance. The validity of this type of marriage has been recognized in a few cases.

There is much guesswork involved in trying to predict whether a proxy marriage or marriage by telephone or mail will be considered valid. Few states have statutes which afford any definite answer so the ultimate decision is in the hands of the courts. Agencies of the federal government too have been called on to determine the validity of purported marriages between two people who were not in each other's presence when the marriage supposedly came into being. A spouse so acquired does not qualify for entrance into the United States under the special and more liberal laws pertaining to the immigration of the husbands and wives of American citizens. The validity of proxy marriages has, however, been accepted in other contexts by the federal government.

The trend is undoubtedly in the direction of more, rather than fewer requirements for getting married. Those state laws which prohibit the marriage of mental defectives, drug addicts, epileptics, alcoholics, and the like are straws in the wind. There is much talk of "marital fitness" tests which psychologists and others are devising to gauge the capacity of prospective husbands and wives to be married in general and to each other in particular. While such tests have, superficially, much to recommend them, it is very doubtful whether taking them or passing them, no matter how ingenious they are, should ever become obligatory as a prerequisite to marriage. For in the realm of personality, especially when the alchemy of two people is involved, finding out what the desiderata are is no less difficult than ascertaining whether particular people measure up to the desiderata. Objective criteria are completely lacking. It is one thing to determine whether a person has syphilis or epilepsy or even whether his mentality is that of a four-year-old. It is quite another to try to judge whether he is "emotionally mature" or otherwise "fit" for marriage.

Certainly some exposure to premarital counseling or education for marriage should be encouraged. But that, at our present level of knowledge, would seem to be as far as we should go. There are enough factors in our mass-production society making for uniformity and centralization of control without vesting still more discretionary authority in the hands of the state. To paraphrase the old saying about censorship: if you ever found anyone wise enough to decide whether or not two people who want to get married, should get married, he'd be wise enough not to make the decision.

CHAPTER 4

Husbands and Wives:

THE PERSONAL SIDE

A STORY is told of Joe Doakes who was arguing with his wife as they walked down the street. In the middle of the argument he took her arm to help her over a particularly icy bit of sidewalk. As he proffered his hand, he said, "Be careful, darling, or you'll break your damned neck."

The story to some extent highlights the legal rights of husbands and wives toward each other. Had Joe gone so far as to lose his temper and push Mrs. Doakes, he would have been guilty in legal terms of a violation of his marital obligations. But nothing in the law required him to proffer his hand and certainly no court would find in his somewhat testy admonition any grounds for legal action by his wife.

An examination of the rights of husbands and wives toward each other reveals that the law is interested only in the extremes. In a very large measure, these rights are the opposite side of the coin which has the laws of separation, annulment, and divorce on the reverse side. Thus, adultery is a ground for divorce; conversely each spouse has a right to expect complete fidelity from the other. Cruelty is in virtually all states a ground for either separation or divorce or both. Conversely, husband and wife each has a legal right not to be maltreated by the other.

Justice Oliver Wendell Holmes pointed out that there is no right without a remedy. By this he meant that unless you can do something about an act that is done unto you, that act

48

does not infringe your rights. Applying this statement to matrimonial rights and duties, it becomes clear that the only rights husbands and wives have in relation to each other are those they can do something about legally. What these are we are setting forth in this chapter. They represent but the minimum framework of a marriage, for many of the important things that make up the difference between success and failure in marriage are not cognizable in legal terms. The law requires two spouses to be physically faithful to each other. It can do nothing to assure them a sex relationship that brings both completion and contentment. The law draws the line at physical cruelty. It cannot do anything about the husband who never helps with the dishes or the children, or who forgets anniversaries. Nor can it do anything about the wife who nags, is bored by her husband's concerns, or who extravagantly spends his money. Though all of us recognize that sexual satisfaction, affection, companionship, consideration, comfort and kindness are desirable elements in marriage, all the law can do is to specify that where extreme lacks of these intangibles are presented, the deprived spouse may leave the home without being guilty of desertion and he may also be entitled to a separation or divorce or both.

One of the essential elements of marriage as a legal relationship is the right to have your spouse live with you and the correlative duty to live with your spouse. If Peter refuses to live with his wife, Janet, no court in the country will send him home with an armed guard to make sure he stays there. In some jurisdictions, his breach of duty is considered sufficient to entitle Janet to a divorce; in others Janet would at least be entitled to a legal separation and to continued support if Peter's leaving was not due to any gross misconduct on her part. If Janet unjustifiably leaves Peter, she may forfeit her right to be supported by him.

The husband usually has the right to choose the place where the couple shall live even if his choice involves a change of citizenship. Thus, a Massachusetts court held that a wife had deserted her husband by refusing to follow him from England to the United States after he had twice sent her passage money. This does not give the husband a right to make grossly unreasonable decisions concerning the place to live or to insist that his wife live in a place which will be injurious to her health. The husband in the Massachusetts case had sound economic reasons for wanting to live in the United States and his wife's refusal seemed based on nothing more than a desire not to leave her native land. Under these circumstances the husband's wish is usually supposed to prevail. But a wife would not be obliged to follow her husband to the African jungle merely because he decided to trade the shoe business for life as a lion hunter. Nor can a man of means insist that his wife live in a slum. The dwelling which the husband chooses must be reasonably suited to the means and circumstances of the parties.

While the husband has the right to choose the couple's dwelling place, the wife has a right to insist that they have a home of their own if that is at all possible. The wife may insist upon being the mistress of her own home and her husband may not require her to live with his mother or other relatives against her will unless this is demanded by economic necessity.

In one case, the husband-to-be, William, told his fiancée, Minnie, that after their marriage they would have a home of their own and that his widowed mother would live with them as their guest. Minnie agreed to this. Shortly before the marriage, however, William (without Minnie's knowledge) transferred ownership of his house to his mother. When William brought his nineteen-year-old bride home she found her mother-in-law in charge of the house. William gave his mother the housekeeping money and authorized her to manage the house. Minnie claimed that her mother-in-law frequently told her that she was an unfit wife for William and accused her of being incapable of managing his household. After a few months Minnie left, saying that she would not return unless she were permitted to take her rightful place in the house. The court held that she was justified in leaving in view of the fact that William's mother was in good health, financially independent and had two other married sons near by to whom she had given property and with whom she was on excellent terms. In these circumstances, the court saw no sound reason why Minnie should have been deprived of her rightful place as mistress of the household. If the mother had been ill or impoverished, her son might have been justified in insisting that she live with him and his wife, but even in such a case he would have no right to permit or encourage her to displace his wife as mistress of the house. The Nebraska court which held that Minnie had been justified in leaving summed up the legal attitude toward the perennial mother-in-law problem by saying, "Whatever his filial obligations may be, a man may not bring his mother to preside in his new home. That place belongs to his wife. Neither may he, without her consent, take her to the home of the mother, there to be under her domination and control and when the wife objects to this, she does not thereby forfeit her right to support and maintenance."

Another essential attribute of marriage is the right to normal sexual intercourse. While it is unquestionably true that the expectation and desire to have children is normally a fundamental motivation for marriage, it is the purely sexual rather than the procreative aspect of intercourse which the law stresses most heavily. This is evidenced by the fact (more fully discussed in Chapter 17 on Annulment) that whereas the sterility of one spouse has no legal effect on the marriage, many states permit a marriage to be annulled if either party is impotent and hence incapable of offering the other sexual gratification. In effect what these states have said is that the right to normal intercourse is so prime a factor in marriage that there can be no true marriage if either spouse is incapable of performing his sexual role.

The law is not able to, and for the most part makes no

attempt to, enforce sexual obligations in marriage except in what we might term the extreme cases of sexual maladjustment—impotence, "abnormal" sex practices, cruelty or refusal to have intercourse at all. In such cases, some states permit divorce and others separation. The cases involving sexual problems between man and wife are replete with references to the "right" of the husband to insist on and the "duty" of the wife to "submit" to "reasonable" sexual intercourse. In broad terms, the word "reasonable" is interpreted to mean any time or frequency which is not injurious to the health of the wife. A husband's insistence on excessive intercourse immediately after his wife has had an ovarian operation or is in the late stages of pregnancy have both been termed unreasonable and cruel by the courts. The more frequent kinds of sexual maladjustment where, for example, the wife is frigid or the couple have for psychological reasons failed to achieve mutually gratifying intercourse, do not usually appear in the courts as such but they nonetheless underlie many of the cases that do get into court. They come masquerading as adultery, cruelty, desertion, fraud or any one of the other "grounds" which the laws specify as reasons for terminating a marriage.

The less tangible rights of husbands and wives vis-à-vis each other are usually summed up by the word "consortium," meaning the right to enjoy what one authority has termed the "person, affection, society and assistance of one's spouse." As part of the rights of consortium, the husband is entitled to the services of his wife. If the wife works outside the home for strangers she is usually entitled to her own earnings. But domestic services or assistance which she gives the husband are generally considered part of her wifely duties. The wife's services and society are so essential a part of what the law considers the husband entitled to as part of the marriage that it will not recognize any agreement between the spouses which provides that the husband is to pay for such services or society. In a Texas case David promised his wife, Fannie, that he would give her $5000 if she would stay with him while he lived and continue taking care of his house and farm accounts, selling his butter and doing all the other tasks which she had done since their marriage. After David's death, Fannie sued his estate for the money which had been promised her. The court held that the contract was unenforceable since Fannie had agreed to do nothing which she was not already legally and morally bound to do as David's wife.

A somewhat different problem may be presented where the wife works in the husband's business. Generally speaking, the wife is not entitled to be paid by her husband even for services rendered to him in a business way unless there is a specific agreement that she should be paid. Some states do not recognize the validity of contracts between husband and wife at all. In such states, a wife who works in her husband's business has no legally enforceable right to compensation if her husband refuses to pay her or if he has creditors who assert a claim to his funds. In one such state, a woman named Eliza worked as cashier and bookkeeper for her husband's store and was apparently paid a regular salary. She was injured in the course of her work and attempted to collect benefits under the state Workmen's Compensation Act. The court held that since the state law did not permit husbands and wives to contract with each other, Eliza could not be considered as her husband's employee. In most states, however, a specific agreement between a husband and wife whereby the wife is to receive a fixed sum or a percentage of the profits for her services in her husband's business can be made and enforced and will be upheld for all purposes including workmen's compensation.

Similarly, when the wife performs services of a domestic character for profit for persons other than her husband and children, the courts have usually held that she is entitled to whatever compensation has been agreed upon.

In one Ohio case, Anna Elizabeth had cared for her mother-in-law, Margaret, for three years with the understanding that she was to be paid for her services. Margaret

lived in a house of her own not far from where Anna Elizabeth
and her husband, Simon, lived. Margaret suffered from gan-
grene and Anna Elizabeth not only kept her house in order
for her but performed nursing services as well. After
Margaret's death, Anna Elizabeth sued her estate for the
sum which she had been promised. The administrator of the
estate claimed that Anna Elizabeth was not entitled to compensation because caring for her husband's mother was
within the scope of her duties as Simon's wife. As proof of
this, the administrator pointed out that the state law would
have required Simon to support his mother if she were unable
to maintain herself. The court rejected this argument and held
that caring for her mother-in-law under these circumstances
was no part of Anna Elizabeth's duty and that she was entitled to collect the sum promised. If, of course, no express
promise of payment is made to a wife who cares for her husband's mother or other relatives, she is not entitled to compensation. The law will not *imply* a promise to pay for such
services.

In addition to her tangible services, the husband is entitled to his wife's love, affection, companionship, and care.
One court summed up this aspect of the marriage relationship
by saying, "The wife does not occupy the position of a servant and her services to her husband are not those of a servant. She makes his home cheerful and inviting and ministers
to his happiness in a multitude of ways outside of the drudg-
ery of household labor. All the work of the house may be
done by hired employees and her services still give character
to the home." While these words were written over fifty years
ago, this is still a fair summary of what, in theory at least, the
law considers a husband entitled to expect from his wife. Her
complete failure in this area may entitle him to a divorce or
legal separation, but here again the law is ill-equipped to help
a husband exact loving affection and attention from his wife
within the framework of the marriage itself. Obviously a wife
is equally unable to use legal process to force her husband to

love, cherish and protect her (as he is, in the eyes of law, bound to do) although his failure in these respects may be sufficiently drastic to entitle his wife to a divorce or legal separation.

There was a time when the husband had one additional remedy available to him by which he could attempt to make his wife conform to his wishes—the power to chastise her or to use physical force to induce her to behave as he wished. There were many similarities between the legal position of a married woman and that of a child, with the child in a somewhat better position because he had at least the hope of eventual emancipation from his father's rule. Today the husband has no greater right to strike or use any other kind of physical force against his wife than he would have against a stranger. But in one respect, even when it comes to physical violence, husband and wife are not in the same legal position as strangers.

Most states will not permit spouses to sue each other for injuries caused by one to the other. In such states, if a husband punches his wife and breaks her jaw, she may have him prosecuted under the criminal statutes prohibiting assault and battery or she may be entitled to a divorce or legal separation, but she cannot sue her husband for the pain or disfigurement or for any of the other damages suffered. This rule is in part a survival of the old common-law theory of the literal unity of husband and wife which regarded a wife's suing her husband in the same light as a man's bringing suit against himself. There is also a considerable body of authority to the effect that lawsuits between husband and wife (or between parent and child) should be discouraged in the interest of preserving family unity and harmony. In many of the states which follow this rule, one spouse cannot sue the other for an injury caused by negligence any more than he can sue for one caused by a deliberate wrongful act. Thus, a wife who is injured because of her husband's faulty driving cannot in many states sue him even though, as a practical matter, he may be insured and would welcome a successful suit by his wife which might, via the insurance policy, cover the expenses of the accident. In some states, however, suits between husbands and wives both for deliberate wrongdoing and for negligence are allowed.

While the law is unable or unwilling in many substantial respects to help husbands and wives enforce their conjugal rights against each other, it is somewhat more helpful when it comes to enforcing such rights against outsiders. If a third party negligently or maliciously causes a husband to lose the society and services of his wife either temporarily or permanently, the husband may have a right to sue for the damage done to him, entirely apart from and in addition to the wife's right to recover for her injuries. Thus, in a Pennsylvania case, Ruth was injured in getting off a train and she recovered damages. Her husband, Henry, sued the railroad company for the loss he suffered as a result of the injuries to his wife. He recovered for the expenses he had incurred in hiring a housekeeper to perform the domestic duties which Ruth ordinarily performed and an assistant to do the work which she had done for him in connection with his flower business, prior to her accident.

In most states the husband has a right to be reimbursed for his wife's medical expenses as well as for the added household costs caused by her incapacitation. The wife, however, is the one who ordinarily can sue for her loss of earning power outside the home since she is by statute generally entitled to her own earnings. In a few states, the courts have held that the statutes which permit a married woman to sue in her own name and to control her own earnings have abrogated the husband's right to sue for loss of consortium or services.

Where the husband is permitted to sue for loss of consortium, the court decisions are divided as to whether he may cite as an element of damages the loss of sexual intercourse with his wife. In a Rhode Island case, a husband whose wife had been injured in an accident sued to recover the money he had laid out for medical treatment and domestic help and asserted a further claim for damages on the ground that he and his wife had been unable to have intercourse for a substantial period because of the injury. The court allowed him to recover for the first two items of damage but rejected the third because the loss of intercourse was temporary. If the injury to the wife had involved damage to her sexual organs which permanently prevented intercourse, the court said that she could sue for this as part of her injuries. But the husband, said the court, had a right to recover for loss of intercourse only if it was the result of such malicious action on the part of a third party as would give rise to a suit for alienation of affections or criminal conversation (both of which are discussed later in this chapter). The courts of other states have taken a contrary position and have held that since a husband is entitled to sexual relations with his wife at all reasonable or mutually agreeable times, he may collect damages from a third party whose wrongful act temporarily or permanently prevents his having intercourse with his wife.

Generally a husband's right to sue for damages which he suffers as a result of injury to his wife is no better than his wife's right to sue for her own injuries; that is, the same defenses are available to a third party against him as would defeat the wife's action. If, for example, it can be shown that the wife was hit by a car because of her own negligence in jaywalking, she cannot obtain damages for her injuries nor can her husband recover for loss of consortium. An exception to this rule is sometimes made where the action of the third party which results in the injury is criminal. In one such case, a wife successfully sued a druggist who had unlawfully sold her husband opium, thereby making him "unfit and incapable . . . to give the aid, support, affection, society, companionship and consortium" which he had formerly given her.

We have referred throughout this discussion to the husband's right to sue for injuries to his wife resulting in loss of consortium without reference to a similar right on the part of the wife. For reasons rooted in the common law which took a rather dim view of women's rights, a wife ordinarily cannot sue for loss of consortium caused by an accidental or negligent injury to her husband. She can, however, sue, as in the case above, for a loss caused by illegal action and for a deliberate or malicious act which results in a deprivation of consortium.

In most states both wife and husband can sue an outsider for a deliberate or malicious interference with the marriage relationship without specific reference to loss of consortium or intercourse. This is the alienation-of-affections suit much beloved of the tabloids. It often goes hand in hand with something known as an action for criminal conversation—interference with a spouse's exclusive right to sexual intercourse with his marriage partner. Recently, suits for alienation of affections and criminal conversation have fallen into disrepute for many of the same reasons as have been discussed in connection with breach-of-promise actions and for some additional reasons as well. A growing number of states have outlawed such suits along with suits for breach of promise to marry, among them Alabama, California, Colorado, Florida, Indiana, Maryland, Michigan, Nevada, New Jersey, New York, Pennsylvania, and Wyoming.

Probably the most potent argument against alienation-of-affections suits is that they rest on the fundamentally unsound hypothesis that a third party has wrecked a marriage which until his advent was perfectly satisfactory. As a practical matter, a marriage is rarely destroyed by a third party. The entrance of the "other" man or woman into the picture is usually the result and not the cause of a disintegrating marriage. The unfaithful spouse has usually taken up with the third party because of a lack already existing in the marriage. It is, moreover, difficult to see what a successful alienation-of-affections suit really accomplishes aside from giving the suing spouse revenge. Certainly the loss of love and marital companionship (if it existed before the advent of the third party) can hardly be compensated in dollars and cents. Like breach-of-promise suits, suits for alienation of affections are less conducive to just compensation for injuries than to spite and blackmail.

In some states, the courts will issue an injunction against someone who, it is claimed, is alienating the affections of a spouse. Not long ago, a Southern court was asked by Mrs. R. to issue against Marjorie, a thirty-six-year-old schoolteacher, an injunction prohibiting her from having anything further to do with Mrs. R.'s husband. Mr. R. was a sixty-four-year-old businessman who had retired and given his business to his son. His wife claimed that he was drinking too much and spending time with Marjorie (though there did not seem to be any evidence that Marjorie was responsible for his drinking). The court granted an injunction. This meant that if Marjorie had any contact thereafter with Mr. R., she would be guilty of contempt of court and subject to imprisonment. The reader, applying his own common sense to the facts of this case as briefly given, can draw his own conclusions as to whether the injunction was likely to make Mr. R. a more affectionate, loving husband or whether he would be all the more likely to become the mainstay of the nearest saloon at which women were not welcome.

Conceivably Mr. R's unrest may have been due to difficulty in adjusting from an active business life to what seemed long, futile, empty days of nothing to do or it may have been a kind of rebellion against growing old or it may have been caused by Mrs. R's own actions or attitudes. Whatever the reason, it does not seem likely that the kind of public humiliation which was symbolized by the injunction would increase his affection for his wife or change him back into the kind of faithful spouse which he had apparently been for years.

In most states a person who is sued for alienation of affections cannot defend himself by proving that there was no affection between the husband and wife to begin with and that, therefore, nothing which he did worsened the relationship. There have been cases where a man has been sued for alienating the affections of a wife who had been separated from her husband for a long time before she even met the other man. In one case a wife won damages from her husband's parents for alienating his affections despite the fact that the couple had quarreled constantly and the wife had locked her bedroom door and refused to have intercourse with her husband some time before her in-laws did the things which she claimed alienated her husband from her.

In another case a husband sued a man whom he alleged to be his wife's lover. The court said that the husband's own immorality and his mistreatment of his wife before she embarked on the alleged affair did not prevent him from recovering damages from the man who he claimed had deprived him of his wife's love. The court added that the jury might see fit to award the husband somewhat less damages than if he had been himself blameless. In this kind of case where it is clear that the third party was not the cause of the disharmony between husband and wife, some states have gone further and have held that there can be no recovery for alienation of affections. In most of the states which permit alienation-of-affections suits, however, the courts have proceeded on the theory that, so long as the marriage legally exists, there is a chance that husband and wife may become reconciled and anyone who does anything to interfere with even a tenuous possibility of reconciliation must pay damages.

Generally, it is not necessary, in order for a spouse to bring a successful alienation-of-affections suit, for him to be able to prove that the wife or husband whose affections were allegedly alienated abandoned the marriage or that the couple were separated as a result of what the third party did. In one case, the plaintiff, Eva, sued Helen for alienating the affections of Eva's husband by enticing and persuading him to have intercourse with her and trying (unsuccessfully) to persuade him to leave his wife. The court held that Eva could recover damages for the diminution of her husband's affection toward her even though they were still living together when the suit was brought.

Some cases of this kind give rise to a suspicion of possible collusion between husband and wife. One reported case, where the defendant was a wealthy man involved a wife who had left her husband briefly (no adultery was alleged) and who at the time of the suit was living with him again. It may be presumed that she was not entirely indifferent to the large sum of money which the husband collected from the other man. There can be little question but that the laws permitting alienation-of-affections suits can be used as a basis for the well-known "badger game." Many a man has made a large and rapid settlement to prevent an "outraged husband" from bringing an alienation-of-affections suit based on evidence prearranged by the husband and wife for that very purpose.

The alleged wrongdoer in alienation-of-affections suits is not always the "other" man or woman. The parents of a husband or wife are not infrequently accused of turning their child against his spouse. The cases take into account the natural concern of parents for the happiness and welfare of their children which does not cease when these children get married. Consequently parents have a certain amount of legal leeway in giving their child advice or counsel aimed against their child's spouse. If, however, they act without what the law regards as reasonable cause or in a malicious manner they may be liable for damages despite the parental relationship.

A Wisconsin case indicates the kind of action which the courts have held goes beyond parental privilege. Charlotte and Frederick were married while Frederick was in medical school. He left school and it is evident that his parents were not happy about the marriage from the outset. After a while the young couple separated and Charlotte brought suit against her mother-in-law for alienating Frederick's affections. She claimed that Frederick's mother had tried to prejudice him against her in a variety of ways, that she had offered to finance his way through medical school if he would leave his wife and had threatened that she and his father would not give him any further financial assistance—in fact would disinherit him—unless he left Charlotte. The court held that these actions went beyond the defendant's mother-in-law's "reasonable parental regard" for her child and manifested "unreasonable ill will" toward Charlotte.

In another case, the wife was allowed to recover damages by showing that her mother-in-law had been prejudiced against her from the beginning because of her religious faith, had disparaged and jeered at her, and had urged that the marriage be abandoned. This behavior, too, the court held went beyond the parental privilege. On the other hand, a parent who shelters or supports a child who has been separated from or who has abandoned the spouse is not guilty of unreasonable interference. Nor is the one who gives his child reasonable advice based on the facts of the case rather than motivated by unreasonable aversion to his child's mate. A father who advises his daughter to leave her husband because he beats her would probably be held to have acted reasonably and could not be sued for alienating his daughter's affections from her husband.

Lawyers and other people to whom matrimonial problems are taken are increasingly appalled by the number of marital split-ups engineered, or at least fostered, by interfering in-laws, especially mothers-in-law. One busy practitioner recently remarked that the greatest single cause of divorce is not adultery nor cruelty nor any of the other conventional "grounds" but rather the in-law problem—parents who are unwilling to let go of their children; children who don't want to grow up. But this type of interference with the marriage relation cannot, except in very rare cases, and should not be made the basis for a suit for an injunction or an action for damages. In the first place, the interference is usually so subtle and unobjectionable in and of itself (just—"Oh my poor daughter, when I think of the men you could have married!" for example) that the difficulties of proof would be insuperable. Furthermore, we have some regard as a society for the natural concern of parents for children. In any event we believe in freedom of speech even in family relations. The solution would seem to be, not legal action, but rather greater availability of pre- and post-marriage counseling services in the direction of teaching the couple themselves how to grow up and be happy though married.

In some states a wife cannot bring a suit for alienation of affections unless her husband has committed adultery with the "other" woman involved—rarely a possibility when the "other" woman" is his mother as in reality she so often is. In most states, however, both husband and wife can sue for alienation of affections even if the element of adultery is not present.

In a number of states the commission of adultery gives rise to a further action called a suit for "criminal conversation." Some states permit only the husband to bring this kind of suit on the ground that, historically, the basis of action is the possibility that the husband will, as a result of his wife's adultery, have spurious offspring foisted on him. Elsewhere, the theory of the action seems to be the destruction of the exclusiveness of the sexual relation, and where that is the theory, the wife may also bring suit since she, too, is entitled to be her spouse's only sexual partner. One court justified permitting the wife to bring suit by pointing out that, while she had nothing to fear from her husband's adultery in terms of having an illegitimate child forced upon her, she did have a different but equally weighty concern arising from the possibility of her husband's becoming infected with a venereal disease which would endanger her health and that of their children. Arguably, too, the husband's adultery might result in his having children by someone other than his wife which might well dilute his resources as well as his interest in his legal family.

As in alienation-of-affections suits, it is not necessary by way of prerequisite to a suit for criminal conversation that the couple be estranged or separated as a result of the adultery. Neither is whether they were in the habit of having sexual intercourse with each other a relevant consideration. Nor does it matter whether it was the derelict spouse or the third party who was the aggressor in the adulterous relationship. As has been stated, the civil action for criminal conversation has been abolished in a number of states along with actions for breach of promise, alienation of affections, etc. But even in such states, adultery may continue to be a crime punishable by fine and imprisonment at the instigation of the state. (See Chapter 14.)

The relationship between husband and wife is a confidential one which the law tries to protect in two ways—by prohibiting husband and wife from testifying against each other in certain cases and by preventing either from revealing confidential communications made during the marriage.

One of the most important aspects of the husband-wife relationship is its confidential character. Underlying our law here is the premise that husband and wife should feel free to "tell each other everything" without risking the possibility of a more general disclosure. In support of this theory, communications between spouses are regarded by the law as "confidential."

The rule which prevents spouses from testifying against each other has an interesting origin. Even at the early common law, husbands and wives were not permitted to testify for or against each other in a court proceeding. This rule, however, does not owe its origin to a recognition of the need for freedom of confidence in marriage but stems rather from the fact that at common law husband and wife were in many ways literally regarded as one person. It followed that one person could not testify either for or against himself; if the testimony was favorable, it would be self-serving and repetitious to permit the spouse to confirm what his alter ego had said. If the testimony was unfavorable, it would be like permitting a schizophrenic witness to testify both for and against himself. The rule persisted long after the law in other respects had begun to regard husband and wife as two separate individuals. Its justification then shifted to the theory that family harmony would be better served if spouses were not permitted to testify for or against each other. However, considerable question was raised as to whether the rule did not on occasion unduly impede the proper administration of justice, particularly in cases where the wife's testimony would help the husband if she were permitted to give it.

Today husband and wife are, for the most part, free to testify for and against each other in civil but not in criminal cases. An exception is made from the general prohibition when the crime for which the spouse is being tried is a crime against the spouse whose testimony is sought to be introduced, such as an assault and battery by a husband on a wife. Occasionally, this limitation can have rather peculiar results. In one case, a husband shot at his wife. The bullet missed her but killed the child she was holding in her arms. She was not permitted to testify when her husband was tried for the murder of the child on the ground that the crime for which he was being tried was not a crime against her.

While one spouse is today not ordinarily prohibited from testifying against the other in noncriminal cases, no such testimony may be given in any kind of case if it involves the disclosure of a "confidential communication." For example, Lewis tells his wife Lila that he has succeeded in tricking his business partner out of several thousand dollars. Lila and Lewis are later divorced. Shortly thereafter Lewis's partner discovers the fraudulent transactions and brings suit against Lewis to recover the money. In court Lewis denies everything. Lila is willing to testify as to his admission to her of what he did. If this evidence were presented to a jury, it might undermine the strength of Lewis's denial and result in a verdict for the partner. Lila would not, however, be permitted to testify to the conversation between Lewis and herself because it falls into the category of what is legally

regarded as a confidential communication which can be revealed only with the consent of the other spouse. The fact
that Lewis and Lila are no longer married at the time of the
trial makes no difference. The purpose of the rule is to give
husbands and wives assurance that their confidences will be
respected no matter what happens to their marriage.

Not everything that a wife can testify to about her husband, or vice versa, is, however, deemed a confidential communication. If Lewis had boasted to a group of people, of
whom his wife was one, of his cleverness in tricking his partner, it would not be a confidential communication and Lila,
like any of the others present, could be called to testify in con-
tradiction of Lewis's stand at the trial. Similarly, some cases
have held that a crime committed in the presence of the
spouse is not a confidential communication nor is profane language or abuse of the other spouse.

Some authorities have queried whether this careful preservation of the sanctity of marital confidence is really worth
the impediment to justice which sometimes results from not
permitting the testimony of the spouse. They argue that practically nobody outside the legal profession knows about the
protection which the law gives to confidential communications between husband and wife so that it is hardly likely
that the rule is doing much to promote a feeling of security
among married people generally. While, however, the general population may not be aware that there is a specific legal
rule which protects confidential communications between husband and wife, the rule has without doubt left its imprint on
our society's way of doing things. In these days of the disintegrating family, we may well conclude that whatever legal
doctrines tend to foster a sense of unity and trust between
husband and wife will, in the long run, do more to prevent
wrongdoing than the abandonment of such doctrines would
help detect and punish it.

CHAPTER 5

Husbands and Wives:

THE PROPERTY SIDE

*I*T IS sometimes difficult to say whether our marriage mores have changed because of the developments in the economic relationship of man and wife or whether the reverse is true. The law relating to family money matters has changed drastically in the United States during the last hundred years and continues to be in flux. Under the English common law, from which our early laws stemmed, a married woman had no right to hold property of her own. Her husband on marriage acquired rights in her real estate which prevented her from selling or otherwise disposing of it. Her personal property (and this term includes money) was subject to her husband's complete control. The husband was not only entitled to his wife's services in his home and in his own business but had an absolute right to claim her earnings if she worked for another. His right to his wife's property and earnings was not vitiated even by his misconduct. A husband who deserted and refused to support his wife was as much entitled to her property as would have been the most devoted spouse.

The American colonies carried over from English law this concept of the complete subordination of the married woman to her husband, but it was not long suited to the trend of marital relationships in this country. Fairly early in the nineteenth century, the states began passing laws permitting married women to hold and control their own property. Statutes giving the wife the right to her own earnings soon followed. Today a married woman can generally exercise the same full control as a man over the property which she inherits or otherwise acquires before or after marriage. Her property cannot be attached by her husband's creditors or used by him without her consent.

A special situation, of course, exists in those states where property acquired by either spouse (except such as is inherited, received as a gift or purchased by one spouse with funds which were his own) is deemed to belong equally to both of them. This situation exists in the handful of states which have community property laws. In one sense, the community property laws make an almost full swing of the pendulum. At common law, the husband became the full owner of his wife's property. In community property jurisdictions, the wife, who is ordinarily not the spouse responsible for the acquisition of property during the marriage since she is not usually the wage earner, becomes in effect the equal owner of the property yielded by her husband's labor during the marriage.

Even in noncommunity property states, separate ownership of property as between husband and wife may be obscured where the spouse in whose hands the property nominally is, received it from the other spouse. If a husband gives his wife a pearl necklace for Christmas, the necklace would be generally considered her sole property. But sometimes gifts between husband and wife are made with the intent that the one receiving the gift is to be only the nominal owner and is not to use the property except as the donor instructs. For example: Leonard transfers his stocks and a large bank account to his wife, Eloise, because his business is on the verge of bankruptcy and he does not want his creditors to attach this property. This gift was obviously made to defraud creditors, and courts generally will set aside such transfers and treat the property as if it were still Leonard's. Occasionally such a transfer will also backfire in another direction. A man who has given his property to his wife to hold for him may find that his wife claims that it was an absolute gift and refuses to give it back to him. In this situation the court will look at all the circumstances to decide what the intentions of the parties were at the time the property was transferred.

In one case Charles deposited $1500 in a bank account in the name of his wife, Lucy. Charles, Lucy and their son managed to run the money up into a sizeable sum by investing it in a little business. With prosperity came dissension and the couple ended up in court to determine which one of them was entitled to the money and its earnings. Lucy proved that at the time Charles opened the account for her, she had the bankbook and was the only person who could withdraw money from the account. These, the court said, were indications that the money was an absolute gift to Lucy and that Charles had given it to her to do with as she wished. There was some evidence that the whole transaction was motivated by Charles's desire to keep the money free of the claims of his creditors but the court gave short shrift to this aspect of the case by saying that if this were true, Charles as a wrongdoer could not come into court and ask judicial help to save himself from the effects of his own fraud. In many cases, however, courts do consider the husband entitled to the return of money which he gave his wife to hold for him no matter what his motivation.

In the reverse situation where the wife gives her property to her husband, the courts tend, in the absence of strong evidence to the contrary, to assume that it was given to the husband to invest or care for, not to use for his own purposes. The particular circumstances of the case as well as the nature of the property involved are relevant in deciding whether the husband is merely holding as trustee or whether the property is his. Generally the larger the property the more the courts tend to assume that there was no absolute transfer. Thus, if Jean inherited $5000 from her father and gave her husband, Henry, $300, a court would be more likely to presume it was a gift than if she give him the entire inheritance.

Nominal transfers from husband to wife or vice versa are apt to be less common in the future than they have been in the past because of recent developments in our tax laws. Until now, husbands would not infrequently transfer a substantial amount of their income producing property to their wives. The result would be that instead of the husband's paying taxes on, say, a $15,000 income, he would pay a lower rate on perhaps $8000 and his wife would pay tax on the remaining $7000 income which flowed to her from securities which her husband had given to her. Since the federal law now permits husband and wife to split their income between them for tax purposes no matter which one of them actually receives it, gifts from husband to wife generally no longer serve any income tax purpose.

A husband must support his wife regardless of whether she has property or earnings of her own. This is considered so essential an element of marriage that the courts will not enforce any agreement between the husband and wife (unless they are separated) which attempts to relieve the husband of his responsibility or to shift the duty of support to the wife. The duty to support includes the obligation to provide the the wife with "necessaries"—food, clothing, shelter, and medical care. The husband's duty cannot be fulfilled merely by providing the wife with the minimum needed for existence; he is obliged to give her what he can afford; furs, jewels and domestic servants have all been held to be "necessaries" for the wife of a fairly affluent man. If the husband fails to provide his wife with necessaries, she is entitled to use his credit to buy them for herself. Thus, if Alan, who earns $4000 a year, refused to buy his wife, Ruth, a new winter coat and Ruth buys one at a department store and has the bill sent to Alan, he will be required to pay for it. If, however, the coat which Ruth selected was a mink costing $2000 it is not likely that it would be considered a necessary for her. Similarly, if Alan could show that he had already given Ruth money for a coat or bought her one, he would not be obliged to pay for another.

In one New York case, Mrs. W. had bought and charged

some clothes at Wanamaker's. The store tried to collect from her husband. Mr. W. showed that he earned $2000 a year and was giving his wife $1500 a year to spend on necessaries. In the circumstances the court held that he was making adequate provision for his wife and was not obliged to pay any further bills incurred by her. A merchant who extends credit to a customer whom he does not know is bound to ask for proof of her authority to use her husband's credit if he wants to look to the husband for payment. Otherwise he is gambling on an unknown factor because he ordinarily has no way of telling whether or not the husband has already made adequate provision for his wife. This is, of course, a gamble which most stores usually take for practical reasons except, perhaps, where very expensive merchandise is involved.

The husband's liability to third parties who supply his wife with necessaries is based on the assumption that they are living together and the fact that the wife as manager of the household is usually authorized by her husband to do the shopping for her personal needs and for the family as a whole. Accordingly, one who supplies the wife with such necessaries as food for the family has a right, even without making specific inquiry, to expect that the husband will pay for them. This is not true, however, if the wife has, to the knowledge of the creditor, been using her own funds to make purchases from him.

A Texas case illustrates this point: Virginia had an income of her own from oil speculation. She bought a diamond pin and pendant costing $3000 from a jeweler, promising to pay for the jewels out of her next profits. The profits never materialized and the jeweler sued Virginia's husband, Joe, for the price of the jewels. Joe brought into court a bill which he had received from the jeweler shortly after the purchase of the diamonds. The bill requested payment for a lamp which Virginia had bought but did not mention the jewels. The account for the jewels was carried on the storekeeper's books in the wife's name. Under these circumstances, the court found that

Virginia had bought the jewels on her own credit and held the jeweler was not entitled to expect payment from the husband. In this case, incidentally, the court indicated that the jewels were not necessaries in the first place. While the couple owned a car and "moved in good society," the husband's total capital consisted of about $8000 worth of merchandise in his retail store. Jewels worth $3000, the court seemed to think, are not a necessity for the wife of a man in these circumstances though they might well be for the wife of a wealthier husband.

Since the right of a wife to use her husband's credit for necessaries arises out of the assumption that they are living together, one frequently sees in the newspapers notices like this: "My wife, Georgiana, having left my bed and board, I shall no longer be responsible for her debts. John Jones." This kind of notice is intended to refute the presumption that the wife has authority to use the husband's credit for necessaries. However, it will only relieve the husband of liability if the wife has in fact deserted him or is otherwise at fault. If they are separated by reason of his fault, she may still be entitled to rely on his credit for her necessaries. Some states also hold him liable if they are separated by mutual consent without either—or with both—being at fault. However, no matter what the reason for a couple's having separated, if the husband is giving the wife a reasonable amount of money pursuant to a court decree or a separation agreement, she may no longer use his credit.

In some situations, a husband is responsible for articles purchased by his wife even though the purchases are against his wishes and are of luxury items rather than necessaries. He may, for example, have so acted in the past as to make a tradesman or other person extending credit believe that the wife is authorized by him to make any purchases she wishes. Take the case of Alma who is in the habit of buying her hats at Madame Mimi's. Her husband, George, after paying several bills sent by Madame Mimi, becomes angry at the high prices Alma is paying for her hats and orders her to buy her millinery thereafter at Field's bargain basement. Alma listens agreeably but proceeds to go back to Madame Mimi's for her spring bonnet. Madame Mimi sends George a bill for thirty dollars and he refuses to pay. It is irrelevant whether the hat is a necessary or not under these circumstances. Since George had previously paid Madame Mimi's bills, the only way he can relieve himself of the obligation to pay further bills which Alma incurs at the same store is to inform Madame Mimi that he will not do so. Even a general notice in the newspaper to the effect that George will no longer be responsible for Alma's debts will not be sufficient unless it is actually brought to Madame Mimi's attention.

A wife whose husband fails or refuses to support her according to his means does not have as her sole recourse her right to pledge her husband's credit in order to buy necessaries. Nonsupport is a ground for legal separation and/or divorce in many states. Moreover, failure to support a wife (or children) is a criminal offense in almost every state. Two different theories animate the criminal statutes dealing with nonsupport. Under one type of law, the husband is guilty of a crime in failing to support his wife only if she is destitute or in danger of becoming a public charge. If the wife has a job or has the means with which to support herself or if her relatives or friends support her, the husband's dereliction may be the basis for a suit for separation or divorce by the wife but it is not a criminal offense. The purpose of this type of statute is primarily to relieve the state of the burden of supporting the wife; if there is no danger that the wife will become a public charge, there is no crime involved. The other group of statutes are concerned primarily with vindicating the right of every wife to have her husband make suitable provision for her. Under these statutes, a husband who fails or refuses to support his wife is guilty of a crime regardless of whether she is capable of supporting herself and of whether her relatives are willing and able to do so.

A criminal prosecution brought under such a statute in-

volved a husband, Jay, who had deserted his wife and child
after they'd been married one year. He left behind him some
horses which the wife sold to support herself and the infant.
Thereafter the wife returned to her parents' farm. They took
her in, gave her and the child a room of their own and supported them both. Moreover, the wife did some part-time
work outside of her parents' home to help pay for herself and
the child. Thanks to her own efforts and the assistance of her
parents, neither she nor the child had been in want since Jay's
desertion nor were they likely to be. Nevertheless the court
found that Jay was guilty of the crime of nonsupport. The
court emphasized that "The law is not a mere poor law. It is
a domestic duty law . . ." A husband who fails to support his
wife is guilty of a crime according to this decision even if
the wife herself or her friends or relatives are able to and do
maintain her in comfort or even luxury.

The great loophole in the support picture has always
been the ease with which husbands can move from one state
to another and effectively avoid the necessity of supporting
their families. If the wife can afford to follow the husband or
to employ legal help in his new state, the courts of the new
state will render her assistance. In most cases, this is not
economically feasible. Some states recognize failure to support as an extraditable offense; that is, the husband can be
returned to the home state by virtue of an agreement to co-
operate along these lines between the two states. Even where
extradition is legally possible, however, it is often not readily
available; it is an expensive procedure for the state and
one which law enforcement officers sometimes prefer not to invoke except where more serious crimes are involved. Recently
reciprocal abandonment laws have been adopted by most of
the states. These laws permit a husband who has deserted his
family to be prosecuted in any state in which he can be found
without the necessity of costly extradition. While these laws
are too new to be judged as yet, their proponents predict that

the disastrous effects of desertion of dependent families may be substantially diminished by them.

While the primary duty to support the family is on the husband, the wife is not free of all obligations in this regard. If the husband dies or if he fails to support the children, the wife usually becomes responsible in some measure for their support. Generally she cannot recover from her husband money which she spends for the family from her own funds, though some states do require the husband to reimburse her for money spent for the support of their children. Many states also make the wife responsible for the support of a husband in certain special circumstances as where he may otherwise become a public charge and this policy may be reflected even in alimony judgments (see Chapter 20).

In one Iowa case the wife, Jenny, was sued by her sister for a debt incurred by Jenny's husband. The husband had gone to the town where his sister-in-law lived and had asked her to take him in as a boarder for a while, agreeing to pay a specified sum for his room and board. He left without paying and the sister sued Jenny for the amount which her husband owed. The court held that she could not collect from Jenny since Jenny would only be responsible for her husband's expenses if he had had an accident away from home or had had to go away for his health or in some similar situation where he was himself incapacitated. Since the wandering spouse seemed to be in fine health, the court considered that the expenses which he incurred on his travels were not family expenses for which the wife was liable within the meaning of the statute which made both husband and wife liable for family expenses.

Under the English common law, the husband was responsible for his wife's torts; that is, for her negligent or deliberate injury of another's person or property. He was not only responsible for the wrongful acts she committed after their marriage but also for those which predated her becoming his wife.

There were actually two good reasons for this rule, a rule
which most of us would find untenable today. One was that at
common law, as we have seen, the wife could not own or control property of her own. If, therefore, she beat her neighbor
over the head in an argument, it would have been futile for
the neighbor to sue her since she had no property with which
to satisfy a judgment. Since the husband owned and controlled
his wife's property, he had to be made responsible for her
torts; otherwise all wives could have gone around committing
torts with impunity. The second rationale of this rule was the
husband's responsibility at common law for his wife's conduct.
He had the right to correct and chastise her in order to make
her behave properly. If she failed to do so, the responsibility
could be placed at her husband's door on the ground that he
had failed to discipline and control her correctly.

Obviously neither of these reasons for holding a husband
responsible for his wife's torts exists today. The old rule persists in only a few states. In at least one of them, the husband
can be forced to pay a judgment obtained against his wife
only if she lacks sufficient money or property of her own with
which to satisfy it. In a few other states, the law is unclear
as to the husband's liability. In the vast majority of states, it
is quite clear that a husband is not responsible for his wife's
torts unless he participates in them or directs or coerces her
to do them. A few jurisdictions have a presumption that the
wife is acting under the coercion of her husband if he is present
at the time she commits the wrongful act. This is something
of a hangover from the old days when the mores of marriage
were such that it could be assumed that the wife was completely subject to the domination of her husband and acted
according to his wishes and directions. In most contexts in
most states today, however, only the wife is held accountable
for the injuries which she occasions to a third party or his
property.

Thus, although there was no formal "Emancipation Proc-
lamation" for wives, the laws as to the personal and property

rights of husbands and wives have so evolved during the decades just passed that today a married woman is as much a first-class citizen in relation to her husband as he is in relation to her. Nor has this development been without its practical aspects; at the present time a large portion of the total wealth of the United States is in the hands of women, many of whom are married—a far cry from the not-so-distant day when they could not call even their clothing their own.

PART II

The Children

PART II

CHAPTER 6

Parents and Children

THE YOUNG father beaming proudly at his small wrinkled son through the nursery window is vaguely aware that the child's noisy entrance into the world has introduced wholly new elements into his life, but he is hardly likely to be fully aware of the extent of his duties and rights as a parent. From the first, the parent is apt to be aware of the fact that he has an obligation to feed and clothe the child; bills for evaporated milk and diaper service start arriving simultaneously with the cards of congratulations. But the full impact of the new relationship is not apt to be felt for some time. The birth of a child automatically sets into operation an elaborate set of laws governing its relationship with its parents. Once the child is born, the state rapidly intervenes as an ever-interested third party, a sort of superguardian which stands behind those to whom the immediate welfare of the child is entrusted.

Every child—even an illegitimate one—has two parents. This fact is not disputed by the laws of any state, but the states do differ in their viewpoint as to which parent is primarily responsible for supporting the child. Some states have ruled that both parents have equal rights with regard to the child and are equally responsible for his support. Others place the primary responsibility for support on the father, on the theory that from a practical economic viewpoint he is the one most likely to be capable of supporting a child. In the case of an illegitimate child, however, the mother is held to have the primary duty of support in some states. Even in states which place the primary duty on one parent, the other parent is not thereby relieved of all responsibility toward the child. The state will look first to the parent on whom the primary duty to support rests—usually the father—but if he is unable or, for any other reason, fails to support the child the mother must assume the duty. In some states, if she does so, she can force the father to reimburse her for the amount she expended on the child's support.

Short of the extreme step of giving out their child for formal adoption, parents cannot usually relieve themselves of the obligation to support the child. For example, Mabel Green gives birth to a child, Anne. For reasons of their own, Mabel and her husband, Steve, do not want the baby. However, Mabel's sister and brother-in-law, Eleanor and Lewis White, are childless and express themselves as willing to take the baby and bring her up as their own. The two couples enter into a written agreement whereby the Greens agree to give the Whites custody of Anne and the Whites agree to assume the full obligation for her support. In some states such an agreement is considered against public policy and the courts will ignore it completely. In others, the agreement will be enforced unless the court feels that it would be prejudicial to the child as, for example, if it could be shown that Anne could not get proper care or medical attention from the Whites. Even if the Whites abide by the agreement and do not try to make the Greens contribute to Anne's support, Anne herself is not bound by the agreement. She or someone acting for her can force her real parents to support her.

The fact that a child does not live with a parent does not relieve the parent of his responsibility to support the child even if the separation from the child is against the parent's wishes. A few states have held that if the mother leaves the father, taking the child with her, the father is no longer under an obligation to support the child. Most states, however, take the position that the wrongdoing of the mother should not be allowed to prejudice the right of a child to be supported by its father.

Food, shelter, clothing, education, and medical attention, all of which are termed "necessaries," are included in the parents' duty to support the child. The common pattern, particularly in the United States, is for parents to lavish on their children not only the best which they can afford but often more than their financial circumstances warrant. The unwanted and unloved child does, however, exist and the law insists that even a reluctant parent provide his child with at least the necessary minimum which his health and welfare require. While the amount of the parent's income is relevant in determining what he must give the child, the law will not necessarily force the parent to give the child the best he can afford. If Mr. Morganbilt, a millionaire, believes that children should be brought up simply, he is under no legal obligation to provide his children with expensive clothing, send them to private schools or provide them with a mansion and swimming pool. So long as he is providing them with adequate basic care and schooling, the law will not disturb his right as a father to decide what is best for his children. If, however, his regime of Spartan simplicity were carried to an extreme where it was endangering the children's health or preventing their proper development, his ability to provide them with better food, clothing, shelter, education or medical care would no doubt induce a court to order him to do better. Where the family is without the requisite means, the state will often step in and supplement the family income.

If a parent, although able, fails to provide his child with necessaries, he may have to reimburse someone who fulfills his duty for him. For example, Mrs. Jones, a kindly neighbor, is concerned about little Jimmy Smith who is running around in the snow with only a thin sweater and trousers and worn out shoes. She knows that the Smiths could provide the child with adequate clothing but don't because they are alcoholics and would rather spend their money on liquor than on clothing Jimmy properly. Mrs. Jones takes Jimmy to the store and buys him a new pair of shoes and a warm overcoat and cap.

She is, in many states, entitled to sue the Smiths for the amount she has spent in giving the child what they were obligated to give him. This does not mean that any busybody who feels that parents are not behaving according to his standards can run around incurring debts for a child which his parents must meet. But parents who have the means and who fail to provide at least a decent minimum for their children may have to reimburse those who do.

In some states a parent is obliged to reimburse a third party for necessaries provided for the child only if the parent *knew* of the child's need and unreasonably refused to do anything about it. In these states if Jimmy's father was in the army or out of town on business during the winter when Jimmy had no good coat or shoes, he would not be obliged to repay Mrs. Jones for what she spent on the child. In other states the fact that the parent failed to provide for his child's needs is enough to make him liable to the person who does provide, regardless of whether the parent was actually aware of the need or not. In still a third category of states a parent is under a duty to reimburse a third party who has provided for the child only in circumstances where it can be assumed that the parent would have done what the third party did if the parent had been present at the time. For example: Mrs. Adams sees eight-year-old Louise fall off her bicycle and break her arm. At the time of the accident, Louise's father is at work and her mother is downtown shopping, Mrs. Adams calls her own doctor and has him attend to Louise's arm. In any state Louise's parents would be obliged to repay Mrs. Adams for the medical care which was furnished at her request since it is assumed that they would have themselves called the doctor if they had been present at the time. Even where no emergency exists, outsiders who provide medical care for a child may be able to collect the cost of that care from the parent if the child needs it and the parents wilfully or negligently fail to give it to him. In some states the parent may also be subject to criminal prosecution for failure to provide the child with medical attention in a case where a prudent person would have called a doctor. Sometimes the parent's refusal to permit surgery to be performed on the child may make the parent guilty of criminal neglect. In one case involving the conviction of parents on such a charge, they had refused to permit the child's adenoids to be removed despite the fact that the adenoids were so badly diseased that they were causing mental dullness and deafness in the child. Where, however, an operation involves a decided hazard to the child or where the benefits to be gained from it are uncertain, the parent has wide leeway in making the decision as to whether to permit it.

Parents whose religious beliefs prohibit or discourage the use of doctors or medicines are not entitled to endanger their children's lives by failing to give them medical care where it is necessary. This is one place where the state as superguardian steps in. It has sometimes been claimed that since the federal Constitution prohibits governmental interference with the exercise of religion, no one should be forced to call in a doctor if to do so is contrary to his religious beliefs. The courts have, however, taken the position that a man may be entitled to kill himself by refusing to get medical aid but that he has no right to kill his child by such a refusal. Nor can a parent do lip service to the law requiring him to provide his child with medical care by calling in a Christian Science practitioner or other "faith healer." The law in virtually every state requires that a licensed medical practitioner be called when, by ordinary reasonable standards, the child's condition demands medical attention.

Some states permit a child (or someone acting on his behalf) to bring a civil suit against a parent who does not support him properly. In other states, such lawsuits between parent and child are discouraged on the ground that they tend to disrupt family ties. It is, of course, questionable how strong these family ties are if the parent is not even fulfilling his minimum obligation to support the child. In many states, if a parent abandons, deserts or wilfully fails to provide the

basic necessities of life for his child, the parent is, as in situations where requisite medical care is not forthcoming, subject
to criminal prosecution.

Like the criminal statutes relating to nonsupport of a
wife, the laws which make it a crime to fail to support a child
fall into two categories. In those states which are primarily
concerned with a burden on the community, the parent is
guilty of a crime only if the child is left destitute and is likely
to become dependent on charity. In states which are primarily concerned with the welfare of the child, the parent is liable
to prosecution in less extreme cases of neglect. In such state
the fact that someone else has taken on the burden of supporting the child is usually no defense for the parent whereas in
states which are primarily concerned with whether or not the
child will become a public charge, the fact that someone else
is taking care of him may free the parent from criminal responsibility.

Whatever a parent's personal hopes may be on the subject, he is not legally entitled to have his child reimburse him
for the expenses entailed in the child's upbringing. Nor can a
parent use the child's own property to defray the cost of supporting him. (We are not here talking of the child's *earnings*.)
If, for example, little Tommy Roe inherits $5000 from his
grandfather, his father cannot breathe a sigh of relief at the
windfall and take a few hundred dollars out of the inheritance
to pay for straightening Tommy's teeth. The parent is the custodian of the child's money and is expected to turn it over to
him intact when he reaches his majority. If, however, Mr. Roe
is financially unable to support Tommy, he may be permitted
to use the child's money for this purpose, but he is safe in so
doing only if he gets court permission. Otherwise the
child may, when he comes of age, sue the parent for
his money and the parent may be hard pressed to prove that
at the time he used the child's funds, his own financial condition was such that he had no alternative.

The parent's duty to educate his child has been simplified

and made less costly since the advent of the public school. It is usually fulfilled by his seeing to it that the child attends the schools provided by the state. He is under no obligation to provide the child with special lessons or to send him to private schools even if his means or the child's particular aptitudes or deficiencies seem to suggest that course. A parent is, however, free to send his children to a private or parochial school if he chooses and if the school has been approved by the state as providing a basic curriculum at least equivalent to that of the public schools. As a matter of fact, any law which forced parents to have children educated only in public school would probably be unconstitutional.

The states take different views as to whether a child may be taught at home instead of being sent to any school at all. In Virginia this can only be done if the person instructing the child meets the qualifications set by the Board of Education for teachers. In New York any "reasonably qualified" parent may instruct the child at home if it is dangerous or difficult for the child to get to school. Among the factors to be considered are: the qualifications of the parent or other person doing the teaching; whether regular hours are set aside for study; and whether the child is being taught the basic skills which are learned in school by other children of his age.

A number of cases have arisen involving Seventh Day Adventists and other religious groups who claim that their religion forbids them to send their children to public school either because the competitive spirit of public education tends to produce pugnacious children or because Bible study is not a sufficiently important part of the curriculum. One particular couple of Seventh Day Adventists were doing their best to educate their little boy at home. The state officials claimed that this was a violation of the state law which required that parents send their children either to a public school or to a private school but made no provision for individual home instruction. The court stretched a point (as courts often do) and held that this child was attending a "private school" despite the fact that he was the only student enrolled with his parents. The court further found that the child was receiving the equivalent of what he would have gotten at a regular school. His father was a college graduate and his mother had had two years of college and some training in pedagogy. Tests revealed that the child was as advanced academically as other children of his age.

A contrary result was reached in a New Jersey case. Mr. and Mrs. B., for reasons which do not appear in the records of the case, took their two little boys out of public school and gave them lessons at home. The court took exception to the qualifications of the parents as teachers, to the irregularity of the boys' school hours and to the calibre of instruction. But the most interesting part of the court's written opinion is the emphasis laid by the judge on an important factor, unrelated to the parents' methods or qualifications, which the court felt prevented the parents from giving the children the "equivalent" of a school education. The court pointed out that the parents "cannot provide for group or class teaching and lack the ability to develop attitudes and create a social setting so that the children may be trained to deal with their playmates and friends as part of a social group," while the schools, on the other hand, stressed "the adjustment of the child to group life and group activity." The court expressed serious doubt as to whether any parent in a cosmopolitan area could give his child the equivalent of what the schools teach in terms of living, playing, and working with other children. There is no doubt that this stress on social adjustment represents the trend in modern education. It may well be that in years to come the courts will be increasingly reluctant to view any home instruction as the equivalent of school attendance unless the parents are unusually ingenious in providing regular opportunities for their children to mingle and work with groups of children. If a child is physically handicapped or mentally retarded, of course, the courts are much more lenient about permitting home instruction.

A parent is usually obliged to permit the child to continue his education until he has either reached a given age or completed the work of a specified grade set by statute; for example, until he is sixteen or has finished high school, whichever comes first. A child, however, is not entitled as a matter of right to compel his parents to send him to college, professional or vocational schools even if they can well afford to do so. As a practical matter, the child of divorced parents may have a better chance of inducing the courts to order his father to provide him with funds for college than a child whose parents are living together would have. The reluctance of courts to interfere with parent-child relationships is less strong where there is already a broken home and where the court has already ruled on or approved of the quantum of support which the father (or mother) must provide for the child.

While parents are in general legally responsible for their child's behavior, the law does not make them absolute guarantors of his good conduct. If Billy Brown and Mickey White get into a fist fight and Billy knocks out two of Mickey's teeth, Billy's father does not have to pay Mickey's dental bills. This is true even though Billy may have previously provoked a fight with Mickey, and it might have been expected that unless drastically restrained he was likely to do so again. As one authority neatly summarized the law: a dog may be entitled to only one bite, but a child may have several. As a practical matter, it is impossible for a parent by any means short of incarceration or constant supervision to prevent his child from ever injuring another.

It is presumed that a parent in giving his child instructions or advice means him to proceed in a lawful manner. If the child violates the law in following advice which could have been lawfully heeded, the parent is not liable unless he clearly advised or authorized the child to commit the unlawful act. Where a father had advised his son to acquire sexual experience before marriage (presumably in a state where fornication is not a crime), the father was not held responsible for the son's going out and committing rape. If a mother sends her daughter to the store for apples and the daughter decides to surprise her mother by saving some money and steals the apples instead, the mother is not herself considered legally culpable. If, however, a parent has expressly or by implication consented to the acts of his child which give rise to injury, he will be held liable for those acts. If, for example, Billy's father had seen the beginning of the scrap with Mickey and had encouraged it by yelling to Billy, "Slug him, kid. Hit him with your fist," he might have to pay for his paternal pride in Billy's prowess by reimbursing Mickey's parents for Mickey's medical expenses.

A parent is also responsible for what his child does when acting under the parent's instructions and he may be held liable for damage by the child when the child is doing work for him even though the parent did not contemplate or authorize the child to do the damage. For example: Mr. Doakes instructs his son, Teddy, to burn the leaves in the back yard. While Teddy is doing so, the fire gets out of control, spreads to the adjoining property and burns down valuable fruit trees belonging to the Doakes's neighbors. Mr. Doakes must pay for the damage because Teddy caused it while acting as his father's agent in burning the leaves.

Where, on the other hand, a child who has been sent on an errand or asked to do some work for his parents takes the opportunity to do some mischief of his own, he is no longer acting as his parents' agent and they may not be called to account for the harm he does. Thus, if Teddy gets bored with the small bonfire of leaves and decides to pass the time by seeing whether he can set the neighbor's cherry tree on fire by pitching burning sticks at it, the law considers that he has abandoned the job he was doing for his father. The result would be different in a situation where the parent, although he did not authorize the child to do the act that caused the damage, is or should have been aware that the child was about to do something that would be injurious and does nothing to restrain the child. Thus a father who sees his child packing rocks into snowballs to pitch at passersby cannot just chuckle nostalgically over the mischievous pranks of boyhood and go on his way. He is under a duty to stop the child. If he does not, any injury which the child causes a passerby is deemed to be done with the consent of the parent and he is accordingly responsible for the damage done.

In like manner a parent who has entrusted his child with a dangerous instrument may be responsible for damage which the child does with it if the parent has not exercised sufficient care in letting the child use the instrument. The liability of a father who gives his fourteen-year-old son a shotgun with which the child accidentally shoots a playmate will depend on the answers to such questions as: Did the father instruct the boy in how to handle the gun and give him adequate information on safety measures? Had the father prohibited the boy from firing the gun except on a shooting range, in the woods or other appropriate places? Did the father have reason to know that the child was careless or not capable of handling the gun properly? If the answers to these and similar questions indicate that the parent exercised due care in permitting the boy to have the gun, he is not responsible for the injuries caused by the boy. If, on the other hand, the child's youth, the nature of the neighborhood in which the family lives, or the child's own carelessness or inability to handle the gun would have warned a reasonably careful man that he was likely to cause damage, the father is responsible for the use to which his son puts the instrument.

The "dangerous instrument" which is likely to cause most trouble in the average American family is the automobile. A child who has been instructed by his parent to drive to town for groceries or to drive the parent's delivery truck is acting as his parent's agent and the parent is responsible for any injury to people or property which the child causes even though the child may be a skilled, licensed driver. This is the general theory, not confined to parent and child cases, that a principal is

legally accountable for acts done by his agent in the course
of the agent's carrying out the job assigned to him. Liability
is also imposed (but on a different theory) when the parent
who knows or should have known that his son is not a competent driver permits the boy to drive the family car for his
own amusement. Here the basis for the liability is the negligence of the father in permitting the son to drive at all. A
somewhat tougher problem is presented where the child is a
careful and competent driver and his father permits him to
drive the family car. Many states have developed what is
known as the "family purpose doctrine" to cover this situation.
The doctrine is to the effect that when a car is kept for the
general convenience and pleasure of the family, a child who
drives it is using it for the purpose for which it was intended
and is therefore to be considered his father's agent. The doctrine is not applicable where the parent has expressly forbidden the child to use the car. There is a split of authority as to
whether it is applicable where the child is using the car
purely for his own purposes as, for example, where a boy uses
the family car to pick up his date and take her driving. Some
states hold that the child's social activities are part of the general pleasure purposes for which a family car is maintained;
others take a contrary view.

Harried parents who have cringed through this enumera-
tion of their duties and liabilities are now invited to perk up
and bask in the assurance that parents, too, have *rights*. For one
thing (though the father who diligently pays out fifty cents
every time he wants his son to mow the lawn will not believe
it) a parent is entitled to the services of his minor children without being obliged to pay for them. This includes not
only the performance of some household tasks but also assistance in the father's business. Moreover, the parents are entitled
to all of the money which a minor child earns by working for
strangers. In some states, if the parent requests it, the employer is obliged to pay over the child's wages directly to the

parent. Sometimes if a minor is employed without the knowledge or consent of his parents, the employer may be forced to pay the parent the amount of the child's wages even if he has already paid the child. Where a parent finds that, without his knowledge, his child has performed work for another at a salary which the parent considers inadequate, the parent may be entitled to sue the employer for the reasonable value of the services which the child performed. The right of the parent to a minor child's earnings is so strong that in many cases the child's earnings can be taken by the father's creditors to satisfy the father's debts.

The parent's right to the child's services and earnings is correlative to the parent's duty to support. Ordinarily the parent on whom the state places the primary duty to support is the one who is entitled to the child's earnings. A parent who has failed to perform his duty of supporting the child (by abandoning him, for example) forfeits his right to claim the benefits of parenthood.

Because parents have a right to the services and earnings of their minor children, they are entitled to collect damages from anyone who maliciously or negligently injures a child so as to deprive the parents of his services. If, for example, twelve-year-old Alice is injured in an automobile accident, the driver whose negligence caused the accident has a twofold liability. Suit may be brought on behalf of Alice herself to compensate her for the pain and suffering caused by the accident and also for any permanent injury which has been done her. Simultaneously, Alice's father may sue the driver, not only for the medical expenses incurred in treating Alice's injuries, but also for the pecuniary damage suffered by her father from the loss of her services or earnings. Perhaps Alice has regularly helped her mother around the house and also earned four dollars a week by baby-sitting for neighbors. In that case her father is entitled to collect the reasonable value of her services around the house and the earnings which she lost during the period when she was incapacitated. Where the child is too young to work or perform any services, the parents can, of course, collect medical expenses in any event.

Ordinarily a parent cannot sue for the mental suffering caused him by an injury done to his child, though where such an injury is deliberate, it might be argued that even punitive damages should be imposed. Consider the action brought by a widow, Margaret T., who sued a druggist for selling her eighteen-year-old son large quantities of heroin, thereby causing him to become a drug addict. The court held that Mrs. T. was entitled to collect from the druggist her pecuniary losses resulting from her son's becoming unable to work or help her in any way; he had even pawned his mother's furniture in order to buy more heroin. But the court held that the druggist could not be made to pay for the anguish which his unscrupulous conduct had caused the mother since a parent's unhappiness is only recognized as a basis for damages in one type of case—the seduction of a minor child. It may well be queried whether seduction is the most horrendous crime which can be committed on a child from the parents' viewpoint or whether they might not suffer at least as much from seeing their child turned into a dope addict. Be that as it may, seduction is usually the only offense against the child which entitles the parents to recover for their mental suffering as well as for actual pecuniary loss.

Parenthood also carries with it the right to discipline the child but this right has been substantially curtailed in modern law. There was a time when a father had the absolute power of life and death over his child. Today that superguardian, the state, steps in here too, to limit the parent's right to punish the child to what is reasonably necessary for the child's welfare. Where a parent behaves cruelly, it is usually presumed that he was not acting for the child's welfare but to satisfy what one authority calls his own "evil passion." In most jurisdictions a parent is criminally liable if he abuses his power and injures his child. In a few states, he is only liable if he hurts the child maliciously or causes permanent injury to him, but even in these jurisdictions there is a tendency to impute malice to the parent if he causes the child serious injury.

Even where, however, a criminal action can be instituted against a parent who hurts his child, the law does not usually permit the child himself to sue his parent. If necessary, the child will be taken from his parents' custody if he has been cruelly treated. So long as the family unit remains intact, the public policy in most states frowns on suits by child against parent. The disability extends not only to the case where the parent has done the child a deliberate wrong, but also to instances of the child's being hurt through the parents' negligence. If, for example, Mr. Barnes is driving a car in which his son, George, is a passenger and has an accident, George has no right to sue his father for his injuries even though Mr. Barnes may have been negligent. The converse is also true: Mr. Barnes couldn't sue George either if George had been driving.

If Mr. Barnes carries liability insurance George may be permitted to sue on the theory that since the parent will not be paying the damages, there is no danger of inducing family disharmony. Other states take the position that the function of an insurer is to pay damages which the insured would have had to pay had there been no insurance. They hold that the fortuitous fact that the parent carries insurance should not create a liability where none would otherwise have existed. These states are also concerned with the possibility of the parent and the child getting together on a fraudulent scheme to collect from the insurance company. Mr. Barnes might say that the accident was his fault even though it was not in the hope that the insurance company would thereby be induced or forced to pay George damages.

A parent does, however, have the right to protect his child from injury by a third party. Just as a man is justified in injuring another in defense of himself, he is similarly exonerated from fault if he injures someone who is attacking his child.

He is not, however, permitted to use more force than is necessary. He may not shoot a man when just pushing him aside would prevent the threatened injury to the child. Nor can a parent assault another in revenge for injury done the child; his right is limited to what is necessary in order to avert injury to the child, not to avenge harm already done. If Mr. Smith comes home from work one night and is told by his small son Bobby that Mr. Jones, their disagreeable next-door neighbor, hit him, Mr. Smith may not proceed to Mr. Jones's house and forthwith lay him low. Since such action is not for the immediate protection of the child Mr. Smith's proper course is to report the assault on his child to the police authorities and to let them handle the situation from there on.

A parent is ordinarily entitled to the custody and company of his minor child as well as to such material benefits as his services and earnings. He has, therefore, a right to sue anyone who wrongfully induces the child to leave home. Nor does the child have the right to leave home before his majority without his parents' consent. In a Louisiana case, for example, a seventeen-year-old girl left home and entered a convent. Her father was granted a writ of habeas corpus for her immediate release.

Theoretically, the child, too, has a right to the company and companionship of his parents. Recently in some jurisdictions this right has been upheld in somewhat questionable contexts as in the following case: Theodore on behalf of his infant children, Charles and Robert, who were respectively two and four years old, brought suit against Lawrence. The gist of the children's suit was that they had always had a happy home and the loving care of both parents until Lawrence, in the guise of a family friend, had intruded himself in the household and enticed their mother, Mabel, to leave them. The parents, Theodore and Mabel, were subsequently divorced and custody of Charles and Robert was awarded to Theodore. "We have," said the children in effect, "been deprived by Lawrence's wrongful conduct of the affection and companionship of our mother and Lawrence should be forced to pay us damages to compensate for our loss." The court held that the children had a good cause of action against Lawrence despite the fact that the particular state whose law was involved had previously passed a statute outlawing suits for alienation of affections. Theodore was permitted on behalf of his children to press the very claim for alienation of affections which he could not have asserted on his own behalf.

There is scant doubt that states which have barred suits for alienation of affection by husbands and wives would also have ruled out such suits by children had the question been called to the attention of the legislature. The fact is that actions on behalf of children for alienation of affections are a new phenomenon and represent a way around the laws outlawing such suits by their parents. For the most part, the state legislatures have not attempted to cope with the problem, and the courts have split as to whether such actions should or should not be entertained. Some courts have refused to let children sue on an alienation of affections theory. Others have held (as in the case discussed) that unless there is a specific statute barring such suits, the children may sue the person who is, on the surface at least, the cause for their being deprived of the companionship of one of their parents. Such a suit may be a satisfying form of revenge for the parent who considers himself injured but it is dubious whether it is of any advantage to a child. On the contrary, such an action might well tend to drive the parents further apart and effectively ruin any chance the children might otherwise have of a friendly relationship with both of their parents despite their separation or divorce. Children of a broken home benefit in direct ratio to the amicability which prevails between their parents; it is this which the law should encourage rather than retaliatory lawsuits.

The interlocking rights and duties of parent and child do not last forever. For the most part, they are terminated when the child reaches his majority or before that if the child has been "emancipated." Emancipation means actions on the part of parent or child, or both, which are inconsistent with a continuation of the legal status of parent and child in terms of the parent's duty to support, his right to the child's services, and so on. The marriage of a child is an emancipation in this sense. His enlisting or being drafted into the army likewise frees him from parental control. Occasionally a child may be emancipated by an agreement with his parent that he may leave home and use his own earnings to support himself. There can even be emancipation if the child continues to live at home where it is understood that the child is free to earn and use his own money and will not look to the parents for support. Or a child can be partially emancipated in the sense that his parents have agreed that he is to be financially self-supporting but that he will continue to live with them and that they will continue to exercise parental control over him. Emancipation is, of course, not possible in the case of a child who is physically or mentally incapacitated. In such a case, so long as the child stays at home and is not institutionalized, the rights and duties of his parents continue even though the child may have passed his majority.

There are two exceptions to the general rule that reaching majority or emancipation terminates the parent-child relationship as far as legal consequences are concerned. Many states provide by statute that a child is responsible for the support of an indigent parent and vice versa. Secondly, the right of parents and children to inherit from each other in the absence of a Will (discussed in Chapter 10) is not abrogated by either majority or emancipation. With these exceptions, once a child reaches the age of twenty-one (or if he is emancipated before that time), he and his parents are in the same legal position vis-a-vis each other as any other adults would be.

From there on, the incidents of their relationship depend not at all on that superguardian, the law, but derive from the love and affection they bear each other and from whatever feelings of obligation they may entertain. Where the parent has done his job well, where there is a satisfactory relationship between parent and child, the chances are that neither will be aware that there is any difference of rights and duties before and after twenty-one. The law can insist on certain minima of family behavior. Only the people on whom the law operates can create happy families.

CHAPTER 7

The Illegitimate Child

*T*HE CHILD born out of wedlock was once known as *"filius nullius"*—the child of no one. During the Middle Ages, the wrath of society seemed directed less against the people who engaged in extramarital intercourse than against the unfortunate children who were the results of the affair. At one time a bastard was considered incapable of taking holy orders or holding any other position in the church. In Germany, the irregularity of his birth made him ineligible to give testimony in court affecting the rights of people born "on the right side of the sheets" or even to earn a university degree. In Scotland a person born out of wedlock could not leave property by Will. The English law, from which our own stems, at one time considered the bastard so completely outside the pale that neither of his parents was bound to support him and neither had the right to his custody or services. One of the first advances toward justice for children born out of wedlock was inspired, not by concern for the children, but by concern for the public money. In the sixteenth century the English law put the duty of supporting children born out of wedlock on both parents in order to take the burden off the parish.

For the most part the American law has indicated a slow but steady advance towards the idea that the sins of the parents should not be visited upon the children. Some few states have gone so far as to eliminate the concept of illegitimacy entirely by ruling that every child is the legitimate child of its natural parents. In others a child born out of wedlock is considered the legitimate child of its mother. In most states a child who is conceived or born out of wedlock is legitimized by the subsequent marriage of its parents. In a few states, if the father is already married but takes his illegitimate child into his own household with the consent of his wife, the child becomes the legitimate child of the father for all purposes. A child who is legitimate as to one or both parents stands in the same position with regard to such parent or parents as a child conceived in wedlock.

Proof of paternity is often prerequisite to establishing the legitimacy of the child vis-à-vis the father or, in states not having the kind of laws discussed above, in order to force the father to contribute to the support of the child. In most states, the father of an illegitimate child can be forced in a semicriminal action to support the child even though the law does not give the child the other rights which a legitimate child may have in relation to its father such as the right to inherit. The maximum amount which a man may be forced to pay for the support of his illegitimate child has been fixed by statute in some states at standards far below the obligation of a father to a legitimate child.

In Florida, for example, even a wealthy man cannot be forced to contribute more than fifty dollars a year for the first ten years of his child's life and need give nothing thereafter. Even in the states which do not prescribe a maximum, the level of support is not likely to be high. Judge Morris Ploscowe, in his book, *Sex and the Law*, recently reported that the average support order in New York City was between four and five dollars a week, substantially less than the twelve dollars a week which the Welfare Department considers the minimum needed for the decent support of a child.

An action to establish that a particular man is the father of a child born out of wedlock is sometimes called a filiation action and sometimes a bastardy proceeding. In recent years, blood grouping tests have become increasingly important in disproving false paternity claims. While there are a variety of blood grouping tests, all are based on the principle that a child inherits certain characteristics of his blood from one or both of his parents. One of the tests, for example, utilizes two blood characteristics known as M and N, one or both being present in the blood of each person. By comparing the blood group of the child with that of the mother and the putative father, it is sometimes possible to determine conclusively that a man charged with paternity could not be the father of the particular child involved.

For example, Enid claims that George is the father of her baby. Blood tests reveal that Enid has type N blood, George has type N and the baby has type MN. Assuming that there is no question as to whether Enid is the baby's mother, obviously George cannot be the baby's father. The father must have been someone through whom the baby could have gotten type M blood. If the child had type N (without the M), the test would not be proof one way or another; it would indicate only that an N factor had come from each parent, and therefore that the man George *could* have been the father. It would not decisively prove that he was the father since many men have type N blood. Thus, while this kind of test cannot prove conclusively that a man is the father of a certain child, it may in some cases prove that he could not be.

The states vary in their attitudes on blood typing tests in filiation proceedings from complete acceptance to complete rejection. In a few states the man named as the father has the right to demand that blood tests be taken. In other states the court may order the tests at its discretion. Some will not order such tests unless all parties agree. In still other states the results of the tests are only admissible as evidence if they prove the accused man *could not* have been the father; it is feared that if the tests prove that he could have been, a jury might misinterpret them and jump to the conclusion that since the man *could* have been the father he was in fact the father.

Scientists believe that the courts in many jurisdictions have given less weight to the tests than they warrant. Cases are not unknown where the blood typing tests have said that the child could not have been the offspring of the defendant but the jury has found nonetheless that the defendant was the father. The trend, however, appears to be in the direction of heeding the tests where they give a definite answer. Thus, in a recent Maine case, a girl, Helen, gave birth to twins eight months after having intercourse with Kenneth whom she claimed to be the father. Blood tests taken of Helen, Kenneth, and the two babies proved that Kenneth could have been the father of one of the children, but could not have been the father of the other. The jury ignored the results of the tests and ruled that he was the father of both. The Supreme Court of Maine reversed the verdict, pointing out that twins must have the same father and if Kenneth were not the father of one, he could not have been the father of the other. The Court went on to say that if blood tests prove a man could not be the father of a child, they are conclusive unless it is claimed that the tests were not correctly made.

No doubt, as the inevitable lag between law and science lessens in relation to blood tests, other courts will follow Maine in ruling that if the test indicates that the putative father could not have actually been the father, the case is to be dismissed. It is believed that a combination of several reliable blood tests could dispose of about half of all false claims of paternity.

In states which do not accept the results of blood tests as evidence in any event, and in cases where the test is inconclusive, that is, where the test indicates merely that the defendant *could* have been the father, other types of evidence are permissible to prove paternity. Obviously the essential thing to prove is that the mother and the putative father had intercourse at about the time when the child was conceived. Sometimes a man who denies his paternity can prove that the mother also had intercourse with other men at about the time of conception. It is not enough for him to show that the mother had at *some* time had other affairs or that she was dating other men around the time of conception. Ordinarily the courts will exclude evidence which has the effect merely of showing that the woman was not chaste in general but which has no direct bearing on the paternity of the child in question. Proof, however, that the mother had intercourse with other men around the time the child was conceived may relieve the putative father of liability by making it impossible to ascertain with any degree of certainty that the child is his.

The claim that a particular man is the father of the child can be bolstered by showing that he has acted as if the child were his. For example: Marjorie claims that Alvin, a married man, is the father of her five-year-old child. Alvin denies it. Marjorie proves that Alvin paid her confinement expenses, visited her and the child frequently for the first year of the child's life and contributed money for the child's support. Unless Alvin can produce strong evidence proving that he was acting out of the kindness of his heart as a platonic friend, a jury is pretty apt to interpret his actions as an admission that he is the father of the child.

A few states permit the resemblance or lack of resemblance between putative father and child to be offered as evidence. It is doubtful whether physical resemblance is ever a very reliable kind of proof as anyone knows who has seen two sets of grandparents each claiming that a grandchild resembles *their* side of the family. Recognizing the hazards of this kind of evidence, many courts restrict offering proof of resemblance to cases where there is a distinct family trait which has been passed on; for example, a characteristic deformity of the earlobe present in both the putative father's family and in the child. In any event, courts tend to admit resemblance evidence only where the child involved is sufficiently grown to have distinctive features.

A married woman is apt to have a peculiarly difficult time in proving that a man other than her husband is the father of a child. Likewise a husband who suspects or even one who is certain that he is not the father of a child his wife has borne may be foreclosed from disclaiming responsibility for the child. This is because the law raises a strong presumption that a child born to a married woman is the child of her husband. In some cases, this presumption can be rebutted by presenting evidence that the husband could not have been the father—by proving, for example, that he is sterile. In other cases the presumption may be irrefutable. Many states will not allow either a husband or wife to testify that there was "nonaccess," that is, that they did not have intercourse around the time of conception.

A California case illustrates the limitations which the law places on a spouse's right to claim that a child is not legitimate. In this case, Diana and Roland moved to California a few years after their marriage. En route they met and became friendly with Robert. After the couple had settled in San Francisco, Robert came and lived with them for many years. During this time, Diana gave birth to three children. Eventually Robert died, leaving a fairly sizable estate. Two of Diana's children claimed an interest in his estate on the ground that they were Robert's children, not Roland's. Diana tried to testify on behalf of the two children. She claimed that she had not had intercourse with her husband, Roland, for many years, that she and Robert shared a room with her husband's knowledge and agreement and that two of her children were the result of this rather unusual arrangement and hence entitled to share in Robert's estate as his children. The court refused to permit her to testify to any of this, ruling that since she and her husband had been living in the same house at the time the children were conceived, unless it could be shown that her husband was impotent, there was an irrebuttable presumption that the children were his.

Not all states follow California in ruling that if husband and wife live in the same house, there is an irrebuttable presumption that the wife's children are legitimate offspring of the husband. Even where the presumption is open to challenge, however, it is difficult to challenge in many states because of the rule that neither husband nor wife may testify as to nonaccess. However, the fact that the child is not the husband's may be shown by proof that the husband is impotent or sterile. Sometimes it can be shown by the testimony of third parties that the husband and wife were living apart at the time of conception or that they saw each other only under circumstances which made it highly improbable that they had intercourse. In some states, the results of blood typing tests are admissible to show that the husband could not have been the father of the child; in other states the use of such tests is restricted to filiation proceedings, that is, where the purpose is to establish paternity not to disavow it.

The child born to an unmarried woman or fathered by a man other than his mother's husband has different rights depending on where he is lucky enough to be born or where his parents reside. Probably the most unnecessary cruelty still imposed on illegitimate children by our laws inheres in our outmoded method of keeping birth records. In some states the fact that a child is illegitimate expressly appears on his birth record and actually or potentially follows him throughout his life. Birth records are generally available to anyone who wants to look at them. Moreover, birth certificates must usually be presented when a child enters school and in connection with application for a passport, for insurance and, in many instances, for a job. The result is that many a mother who has gone to considerable sacrifice to keep her illegitimate child rather than give it out for adoption has whatever story she has invented for both their protection shattered when any situation arises in which her child's birth certificate has to be produced.

In recent years the trend has been toward protecting the child born out of wedlock from this kind of publicity. Some states have sought to remedy the situation by having all their birth certificates state simply the mother's maiden name and the name of the father without any indication as to whether the two were married. Other states require full disclosure of the facts in records which they keep sealed but issue short form certificates noting only place and date of birth without any information as to parentage or legitimacy. According to the Federal Security Agency, the only states which still include the fact of illegitimacy on the main body of the certificate are Pennsylvania, Rhode Island, Texas, and Vermont.

Ordinarily the mother of a child born out of wedlock has a right to custody of the child superior to that of the father. This is sometimes explained in terms of the mother being sure that the child is hers while the father may have doubts. Realistically, an illegitimate child is usually unwanted by both parents in the first instance. But it is more probable that the mother, who actually carries and bears the child, will develop some feeling of love for it than the father whose connection with it after the initial conception is apt to be as slight as he can possibly make it. The mother can, however, waive her right to custody by appointing a guardian for the child or by giving it up for adoption. If the child is adopted through legal channels, the mother has no further right to claim it. But where the mother merely transfers custody to another without a formal adoption, the courts will often permit her to reclaim the child.

An interesting West Virginia case involved Phyllis, the unmarried twenty-two-year-old daughter of a Southern minister, who gave birth to a baby boy in a town some distance away from her home. Her parents had not even known she was pregnant. After the birth of the child Phyllis got a job and hired a nurse to care for the baby while she was working. After several months, the nurse had to leave town and Phyllis decided to take her baby home. She was ashamed to go directly to her parents and confess that she had had a child and felt that, if her parents already knew and loved the baby, the way would be paved for her to tell them what had happened. One night she boarded a train with the baby and arrived at her parents' home in the early hours of the morning. She placed the baby in a basket outside the door and hid herself behind some trees until she saw her father discover the crying baby and take him into the house. She then went away, intending to return in a few weeks after her parents had come to love the little boy and might even be happy to hear that he was their own grandchild. Unfortunately, the romantic little plot did not work out as expected. Phyllis's parents, not knowing who the child was and apparently not eager to assume the burden of caring for a little foundling, gave the child over to some neighbors who were anxious to have a child. A few weeks later Phyllis learned what had happened, rushed back and demanded her child from the neighbors. The little boy was apparently as beguiling as his mother had thought him, judging by the fact that the neighbors refused to give him up. Phyllis brought suit for the custody of the child. The court awarded the baby to his mother, saying that although she had been guilty of foolish conduct and lack of courage in her little scheme, she had not evidenced any intent to abandon the child. The court also rejected the claim that she was morally unfit to rear him; the fact that a woman has had a child out of wedlock does not of itself render her unfit to have custody. Nor was the court moved by the fact that the neighbors were richer than Phyllis and her parents and able to give the child more material advantages.

A mother does not, however, always have the right to reclaim her child. A woman, for example, who had never shown the slightest interest in her illegitimate son until he became heir to a large amount of money was not permitted to take him away from the family with whom he had lived since birth. Sometimes if a child has been left with strangers for a considerable length of time, the courts will refuse to return him to his mother if she is a stranger to him and if the welfare of the child will be best served by leaving him where he is. Usually, however, if the mother has not completely ignored the child and if she claims him at the earliest possible moment when she is in a position to take care of him, her superior right to custody will be respected.

While the father's right to custody is usually inferior to that of the mother, it is stronger than that of any stranger. If the mother turns the child over to him, she will in most cases not be permitted to change her mind and reclaim the child. If the mother dies, the father's right to have the child is superior to that of any person including the mother's relatives to whom she may have entrusted the child. In some states, if the father of the child is already married and both he and his wife are willing to take the child, he may be given custody over the protests of the child's mother. While the child would become the legitimate heir of its father in this way and have the advantage of a more normal home life than the mother alone could ordinarily give it, it is questionable whether the best solution can be one which, against her will and desires, deprives a mother of the custody of her child. Moreover, even if the mother is unwilling or unable to keep the child herself, the child might be better off being adopted by strangers than left in the care of a woman to whom he may be a constant reminder of her husband's infidelity.

In those states in which every child is deemed to be the legitimate child of its natural parents, both parents have equal right to custody. As a practical matter, however, unless the mother is unfit or doesn't want the child, the courts will ordinarily leave a young child with her. And the fact that the child is considered the legitimate heir of its father does not in any event give the child the right to live with the father if he is already married and does not want the child.

In most states the primary duty to support an illegitimate child rests with the mother and she has the correlative right to the child's services and earnings. The father, however, can be forced to contribute to the child's support and usually to pay the mother's confinement expenses as well. In most states the fact that the father voluntarily agrees to support the child or is bound by a court decree to do so does not increase his

right to custody. In a very few states, however, the father's
support of the child can, under some circumstances, make his
right to custody superior to that of the mother.

The illegitimate child's right to inherit from his parents
and from collateral relatives varies from state to state. If the
people concerned are careful to make Wills, litigation pointing up the child's illegitimacy can usually be avoided. A few
states limit the amount which a man may leave to his illegitimate child if he has legitimate children as well. For the
most part, however, both parents can provide for the child as
they see fit in their Wills. No question as to relationship or
legitimacy need arise if the child is simply referred to by his
full name; it is not necessary that the testator specify the relationship.

If the mother or father dies without a Will the states
have different rules as to what the rights of an illegitimate child
to inherit are. In many states the child inherits from the
mother in the same way as any legitimate child. In others he
can inherit from the mother only if she has no legitimate children. On the other hand, there are some jurisdictions where
the child can inherit from both its parents regardless of
whether it was born in wedlock or not. In some few, the
child can inherit from the father only if the paternity was established during the father's lifetime as, for example, where
there has been a filiation proceeding ending in a decision that
the man was the child's father or where the father has, during
his lifetime, recognized the child as his own.

The right of an illegitimate child to inherit from his
mother's or father's relatives depends not only on the law of
the state but also sometimes on the wording of a Will and the
circumstances surrounding it. If, for example, a woman makes
a Will leaving her estate to "the children of my nephew, Bill
Stokes" and it is shown that Bill had two little boys by his wife
and a little girl by another woman of whom his aunt knew
nothing, the little girl might not be entitled to inherit under the
Will. If, on the other hand, the little girl was the only child of

Bill Stokes born at the time the Will was made, the court might assume that his aunt knew of the child's existence and wished her to share in the estate.

It is believed that the greater number of illegitimate children are given out for adoption. Once adopted, neither the stigma nor any of the attributes of illegitimacy attach to them any longer. A much smaller number of illegitimate children are legitimized by the subsequent marriage of their parents, so that they too escape the detriments that might otherwise attach. For the rest, the courts in general have tended, where possible, to give to such children the maximum protection they can accord without interfering with the security or expectancies of regularly constituted family units. From being *filius nullius,* the child of no one, the illegitimate child has to a considerable extent become the child of everyone. The twentieth century State, as such, is coming to accept the responsibility for seeing to it that such children are given the same chance as their contemporaries fortunate enough to be born to a mother and father who took the trouble to become husband and wife before they became parents.

CHAPTER 8

Artificial Insemination

THE DOCTOR looked sympathetically at the young couple sitting tensely on the other side of his desk.

"Have you considered adopting a child?" he asked gently.

The man nodded.

"We've been making the rounds of the adoption agencies the last couple of weeks," he said. "Just in case your verdict turned out to be—what it is. They weren't very encouraging. We'd have to wait two or three years for a baby. Maybe more. They say they've got eleven couples who want to adopt a child for every child they get for adoption."

"Isn't there any chance at all that we could have a baby of our own?" the woman asked.

The doctor shrugged.

"Miracles sometimes happen, but in this case, I wouldn't count on one. I've done very careful tests and they indicate that your husband's semen is so defective in number and motility that it's unlikely that you will ever conceive."

"But there's nothing wrong with my wife, is there? asked the husband. "I mean—if she were married to someone else, she could have children, couldn't she?"

The doctor acknowledged that this was so. The eyes of the young couple met for a moment. Then the wife smiled encouragingly at her husband. He turned back to the doctor.

"Then we'd like to have a baby by artificial insemination. Can that be done?"

"Medically, it's not very complicated," answered the doctor. "It's simply a process of taking the healthy sperm of an anonymous donor and inserting it in the vaginal tract of the woman at what we believe to be her most fertile period. If you have a little patience and you're willing to keep trying for several months, the chances of conception are very good."

"Then that's what we'd like to do," the woman put in eagerly. "We've talked it all over and we've decided that we'd rather have a child that was half ours than one who wasn't ours at all or no child."

"But," said the doctor, "it's not quite so simple. I can tell you with some degree of certainty that, from a medical and eugenic standpoint, the results of artificial insemination would be entirely satisfactory. In fact, because your donor will be carefully selected, you are likely to have a better-than-average child, both physically and mentally. Some doctors even believe that it can be predicted that you are more likely to have a boy than a girl."

"Well, that all sounds fine," the husband remarked. "Even the part about the boy."

"Unfortunately," the doctor continued, "I can't tell you what legal complications may ensue from your having a child by artificial insemination. And I'm afraid that your lawyer won't have most of the answers either. The law hasn't evolved to anywhere near the same extent with regard to artificial insemination as medicine has so that we're all operating in the dark." The young couple looked puzzled.

"What do you mean by 'legal complications,' doctor?" they asked.

"Well, I'll give you an idea of some of the questions neither your lawyer nor I know how to answer. We don't know whether you," pointing to the husband, "will be considered the legal father of the child, or whether you would be legally responsible for its support or whether you could at some later time claim that your wife had committed adultery because she had been impregnated with the semen of another man.

Or whether the donor's wife, if he has one, could sue him for a divorce on the ground that he had committed adultery. Or whether the child would legally be the child of the donor and could claim the right to be supported by him. Or whether . . ."

The good doctor could go on for at least half an hour just outlining the questions to which the law has given us no answers. It is estimated that there are at least 20,000 babies in the United States who have been born as a result of artificial insemination. No state has passed legislation defining the status of these children and there are only a few judicial decisions in the United States and Canada combined in which any of the problems have even been discussed.

Not every artificial impregnation raises legal problems. At least half of all artificial inseminations utilize the sperm of the mother's husband. This is commonly done where neither party is sterile, but where, for physical or psychological reasons, the husband's sperm does not reach the uterus in normal intercourse, or where the number of spermatozoa may be too small for normal impregnation. The doctor injects the husband's semen into the wife's vaginal tract at the time of ovulation. The child born of this type of impregnation obviously is as much the child of both husband and wife as if it had been conceived in the normal manner.

The only legal question raised by this procedure is whether, if the husband's disability amounts to impotence, the fact that the wife has been artificially impregnated is a waiver of her right to divorce or annulment in those states where impotence is considered sufficient ground for dissolution of the marriage. There have been no American cases on this question, but one arose in England. The husband was impotent, not for physical, but for psychological reasons. The couple tried every means to bolster their marriage including the attempt to artificially impregnate the wife with the husband's semen in the hope that having a child would unite the couple sufficiently to overcome the absence of any sexual relationship. Subsequently the wife came to the conclusion that the marriage was untenable, left her husband and started suit for annulment of the marriage on the ground that it had never been consummated. Shortly afterward, she found that the last insemination had taken effect and that she was pregnant. Faced with the problem of whether a wife, admittedly pregnant by her husband, could claim failure to consummate the marriage, the court held that she was nonetheless entitled to the annulment.

Implicit in this case—as in many of the problems raised by artificial insemination—is the basic question of *why* the law regards sexual intercourse as an essential ingredient of marriage. If, as some claim, marriage presupposes intercourse because intercourse leads to reproduction, then the English court's decision is wrong. This couple, despite the fact that they could not have normal intercourse, could reproduce. Witness the pregnancy of the plaintiff. The court's decision is obviously a tacit recognition of the fact that, completely aside from its reproductive aspects, intercourse for the mutual gratification of the spouses is a right to which married people are entitled. This line of thinking is also reflected increasingly in the American law in matrimonial cases. In many states, for example, impotence is a ground for annulment; sterility is not. (See Chapter 7.) It is interesting to speculate whether this trend of the law will some day go so far as to recognize a right of a spouse to seek dissolution of a marriage, not on the ground of complete impotence, but on the ground of sexual incompatibility of a particular man and woman.

Artificial insemination with the semen of a man other than the wife's husband presents many more problems. In the absence of guidance from legislature or courts, the relatively few doctors familiar with artificial insemination techniques have worked out their own sets of rules to protect themselves, the child, the donor, the wife and her husband. Because they can only guess at how the courts will react to the legal questions raised by artificial insemination, doctors try to restrict inseminations to people who, so far as can be seen, have an otherwise satisfactory marriage.

Most doctors will not agree to employ this procedure unless convinced that the couple are of average intelligence or better, that they are both emotionally stable, that their marriage has an excellent chance of survival, that they have reasonable ability to support the child and that both the husband and wife really want the child. The amazing success of the doctors in making their judgments would seem to be indicated by the fact that of all the artificial inseminations performed in the United States there seem to be only two cases which have actually come to court. There is no way of knowing whether other couples who have had a child by this method have subsequently been divorced. But if they have, the lack of mention of artificial insemination in the court records would seem to indicate that the child was so far regarded as their own that neither attempted to make any special issue of the fact that the child was not actually the child of the husband. This in itself suggests that the doctors have accurately gauged the emotional maturity of the couples to whom they have made available the technique of artificial insemination.

The donor is chosen even more carefully. He must be healthy, with no bad hereditary traits; he must have a high spermatozoa count and motility index; above all, he and the couple requesting the artificial insemination must remain totally unknown to each other. Generally the doctors also try to choose a donor who, as far as possible, resembles the husband in racial, physical and emotional characteristics. If the husband is short, stocky and volatile, he is more likely to feel kinship with a child of the same general type than with a tall, lean, placid child. Some doctors prefer to use as donors married men with children of their own. This has two advantages. The donor's own children serve as a check of physiological factors. More important, the donor's own children are a focus for his parental affection. He is less likely than a childless man to become wrapped up in the idea of the unknown children he may have fathered and to try to find them. Other doctors prefer not to use married donors since this introduces the additional problem of a possibly adverse reaction by the donor's wife.

Although doctors are frequently asked to use the sperm of the husband's brother or some other relative they rarely if ever do so. Whatever advantages there might be in having the child of the same blood line as the husband are more than outweighed by the emotional hazards of such a mixed family relationship. The husband's brother could hardly fail to regard the child he fathered with special interest. The mother might very well find herself focusing her attention on her brother-in-law rather than on her husband, where it belongs. Every meeting with his brother might serve to remind the husband anew of the fact that the child is not biologically his.

In cases where the husband has even a few active spermatozoa in his semen and has no undesirable hereditary traits, some doctors inject the wife with a combination of her husband's semen and the semen of an anonymous donor. This makes it harder legally to prove that the child was not the child of the husband if the question of legitimacy is ever raised. But this procedure has a psychological advantage as well. The husband knows that there is some possibility at least that the child is his. If the donor has been well chosen for his resemblance to the husband, it is easy for the husband to accept the child fully as his own, even though the artificial insemination would not have been performed with semen other than his had not the doctor in charge concluded that he was sterile.

Some doctors prefer to have no written records at all in connection with the impregnation. They reason that if there are no records, it may be *suspected* that the child was what is popularly known as a "test-tube" baby but there is no way of proving it and no legal complications as to the legitimacy of the child can arise. The doctor, of course, could not in any event be forced to testify unless his artificially inseminated patient wanted him to, since the law regards as confidential all communications between a doctor and his patients and will not force a doctor to reveal anything about his treatment or diagnosis of a patient without the patient's consent. In any case, keeping no records will not help to solve many of the problems that may arise.

Conceivably, the question of whether the wife has committed adultery in permitting herself to be impregnated with the semen of another man may hinge on whether or not the husband consented to the procedure. The best way to prove that he did would be to have a written record of his consent. The majority of doctors do require that both husband and wife sign a written consent to the artificial insemination. Some insist that the fingerprints of both parties and a picture of the husband be attached to the consent. This is to ward off the possibility that a wife whose husband was opposed to the idea of artificial insemination might bring some other man to the doctor's office with her to pose as her husband. Since, however, most doctors insist on checking the husband's sterility themselves, this is not a very likely occurrence. The success, from a social standpoint, of artificial insemination is attributable to a large extent to the doctors' insistence, as a prerequisite to artificial insemination, that the husband be sterile and that husband and wife consent in writing to the wife's being artificially inseminated with live sperm from some other male.

Some doctors go so far as to insist on the written consent of the donor's wife, if he is married, so that she may not later claim that her husband committed adultery by permitting his semen to be used to impregnate another woman. Of course, if his anonymity is carefully preserved as it should be, the risk here is minimal. Although the very idea that a man and woman can commit adultery without ever having met may seem fantastic, the question has actually been discussed in two court cases and doctors are constantly aware of the fact that it may arise again. Of course, our adultery statutes were written years before artificial insemination was ever used. However, until we have laws designed specifically to cover artificial insemination, the question whether this procedure can be considered adultery must unfortunately be decided by analogy in the light of laws never intended to apply to this kind of situation. In some states the purely accidental wording of the adultery statute eliminates the possibility that artificial insemination could be considered adultery. This is true of those states whose statutes talk in terms of sexual intercourse, fornication or living together out of wedlock. But in other states the statutes are so worded that artificial insemination might be found to be adulterous.

An interesting case was decided in Canada some years ago. A husband sued his wife for divorce on the ground that she had committed adultery and cited as evidence the child conceived and born while the couple were separated. The wife claimed that the child was conceived by artificial insemination and that she was therefore not guilty of adultery. The court found that the child was the result of extramarital sexual intercourse but in his decision the judge gratuitously offered the opinion that even if the wife had been telling the truth and the child had been conceived by artificial insemination, she would nevertheless be guilty of adultery. The court's rationale was that the essence of the evil of adultery was not the physical contact but lending the use of the reproductive organs to one other than the spouse and the consequent possible pollution of blood lines. Of course, if this were the only reason behind the ban on adultery, query whether it would be adulterous at all for a sterile woman or a woman past her menopause to have intercourse with a dozen men if she chose. On this theory, would it be adulterous for a young married woman to have intercourse with a lover during the sterile period of her monthly cycle or while she was pregnant? Logically, under the theory of the Canadian judge the use of contraceptives would negate adultery in any situation where they worked.

It is not likely that this Canadian case will find acceptance in the United States. The one court which has considered the question in this country—an Illinois tribunal—offered the opinion that where the husband had consented to the artificial insemination (the husband's consent was not even alleged in the Canadian case) it could not be considered adultery or used as a ground for divorce.

Actually, if the husband's written consent has been obtained and can be proved, the question whether the wife has been guilty of adultery because of artificial insemination with a donor's sperm is of no importance because in most states the husband's consent would waive his right to complain of adultery even if the impregnation were so considered. The law will not allow a man to divorce his wife for conduct which he has condoned and encouraged. The written record is a continuing protection to the wife against the possibility that her husband might change his mind about wanting her or the child and deny that he ever knew of or agreed to the artificial insemination.

Careful planning is essential at every stage to protect the child born of artificial insemination. Authorities generally agree that an adopted child ought to be told early in life that he was adopted. But the same reasoning does not apply to a child who is the result of artificial insemination. Since the mother actually bears the child, there is no reason why friends and relatives need know that the child was conceived in any but the normal manner. When a child is adopted there is a danger that an outsider may break the news to the child. This problem need never arise for the "test-tube" baby. Moreover, in the case of the adopted child, the parents can explain to the child that both of them voluntarily chose him though neither had any part in his birth. The child's attitude is, therefore, likely to be the same toward both his adoptive parents. But if the child knows that his mother is his natural parent and her husband is not, he may be drawn to his mother to the exclusion of the man who is his father in every sense save the biological one. Such a situation would not make for a happy or a unified family.

There is even less reason why the world generally should know of the facts of the child's birth. He should, for his own protection and for the protection of the husband's sensibilities, be presented to the world as the natural child of both spouses. Here again, however, difficulties arise from the failure of the law to recognize that such a thing as artificial insemination exists.

The first of them comes with the ordinarily simple matter of filling out the birth certificate. In many states, the law requires that the birth certificate state the name of the child's father. If the doctor who performed the artificial impregnation were to fill this out honestly, he would have to insert the name of the donor of the semen. Obviously this would be cruelly unfair to everybody involved. Yet if the doctor were to put down the name of the mother's husband, he would be knowingly submitting false information and might be guilty of perjury and perhaps of unprofessional conduct as well.

In Wisconsin the question of what doctors should do in this situation was presented to the Attorney General of the state. He answered that in his opinion a doctor would be justified in giving the name of the husband as the father even though a donor's sperm had been used. In other states where the question as to proper entry on the birth certificate is as yet officially unresolved, the doctors have worked out various ways of avoiding it. Sometimes the doctor who performs the insemination refuses to deliver the child. As soon as the wife becomes pregnant he advises her to go to an obstetrician who knows nothing of the fact that the child was conceived by artificial insemination. Thus, the obstetrician who delivers the child can with a clear conscience put down the name of the husband as the child's father. Some doctors feel that this serves a double purpose. Having another doctor around at the time of the birth of the child may help the husband to forget that he is not really the natural father, whereas the presence of the doctor who did the insemination might serve to emphasize in the husband's mind his lack of biological connection with the child.

No conscientious doctor will perform an artificial impregnation unless he is convinced that the mother's husband genuinely wants the child and is emotionally prepared to regard the child as his own. But what if the husband later changes his mind? Even marriages which look sound sometimes deteriorate. Parents sometimes develop strong antagonisms even toward their natural children. Can the husband later claim that he has no obligation to support the child? Is the child entitled to inherit from the husband? Can the child be declared illegitimate? We have seen that in some states a child born out of wedlock acquires all the rights of a legitimate child with reference to both parents. In an artificial insemination case, this law, strictly applied, could give the child rights vis-à-vis the donor—the last person in the world whom one would wish to involve. But it is possible that if and when the question arises, the courts may hold that the acceptance of the child by the mother's husband has the effect of legitimizing him as the husband's child.

It has been suggested that greater protection can be given to the child through formal adoption by the mother's husband. In most states an adopted child automatically is entitled to all the rights which the natural child of the adopting parents would have. But the grave disadvantage of this course is that it almost inevitably publicizes the origin of the child which would otherwise be unknown. An adoption virtually assures that the community and therefore eventually the child will know that he is the product of artificial insemination. The potential hurt to the child, the husband, and the whole family situation probably outweighs any advantages of an adoption.

Fortunately, the lack of normal adoption will not necessarily leave the child without protection. In the one American case in which the status of a child resulting from artificial

insemination was at issue, the court waved aside the technicalities of the situation to reach a just and humane result. The
case was a custody proceeding between a husband and wife
in New York State. The wife claimed complete and exclusive
custody of the child and urged that her husband should not
be granted any visitation rights because the child was not his
but had been born of artificial insemination with a donor's
sperm. The court rejected this argument, treated the husband
as if he were truly the father of the child, and granted him the
right to see the child at least one day a week. While there had
been no formal adoption, the court found that the husband
had consented to the insemination and had treated the child
as his own. From these facts the court deduced that the child
had been "potentially adopted or semi-adopted" by the husband and that he was therefore entitled to at least the same
rights as a foster parent who had formally adopted the child if
not to the same rights as a natural father. The judge went on to
deny flatly that the child was illegitimate. "Logically and realistically," he said, "the situation is no different than that pertaining to the case of a child born out of wedlock who by law
is made legitimate upon the marriage of the interested parties."

This case clarified somewhat the law in New York State.
It is to be hoped and expected that the reasoning of the New
York court will be adopted by other jurisdictions. Until the
law is settled, however, there are some steps which can be
taken to protect the child. It has been suggested that husband
and wife should enter into a contract before the child is born
in which the husband agrees to adopt the child, support it
and provide for it in his Will. The agreement to support the
child is undoubtedly enforceable during the husband's lifetime.
If he dies without having adopted the child or providing for it
in his Will, there is some doubt as to whether the courts will
force his estate to provide for the child if it can be shown that
the child is not his. Some authorities feel that the promise to
adopt even though not fulfilled in the husband's lifetime will
induce the courts to treat the child as adopted for inheritance

purposes. Some states have so treated a child whom foster parents promised to adopt or thought they had adopted. (See Chapter 9.) The entire question whether the child born of artificial insemination can inherit from the husband can be bypassed if the husband makes a Will providing for the child. However, if the husband and wife have been scrupulous in keeping the child's background a secret even from their relatives, the chances of the child's share being challenged would be small even if the husband should die without a Will.

The child is protected to some extent by the presumption of legitimacy discussed in the preceding chapter. The law assumes that any child born to a married woman is the child of her husband. The burden of proving that the child is not legitimate is on the person who makes such a claim. Where the husband has consented to the insemination of his wife, the question of the child's legitimacy is likely to arise in only two ways—an attempt by the husband to evade responsibility for the child's support, or an effort by relatives of the husband to deny the child any share in the husband's estate or the estates of the husband's relatives. Where the semen of the husband has been used together with that of the donor and where the donor is of the same blood group as the husband, it is difficult to overcome the presumption of legitimacy. Where feasible both these precautions should be taken. The presumption of legitimacy may, however, be overcome by showing that the husband was completely sterile or that there was "nonaccess" (that is, that the husband and wife could not have had intercourse at any time around the time of conception) or by proving the artificial insemination itself. It can readily be seen that this kind of proof would be hard to adduce without the cooperation of the husband. The risk of relatives successfully challenging the legitimacy of the child is, therefore, not great—particularly if the fact of the artificial insemination is known only to the husband, the wife, and the doctor. If the husband has consented in writing to the insemination, it is doubtful that a court would permit him to "bastardize" the child that resulted. And, as previously stated, the doctor would, in any event, be disabled from testifying to the artificial insemination without the consent of his patient, the mother.

Many states have laws designed to protect the child born out of wedlock which might have unfortunate repercussions if applied to the child born of artificial insemination. These states impose the responsibility for the child's support on the biological father even if he was not married to the child's mother. This may make sense where the child is born of an affair between two unmarried people or of an adulterous relationship in the usual sense. No such responsibility should be imposed on the donor of sperm used for artificial insemination. Again here, we can only hope that if and when the question of whether the donor should be forced to contribute to the child's support is presented to the courts, they will meet it with the same good sense and awareness of the intentions of the parties which the New York court exhibited in the case previously discussed. In the absence of statutes or judicial decisions exempting the donor from the obligations of a parent, the best protection for him is his complete anonymity. The responsibility for seeing that the donor and the couple do not know each other and have no way of learning each other's identity is the doctor's. The couple serve their own interests and the child's by following their doctor's instructions and not making any attempt to gratify their natural curiosity as to the identity of the donor. If the donor and the child do become known to each other, the strict letter of the law in some states might give them all the rights and duties of natural parent and child, unless the courts, like the New York court, refuse to follow the letter of the law in such a situation as this where it was never intended to apply.

It has been estimated that one marriage in ten in the United States—some three million marriages altogether—are barren. It is further estimated that in about one third of these cases, the husband may be the sole or a contributing cause of the sterility. This means that there are more than half a million

couples for whom artificial insemination may be the alternative to childlessness or adoption. Nobody knows how many
live births resulting from artificial insemination have taken
place. The twenty thousand figure we have given would seem
to be conservative. Probably many more people will resort to
artificial insemination as the medical profession as a whole
becomes more familiar with the technique and as the public
assimilates and accepts it. Yet the laws now on the books fail
utterly to provide for children born as a result of artificial
insemination with a donor's sperm, or to define the rights and
duties of the people involved.

In New York and Virginia, bills were introduced in the
legislature which would have given such a child all the rights
and duties of a natural born child of the husband where he had
consented to the insemination. Both bills died in committee.
A similar bill was introduced in the Wisconsin legislature and
was withdrawn. The people who submit to artificial insemination are not likely to form a pressure group and demand
legislation, for they are primarily concerned with protecting
their own privacy and that of their child. Yet the problem
can be satisfactorily resolved only by carefully thought out
legislation which will at one and the same time protect all the
interested parties and keep secret the fact of the artificial insemination.

There is, however, some potentially well organized opposition to the practice of artificial insemination. The Catholic
Church apparently opposes it as a violation of the spirit of
the marriage. Even the husband might be considered morally
guilty of adultery in consenting to his wife's being impregnated with the sperm of another man. Some non-Catholics also
feel that there is something immoral about artificial insemination. Clearly anyone who holds such views should not avail
himself of the technique. But those for whom it poses no
moral or ethical issue and the children who have been born
of artificial insemination, as well as those who will undoubtedly be born as the practice spreads, are in any event entitled

to protection. The law might provide that the sealed consent of the husband to the impregnation of his wife by a donor should be filed with the county clerk and produced only on a court order; that the child has all the rights and duties of a natural child vis-à-vis the mother's husband and no legal connection whatever with the donor. Until some such legislation is on the books, however, we must continue to look primarily to the ingenuity of the medical profession to safeguard all those involved in an artificial insemination procedure and to the legal profession—both lawyers and judges—for wise resolution of the problems that arise.

CHAPTER 9

Adoption

*I*N A Tennessee court, two women fought for a bewildered little boy. One was his mother who had consented to the child's being adopted shortly after he was born out of wedlock. He had been adopted by the husband of the other woman with her full consent and approval. The little boy had lived with his foster parents for seven years until the death of his foster father. The real mother, who by this time had married and wanted the child back, claimed that the foster mother had no right to keep him because it was her husband and not she, who had adopted him and the husband was now dead. According to the letter of the law, she was right: the foster mother who had cared for and loved the little boy for seven years had no right to keep him.

A California widower was just recovering from the shock of his wife's death when a social service agency representative appeared to claim the younger of his two small sons. The child had lived with the couple all his life and they regarded him as their own to such an extent that the wife had made lavish provision for him in her Will. But he had never been formally adopted. The rules of the social service agency which had placed him prohibited leaving a child in a motherless boarding home and the boy had never technically been adopted.

A childless farmer told his friends how happy he was that he had an adopted son to whom he could leave his farm. But after the farmer's death, greedy distant relatives found a flaw in the adoption proceedings and brought suit to oust the young man from the farm which they claimed was legally theirs.

Cases like these could be cited ad infinitum. The law books are replete with evidence that the failure to seek competent legal advice in connection with an adoption can bring tragic results. Fortunately, the tendency of the courts in recent years has been to decide cases with a view to the best welfare of the child involved. In many instances they have refused to separate foster parents and children, although technically such a course was indicated. People who plan to adopt or who have adopted children should, however, be certain they have complied with all the relevant legal rules rather than rely on the mercy of the courts not to wrest their adopted children from them.

While adoptions usually involve young children, adults can also be adopted in most states. Such adoptions are rare and usually are made for sentimental reasons. Occasionally, however, the adoption of an adult may be motivated by practical financial considerations. Suppose, for example, that Miss Doe, an elderly spinster is beneficiary under the Will of her deceased father who provided that a trust fund of $50,000 was to be set up and that the income was to be paid to Miss Doe for life and at her death the principal was to be paid over to her children or, if she had none, to an educational institution. Miss Doe, contrary to her father's expectations, has never married and does not expect to. She, however, has a grown niece of whom she is very fond and she would rather her niece got the $50,000 than have it go to an institution. Under the laws of some states Miss Doe, by adoption, may make the niece her "child" so as to entitle her to the legacy.

The usual adoption proceeding, of course, involves a young child and is considerably more complicated than where the subject of the adoption is an adult. The state here, as in many other contexts, is a superguardian of minor children. It asserts a direct concern with their welfare, and insists on scrutinizing all adoptions with a view to seeing whether they will serve the best interests of the child sought to be adopted.

The state exercises its rights as superguardian not only through the courts which pass on adoptions but also by means of the child-placement agencies which are either established or approved by the state as qualified to select suitable adoptive parents for children. In almost half the states the law has made some attempt to channelize all adoptions through such agencies and have (with some exceptions discussed below) prohibited anyone other than an approved agency from participating in child placement.

The usual course of events leading up to an adoption runs something like this. Sam and Sally Green, themselves unable to have children, wish to adopt an infant, Betty. In some states, Betty must have lived with the Greens for a period of months before the court will even consider a petition for her adoption. At the proper time the Greens file a petition to adopt Betty which sets forth facts showing that they meet the state's requirements as to age and residence of adopters and so forth. They must also set forth the circumstances which made Betty available for adoption: her parents have consented to the adoption or they are deceased, or they have in some other way relinquished their right to their child. In most states an investigation of the Greens is made either by the social service agency which gave Betty out for adoption, by the state welfare board or by someone appointed by the court which passes on the adoption. The investigator submits a recommendation to the court as to whether or not the adoption should be permitted. In some states if the judge approves the petition, the adoption becomes final immediately. In other states (usually those which do not require that the child have lived with the couple that wishes to adopt it before the petition for adoption can be filed) the court issues an interlocutory decree which becomes a final order of adoption some months later.

The legal procedure of adoption is usually fairly simple. The real problem for husbands and wives who desire an adopted child is finding a child to adopt. There are many more people who want to adopt a child than there are children available for adoption. The over-all national average has been estimated to be eleven couples looking for a child to adopt to every available child. In some areas the ratio is reported to be as high as thirty to one.

Ideally, all children should be placed for adoption via accredited social-service agencies set up to take care of them until they are adopted. Such agencies have facilities to check on the general fitness of the child for adoption and the fitness of prospective parents in general and in terms of that particular child. The trend is in the direction of requiring that all adoptions be channelled through such agencies. However, as happens in any case where the demand far exceeds the supply, a "black market" and a "gray market" have come into being. Children are said to have come from the "black" or "gray" market when their adoptive parents have obtained them from sources other than the social service agencies licensed by the state to supply children for adoption and to protect their interests.

The "black market" is involved when a source like a maternity home for unwed mothers or a partnership of doctors and lawyers buys children for cash from a parent or parents who are willing or anxious to be rid of them and then turns the children over for adoption to people who are able and willing to pay well for them. It is quite a profitable business not unreminiscent of the slave trade.

Actually, comparatively few children come from the black market. Far more are placed from what has been called the "gray" market where the transactions are not for cash but where they are outside the ordinary social service agency setup. Thus, Dr. A., an eminently respectable physician, informs Miss B., his patient, that she is pregnant. Miss B. is distraught. She tells the doctor that the father of the child is already married, that she has no way of supporting a child and that she must get rid of it immediately after its birth. Dr.

A. knows of a fine couple, Mr. and Mrs. C., who want a child and cannot have one of their own. Out of the goodness of his heart, he puts Miss B. in contact with Mr. and Mrs. C. or their lawyer and they agree to adopt Miss B.'s child. Dr. A. gets nothing out of the transaction except his usual fee if he delivers the child and the satisfaction of knowing (or at least believing) that he has done a good turn for Miss B., for the hitherto unwanted baby who will now have a fine home, and for the nice couple who now have the child they so badly wanted.

Many doctors who have done what Dr. A. did in this hypothetical case are heated in their arguments justifying the part they play in placing children. Often, they claim, their help in making such arrangements for a child has deterred pregnant women from seeking the services of an abortionist. They admit that there are many social agencies whose job it is to help unwed mothers but, they point out, many women flatly refuse to avail themselves of such a public form of assistance. In some cases the couple whom the doctor finds to adopt the child contribute to the support of the mother in the last months of her pregnancy when she may be without means and unwilling to approach family or friends for help.

Sometimes an unwed mother prefers this kind of private arrangement because she wants to get out of town in order to conceal her pregnancy from her family and the couple who is to get the child makes it possible for her to do so. In such a situation the mother cannot usually get help from local agencies if she leaves town and agencies in the city to which she goes may consider her ineligible for help because she is not a resident. Sometimes an unwed mother who knows and trusts her doctor finds it easier to accept his choice of a home for her child than the more impersonal designation of an agency.

Not infrequently the agencies themselves are blamed for the existence of the "gray market" in babies. Because they cannot make up special rules to meet every situation, they sometimes reject applicants who appear to be fine prospective parents by any reasonable standards. Sympathy for such people often motivates doctors, lawyers, ministers, and others who in the course of their work hear of children who are or are going to be available for adoption.

In one case, for example, a couple was turned away by the only social agency in their city on the ground that the woman was "too old" to adopt a child; she had reached the ripe old age of thirty-four and the agency had a blanket rule against placing a child with people who had waited that long before deciding they wanted a child. A doctor who had been treating the woman knew that for six years she and her husband had undergone expensive and often painful medical and surgical treatment in order to have a child of their own. Indignant at their cursory dismissal by the agency, he arranged for them to adopt the child of an unwed mother who shortly thereafter became his patient and who wanted to give her child up for adoption. The agencies' answer to this type of situation is that their primary function is not to provide children for childless couples but to make the best possible arrangements for each child under the agency's care. They consider their first duty to be to the child; this being the case, they feel that apparent injustice to some couples seeking a child is unfortunate but inevitable.

Despite all of the arguments that are advanced for nonagency placements, the fact remains that they are generally not as successful as those handled by a good agency. Often adoptions made possible by the intervention of private individuals like doctors or lawyers lack the anonymity which is so essential to the security of both parents and children. In a well handled agency placement, the real parents do not know who the adoptive parents are; hence the chances of subsequent interference on their part are considerably less than they are in the average independent placement. Moreover since an agency has a fairly large number of children and prospective parents to deal with, it can study and attempt to match the child to the adoptive parents. Furthermore, a good agency knows that a child it offers for adoption is mentally and physically sound. It has had the child examined thoroughly in order to ascertain whether there are any weaknesses of which prospective parents should be told. Often an agency will place a child in a temporary foster home for a few months in advance of offering it for adoption, so that it has a chance to learn what kind of child it is and choose its prospective parents accordingly. The agency can also become thoroughly acquainted with the prospective parents and can reject those who want the child for reasons not conducive to its best interests, as, for example, where the prime purpose of adoption is to bolster a weak marriage.

A study made in Connecticut in 1945 showed a rather shocking difference in quality between agency and independent placements. Dr. Catherine S. Amatruda of Yale studied one hundred adoptions which had been arranged by agencies and one hundred which had not. In order to be classified as desirable the parents and their adopted children had to measure up to certain minimum standards. The child had to be mentally normal and without serious personality defects. The adoptive parents had to have a stable marriage and neither of them could be a psychiatric case, chronic alcoholic, or drug addict. The husband couldn't be a wife beater nor the wife a prostitute. So tested, only forty-eight out of the one hundred independent placements were classified as desirable, twenty-eight were considered definitely undesirable and twenty-six questionable. While the adoptions arranged by agencies were not uniformly good, they did score substantially higher. Seventy-six of the agency adoptions met the test of desirability; only eight were definitely undesirable and sixteen were questionable.

These figures should not be taken as definite. As one adoption expert pointed out, the success of an adoption can really only be gauged ten or twenty years after the child has been placed. At a minimum, however, it can be said that Dr. Amatruda's figures indicate that the people involved in independent placements do not seem as frequently to have the characteristics necessary for successful adoption as those involved in agency placements.

Yet, despite all the obvious advantages of agency placement and the fact that almost half the states have laws designed to curb independent placements, it has been estimated that (excluding adoptions by stepparents or other relatives) about as many children are placed by private individuals as through agencies. Many of the laws designed to assure agency placement are ineffective because, while they prohibit anyone other than a licensed agency from placing a child for adoption, they make an exception for parents. In most cases even where a third party is involved, the transaction can be made to look as if the mother herself had placed the child.

Somewhat more effective are laws which prohibit all independent placements except where the child is placed with a relative of one of its parents or which require the approval of a court or of the state welfare department before a child can be placed in a home in contemplation of adoption. Colorado, Georgia, Indiana (if the child is under three), Iowa, Kentucky, Maine, Michigan, Missouri, New Jersey, Ohio, Rhode Island, Tennessee, and Utah are among the states having these types of laws. A few other states require that the state welfare board be notified immediately when any child is placed for adoption. Massachusetts, New Hampshire, and Rhode Island require such notices. Notice is not usually required if the child is placed with relatives, however.

Some states have attempted to curb nonagency placements by prohibiting the giving of money in connection with the placement of a child except for fees to a licensed agency, medical expenses or legal fees in connection with an adoption. Such laws are difficult to enforce and for the most part affect only black market transactions. The New York statute, however, is so worded as to make it illegal for the adopting parents in a gray market transaction to pay the mother's living expenses or anything other than her actual confinement costs.

The traffic in children for adoption is to a small extent interstate and here it is questionable whether even an agency placement can be expected to comply with approved standards. In recent years, many people living in areas where children are particularly hard to obtain have gone to other states to get them—particularly to certain southern states where there are fewer applicants in relation to available babies than there are in the rest of the country. However, pressure has been exerted on the southern agencies involved so that it has become much more difficult to secure a child simply by making a quick trip down south. Many couples, for example, used to find it easy to get a child from Tennessee. A new law which became effective in 1951 now prohibits sending a child out of the state to anyone except a relative without the consent of the state department of public welfare.

Many states require that anyone who brings a child not his own into the state must secure the permission of the state welfare department and post a bond to guarantee that the child will not become a public charge. In a few states the permission of the state welfare department must be secured in order to take a child out of the state. These legal requirements are not difficult for responsible people to meet. The chief deterrent to getting a child from an agency in another state remains a practical one. Most agencies take the position that they are not at liberty to accept applications from people outside of the state—or, in some cases, outside of the particular community they serve—as long as there are applicants from their own locality whose request for a child they cannot fill.

All of the states specify minimum requirements which prospective adopting parents must meet. Since by and large these are less exacting than the rules which govern the operation of social agencies, they do not give a realistic picture of the situation at least as far as agency adoptions are concerned. Thus, under the law of most states, a single person can adopt a child. Generally speaking, agency rules tolerate such adoptions only when the adopter is a relative. If, for example,

Anne dies when her son Charles is born and her husband Roger is unwilling or unable to undertake the responsibility of raising the child alone, Anne's sister or her widowed mother would probably have no difficulty in obtaining court approval of her adopting Charles if Roger consented. No agency would be involved. Where, however, a single person tries to adopt a child unrelated to him, he may find himself unable to do so despite the fact that the law says he may. The demand for children is so far greater than the number available that the agencies can afford to be rigid in insisting that anyone who wishes to adopt a child not related to him must be able to provide it with a full normal home background including the usual number of parents. Hence they will not give a child out for adoption by a single person. If such a person succeeds in locating a child anyway ("black" or "gray" market) he may find the agency policy mirrored in the action of the court passing on the adoption even though no legal disability to adopt attaches to him. If there are other available alternatives for the child he may find his petition denied. Even in the absence of present alternatives, the court's investigating agent or the state social welfare board may recommend that the adoption petition of a single person be refused on the ground that if the child is turned over to an agency, the agency will find a couple to adopt it.

In most states, a married person can adopt a child only if his spouse consents. While this does not mean that both husband and wife must adopt the child, it is always advisable for them to join in the adoption petition. If they do not, the child is considered to be the adopted child only of the spouse who actually was named as the adoptive parent, no matter what the facts of the relationship between the couple and the child.

In the Tennessee case referred to at the beginning of this chapter, the widow had clearly always considered the little boy to be as much her son as her husband's; yet her failure to join in the petition for adoption resulted in her having no legal status as the child's adoptive parent. In the particular case, the court decided that notwithstanding the legalities of the situation, the welfare of the child demanded that he be left with the widow whom he regarded as his mother rather than returned to his real mother who was a stranger to him. An inordinate amount of anguish would undoubtedly have been prevented if the widow had been, as she should have been, a party to the adoption proceedings.

If only one spouse adopts a child, the fact that the other consented to the adoption gives the child no rights vis-a-vis the consenting spouse. Thus, if George adopts a child with the consent of his wife, Amy, the child is not legally entitled to inherit from Amy nor is she obliged to support him. Neither does she enjoy the rights of a parent with respect to his custody, earnings or services, whatever the affection they may have for each other.

The mere presence of a law on the statute books permitting adoption by single persons probably is not conclusive one way or the other as to what is the practice with reference to adoptions in a particular state.

There is likewise a variance between theory and practice in connection with the question whether the adoptive parent and child must be of the same racial stock. Only a few states have such a statutory requirement. Yet even in states that have no such law, interracial adoptions are often disapproved by the courts. Georgia, for example, has no statute specifying that the adoptive parent and child be of the same race, but it is highly improbable that one could find a Georgia judge who would approve the adoption of a white child by negro parents or vice versa.

Similarly, comparatively few states demand by statute that the foster parent and child be of the same religion. Some states, including Illinois, Iowa, Pennsylvania, Maryland, and Connecticut require that information as to the religion of the child and the prospective parents be included in the petition for adoption. Others, including Delaware, Georgia, New Hampshire and Ohio require that the investigation include a report on the suitability of a proposed adoption in terms of the similarity of religious faiths of child and prospective parents. New York, Maryland, and Tennessee require agencies to place children with foster parents of the same faith. (In Maryland this requirement may be waived if the parents of the child indicate another preference.) New York and Rhode Island further require the court hearing adoption proceedings to permit adoption of a child only by people of the same faith, when practicable.

A recent New York case raises the question of how much weight a state may constitutionally accord to religious background in adoption proceedings. The case involved two little girls, apparently Jewish, who had been committed by the New York City Children's Court to a Jewish adoption agency. The agency, in turn, had placed them in a Jewish home. It was subsequently discovered that the children had been baptized Roman Catholics. The New York courts ruled that the adoption law required the religion of the little girls to be considered to the exclusion of all other factors. The children were then withdrawn from the Jewish home (though they were apparently fully adjusted there) and transferred to a Catholic agency. The Jewish agency thereupon appealed to the United States Supreme Court, contending that this ruling converted the Children's Court from a guardian of the welfare of the children to an agency serving religious groups. This, it said, is a violation of the principle of separation of church and state. The agency maintained that religion should be considered in placing children for adoption, but only in conjunction with all other facts bearing on their health and well-being. This view is supported by the American Civil Liberties Union The case will probably be decided by the Supreme Court before the end of 1952.

Even in the states which do not require the adopting

parents and the child to be of the same religious faith, it is often, as a practical matter, very difficult for a couple to adopt a baby whose parents were of a different religion. For one thing, many of the licensed agencies are set up along religious lines. A Catholic placement service will not consider applications by Jews or Protestants, nor will Protestant or Jewish agencies supply children to Catholics or people of other faiths. Even agencies which are not strictly denominational in character will often as a matter of policy make children available only to persons of the same religious background. This practice is by no means confined to cases where the natural parents desire the child to be brought up in their religion. The policy is frequently invoked even in cases where the child's parents didn't practice any religion or had expressed a definite preference against the child's being brought up in their religious faith.

This matching of religions sometimes entails extreme hardship to husbands and wives who do not happen to be of the same religious background. Not long ago the story was reported of a young couple who had been on an agency's list for an unusually long time without being offered a child and who finally asked in desperation when the agency thought they could expect to get a child. "Oh," said the agency social worker cheerfully, "as soon as we get a child who had an Episcopalian mother and a Jewish father, the same combination as you."

Assuming that a husband and wife do manage to get a child of religious origin different from their own and that the state has no specific statutory requirement on the subject, there still is no guarantee that a court will approve such an adoption. Some judges in the absence of statute refuse to consider the religious element in determining the suitability of an adoption; others are reluctant to permit an adoption where divergent religious backgrounds are involved. A couple contemplating the adoption of a child with a religious origin different from their own would be well advised to get legal advice as to the practice of the courts of their state with regard to mixed adoptions as well as with respect to the applicable law on the books.

Almost all states require by law that couples wishing to adopt a child be "fit" and "proper" and "able to provide" for it and here particularly the generalities of the law are apt to yield to specific agency practice. With respect to nonagency placements (where these are permitted) the court may appoint someone to investigate and report or the state welfare department may be entrusted with the investigation. Where the child is obtained from an agency, the approval of the agency is ordinarily accepted by the court passing on the adoption. Some agencies judge applicants on an individual basis, others tend to adhere to hard and fast rules of their own. Thus, the laws of some states are silent with respect to what age adopting parents must be; many merely require that the would-be adoptor be over twenty-one; still others specify merely that he must be a certain number of years older than the child to be adopted. Yet many agencies will automatically rule out adoptions by couples where the wife is over thirty-five or the husband over forty. Others approve the adoption of older children by such couples but not of infants. There is no question that as long as there are more people who want to adopt children than there are children to adopt, the age of the adopting couple will be a relevant factor no matter what the laws of the particular state say or don't say about it.

Similarly, although the state laws do not require that a couple be well off in order to adopt a child, the agencies rarely give a child to husbands and wives who don't have a reasonably steady source of income and at least some capital—a few hundred dollars in the bank, or some government bonds or a reasonable amount of insurance. For the rest, the child is expected to share the economic ups and downs of its adopted family.

Some agencies will not give children to couples who have a child of their own. Some require medical proof that the couple is physically unable to have a child. Others refuse couples who have two or more adopted children.

Just as the agencies differ in their standards of who is an eligible parent, they vary in their appraisal of what constitutes an adoptable child. Some do not consider any child with a poor hereditary background adoptable. Others will offer such children for adoption if study of the child himself shows no defect and if the adopting parents know of and are willing to take a chance on the undesirable heredity.

While some agencies consider only infants as suitable for adoption, the trend is to try to place older children for adoption as well. In some areas it is easier to find an older child to adopt than an infant since most people want a small child whom they can raise from the beginning of his life rather than an older one who may have memories of his own parents and who may already have emotional or psychological difficulties because of the death of his parents or their abandonment or mistreatment of him. Hence the couple who want a six-year-old boy may sometimes have little trouble in getting one compared to the couple who will settle for nothing short of a one-month-old baby. However, there are, by and large, fewer older children available for adoption than infants. Most of the babies offered for adoption are illegitimate and their parents' families usually want no part of them. An older child whose parents cannot care for him or have died often is forced to stay in an institution or a temporary foster home because his relatives refuse to consent to a formal adoption which would give the child a permanent home but which would take him out of the orbit of his natural family. Thus, while the demand for older children is less than that for infants, the supply may likewise be considerably smaller. In some areas, agencies have felt it necessary to conduct intensive campaigns to induce people to consider adopting older children; in others a couple who wants an older child may have as much (or more) trouble finding one as a couple who wants an infant.

Ordinarily the consent of the child's natural parents must be obtained before a child can be adopted. Where the child is illegitimate (one half the adoptable children at any one time are), the mother's consent alone will suffice. In some states if the father has recognized the child as his and contributed to its support, his consent is also necessary.

A parent can lose his right to be consulted as to the adoption of his child if he has acted in such a way as to forfeit his parental rights. A father or mother who abandons or neglects his child will not usually be allowed to oppose a proposed adoption which will make better provision for the child. The fact that the custody of the child has been awarded to someone other than the parent does not mean that the child can be placed for adoption without the parent's consent unless the reason for his not having custody is his abandonment or neglect of the child. Thus, if a child's parents are divorced and the custody of the child has been granted to the mother, she cannot give the child up for adoption without the father's consent except possibly in a case where the divorce was granted on the ground that the husband had deserted and failed to support his family. If a parent is mentally incompetent, his consent will not ordinarily be required. In some states the parents (or the mother of an illegitimate child) can transfer their right to consent to an adoption by transferring custody to an authorized social service agency; in such cases the consent of the agency is required for the actual adoption rather than that of the parents.

In connection with this problem of consent, one of the great advantages of adopting a child through a reputable agency rather than from the "black" or "gray" market becomes evident. The law in most states is very liberal in allowing a parent who has consented to an adoption to change his or her mind and revoke the consent at any time before the adoption decree becomes final. This may not be for six months

or a year or more after the child has been living with the
adoptive parents. Such a change of mind is not uncommon
and it can involve much heartbreak and disappointment.

Recently a Midwestern couple who wanted a child badly
became impatient at the delays in getting one from an agency
and were delighted when a friend told them of an unmarried
girl who was pregnant and wished to give her child over for
adoption. The couple agreed to and did pay all the girl's confinement expenses and, in addition, paid all her living expenses for the last five months of her pregnancy in a city far
removed from her home so that her pregnancy would not be
known to her friends and family. Immediately after the birth
of the child, the girl signed papers consenting to the adoption
of the child. Within a week, however, she had changed her
mind and decided that she would keep the child. She was permitted to do so. Aside from the acute disappointment involved,
the couple had expended almost $2000 in what turned out to be
a futile effort to obtain a child.

While adopting a child through an agency does not give
an absolute guarantee that the child's parents will not change
their minds before the adoption becomes final, the possibilities
of such a contingency are reduced enormously. To begin with,
a good agency explores the possibility of keeping the parent
and child together before offering the child for adoption. In
the case of unwed mothers, a social worker will usually be
assigned to the case and will explore the situation fully, usually
over a period of months, with the mother. If the mother wants
to keep the child, a sound agency will do its best to help
her with arrangements to do so. When a mother who has had
the benefit of such consultation and help during her pregnancy
decides to consent to the adoption of the child, the chances
are fairly good that she will not subsequently change her mind.
Moreover, if, in connection with the decision to give up her
child for adoption, the mother has turned the child over to the
agency, the agency in many states has the legal right to con-

sent to the adoption in her stead in the formal court proceeding; the mother is not involved at all.

While many states still permit a parent to revoke his or her consent before the adoption becomes final, the trend seems to be toward allowing such revocation only if the parent has changed his mind for sound reasons or if the child's interest will be served by returning him to his parents.

Two New York cases illustrate the trend of the courts. In the first case, decided during the thirties, Marion had been abandoned by the father of her child soon after it was born. In these circumstances, she signed a document consenting to its adoption. Shortly thereafter she recovered her health, got a job and tried to reclaim the child. She told the court that she had been desperately ill at the time she signed the consent, and thought she might die. She claimed she had been told that, if she wished, she could revoke her consent at any time during the six month period during which the New York law requires that the child live with the adopting parents before the adoption can be finally approved. The court held that her action in signing the consent to adoption did not constitute an abandonment of the child so as to make any further consent to its adoption unnecessary. Marion was permitted to revoke her consent on the ground that the whole purpose of the law requiring a child to live with the adopting parents for six months before formal adoption was to give everyone involved a chance to reflect and to change his mind before the adoption actually takes place.

In a case decided in 1949 the court seemed less concerned with the rights of mother love than with the welfare of the child. A woman whom we shall call Betty, was about to be divorced from her husband. She came to New York from her home in a nearby state and, after consultation with her relatives, gave her consent to an agency for the adoption of her nine-month-old son. Both she and her husband signed the requisite consents permitting the agency to place the boy for adoption. Two weeks later the agency gave the child to a couple whom it considered well suited for him. A few weeks later Betty changed her mind and appeared at the agency office demanding that her baby be returned to her. After consultation with the agency social worker she changed her mind again. During the next few months she wavered constantly and had numerous conferences with the agency. About five months after she had given up the boy, she definitely decided she wanted him back and brought suit against the agency to compel his return.

At the hearing, conflicting psychiatric testimony was offered as to whether Betty was a psychopathic personality and unfit to rear the child. The court decided that her indecision over a period of months as to whether she wanted her child was strong evidence of emotional instability. Her letters and conduct showed that her decision to give the child away was not motivated by health or financial consideration (she had $2500 in the bank when she gave the child for adoption) but by a desire to start life again as a single woman. The court pointed out that the law gives preference to a mother because it is presumed that the love she feels for her child is stronger than any nonmaternal affection could be, but that Betty obviously did not have this kind of feeling for her son. By contrast, the adopting parents had clung to the boy even though the agency had warned them a few weeks after the child had been taken into their home that the mother was wavering and they might lose the child. Under the circumstances the court felt that the child would be better off with the adopting parents. It is worth noting that at the time this case was decided, New York still required that the child live with the adopting parents for six months before a formal adoption could be made. Yet the court which refused to return Betty's child to her ignored this requirement completely, probably on the theory that the waiting period was for the protection of the child and adopting parents, rather than a grace period for the natural parents.

In both cases just discussed a short period elapsed between the time the mother gave her consent and the time she attempted to withdraw it. The longer the time that intervenes, the more reluctant are the courts to permit a change of mind or heart by the real parents and the stronger must be their reasons for doing so. In one case, for example, the adopting parents delayed initiating formal adoption proceedings for two years after the child had come to live with them. The child's mother consented to its adoption at the time the couple took the child. The couple delayed adopting the boy, not because they were uncertain as to whether they wanted to keep him, but because they wished to protect the mother from publicity. The court refused to allow the mother to revoke her consent at the end of the two-year period.

It goes without saying that a parent will be permitted to revoke his consent and even to have an adoption annulled where the consent was fraudulently obtained. A mere mistake of fact is not fraud. In one case, both parents of the child involved were tubercular and were in a sanatorium. The father died and the mother believed that she would die too. In this belief, she signed papers giving a named couple the right to adopt her child. After the adoption she recovered and found herself able to work and capable of supporting the child. The court held that she was not entitled to revoke her consent even though she gave it in the mistaken belief that she was dying. A different situation would have been presented, of course, if the people who wanted the child had known that she would recover but had deliberately deceived her in order to obtain her consent to the adoption. In such a case, even if the adoption had become final, the mother would probably have a right to have it annulled.

In some states a consent to adoption given before the birth of the child is in the same class as any other consent. Other states take the position that a parent isn't in a position to know whether he wants to give the child up until after the child has been born. A recent amendment to the Tennessee law, for example, provides that the mother's consent to the adoption of her child before it is born is not a binding consent. She can also withdraw a consent given after the child is born (unless such consent was given before a judge) provided she does so within thirty days after its birth or within thirty days from the time of her discharge from the hospital, whichever comes later. This statute is designed to counteract the undue pressure often put on unwed mothers to give up their children and to give them a chance to figure things out calmly.

The courts seem not to find any implication of fraud or any evidence that the consenting parent did not know what he was doing in the fact that the name of the adopting parent is left blank in the consent signed by the parent. The courts seem to assume that anyone who signs such a blank consent waives his right to know about the adopting parents or to make an independent judgment as to their fitness. Consents in which the names of the adopting parents do not appear are frequently used in nonagency placements to minimize the possibility of later interference by the natural parents. In the case of agency placements the consent usually runs to the agency.

A more difficult question as to whether there has been fraud arises in the cases where the parent has definitely been told that he may revoke his consent within a given period without objection on the part of the adopting parents, but finds when he attempts to do so that the adopting parents do object. If such a promise is made without any intention of keeping it, the parent would seem entitled to revoke his consent or even to have a completed adoption annulled. Whether he will be permitted to do so, however, seems to depend somewhat on whether the child's welfare will in fact be best served by permitting the parent to reclaim him.

One rather curious case of this sort involved a famous child actor. The boy was the youngest of three children of fairly poor parents. When he was about three, his parents were told by doctors that he could not survive if he remained in the

city slum where his parents lived. They forthwith sent him
to his grandparents' home in the country and regularly sent
money to pay for his upkeep. He was reared largely by an
unmarried aunt who lived with the grandparents and who discovered as the years went by that the little boy had a decided
flair for acting. She managed to get the child to Hollywood
and into the movies and then convinced the father that his
career would be best fostered if he could be at least nominally
adopted by her. She gave the father written assurance that
he could revoke his consent to the adoption within six months
after it was given. The father attempted to revoke during this
period. Despite the aunt's admission that she had never had
any intention of allowing the father to revoke his consent, the
court ignored the father's objections and permitted her to
adopt the child.

This is one of the rare instances where parents who had
never abandoned or neglected their child were deprived of
parental rights against their will because of a conditional consent given prior to actual adoption. The court indicated that
it was influenced by the fact that the child wished to be
adopted by his aunt. The ability of the aunt to handle and
further the child's acting career may also have been a factor
in the court's decision that even though there had been deliberate fraud in procuring the parents' consent, the adoption
would be permitted to stand because it seemed to serve the
child's best interests.

In most states if the child to be adopted is of an age where
he can be expected to have a reasonably intelligent opinion on
the subject of his own adoption, his consent is also required before the adoption is approved. Different states specify different
ages. In some, the consent of the child must be obtained if he
is over ten; in others, not unless he is over twelve or even
fourteen.

A valid legal adoption transfers all of the rights and duties
of the natural parents to the adoptive parents and gives the
child the right to look to them for those benefits to which a

natural child would be entitled. This usually includes the right to inherit from the adopting parents in the same manner as natural offspring would if they die without a Will. The states are not unanimous as to whether (unless he is specifically named in their Wills) an adopted child can inherit from his adoptive parents' relatives as if he were their natural child. In any event, adoption usually terminates the child's right to inherit from his real parents; in some few states only, can he inherit from both sets of parents. The adoption of a child does not destroy, however, his rights in the estate of a parent or other relatives who died before the child was adopted.

A desire to inherit is often the moving factor behind efforts to establish what the law calls a "quasi-adoption," that is, a situation where the child was legally entitled to be adopted but for some reason was not. In one such case, May N. had agreed by written contract to give the custody of her baby daughter to Mary and Edward B. who, in exchange, promised that they would adopt the baby and give her all the rights of a natural child including the right to inherit from them. For some reason, no formal adoption was ever consummated. Mrs. B. died leaving a fairly valuable piece of real property which was claimed by her three natural children. The girl claimed that she was in effect an adopted child whose rights were the same as theirs and that she too was entitled to share in the property. The court agreed with her.

Even where there is no such specific written agreement as the one whereby the B.'s promised to give the child the right to inherit, the courts sometimes accord the rights of an adopted child to a child who should have been but was not actually adopted.

A Michigan farmer, Phineas, and his wife took a boy, Frank, from a county home when he was one and a half years old. As time went on, they became fond of him and they went through a formal proceeding looking toward his adoption when he was eight. Frank, who was twenty-two at the time of Phineas's death, had worked on the farm all of his life without compensation exactly as if he had been Phineas' own son and it was understood by all that the farm would be Frank's when his adoptive parents died. Phineas had spoken lovingly of the boy to his friends and neighbors and had said how happy it made him to think that he had a "son" to inherit his farm. Unfortunately, after Phineas died, his sister and the children of his deceased brother turned up and proved that the law under which Frank had been adopted had been declared unconstitutional and that Frank had never, therefore, been legally adopted. They brought suit to oust Frank from what they considered *their* farm. The court waved aside technicalities and held that there was an "implicit" contract between Phineas and Frank to the effect that Phineas would leave the farm to Frank and that this contract could and would be enforced by the court.

In some states a child who has not been legally adopted cannot inherit from his foster parents, unless there is an express agreement such as there was in the first case described. Most states, however, will follow the Michigan case in allowing a child adopted in every sense but a highly technical one to inherit, even in the absence of an express contract, on a theory of quasi-adoption. This theory of quasi-adoption has also been applied in at least one state to describe the relationship of a child born of artificial insemination and the husband of the child's mother. (See Chapter 8.)

Once a child has been legally adopted, both the child and the parents are usually expected to assume the risks and shoulder the burdens which natural parents and children have in relation to each other. Thus, if Mr. and Mrs. Martin adopt a child, Laura, and Mr. Martin subsequently becomes incapacitated and Mrs. Martin has to go to work to help support the family, Laura will not be taken away from them even though they might not have been permitted to adopt her if those had been the circumstances at the time of the adoption. Laura must accept the misfortunes as well as the fortunes of her new family just as if she were their own child. Similarly, if

Laura turns out to be a sickly child whose medical expenses cost more than the Martins can afford, they cannot rid themselves of her any more than they could if she were their own child. In certain extreme situations, however, the law of many states does give the child or the adopting parents an escape from the adoption. In some, the adoption can be annulled if the adopted child turns out to have certain named serious defects which were unknown to the adoptive parents at the time of the adoption. In Illinois, for example, the adoption can be annulled if the child develops mental illness or mental deficiency, epilepsy or venereal disease as a result of conditions arising prior to the adoption. In such a case, the child becomes the legal ward of the State Department of Public Welfare.

Statutes permitting adoptions to be annulled on such grounds can probably be justified on the general principle that they give prudent prospective adoptors security and confidence without which adoption might become a hazardous proceeding. Somewhat more questionable are statutes and cases which permit an adoption to be abrogated if the child behaves in an unfilial way.

In one New York case a six-year-old girl, adopted from a foundling home, developed about a year later a disease which resembled St. Vitus Dance but which did not completely respond to medical treatment. The child rapidly became what might be mildly termed a behavior problem. She threw stones at her adoptive mother, lay down on the road in front of cars, started fires in the house, cut the bedding, and generally behaved in a way which undoubtedly did not coincide with the adoptive mother's dreams of an angelic little daughter. After six years of this, when the little girl was twelve, the adoptive parents went to court and asked for an annulment of the adoption. The court admitted that real parents could not have cut off their own child in similar circumstances but granted the annulment nonetheless on the ground that love between the adoptive parents and the child was already lost and that compulsory continuation of the relationship would only engender hatred on both sides.

Compare with this an Alabama case where the adoptive parents also tried to cast off a twelve-year-old girl. In this case, John and Mary B. had adopted Dorothy when she was twenty months old. When she was twelve they came to court with a long list of grievances against her and claimed that she was disrespectful, disobedient, incorrigible, and recalcitrant to her father's wishes. The court refused to revoke the adoption, pointing out that respect and obedience were the results and rewards of good care and training of a child and that the parents' complaint was "rather a confession of failure on the part of the parent than a grievance against the child." The court also considered that a child of twelve was not old enough to be considered responsible for its own misdeeds. While the court's allocation of responsibility was undoubtedly correct, we might query the wisdom of forcing to stay together parents and a child who clearly have no use for one another.

The difference in the results in the two cases just cited may be partly due to the different ages at which the child came under the influence of the adoptive parents. Dorothy was less than two years old when adopted. The little girl in the first case was six. Generally the adoptive parent can be held to a higher degree of responsibility for the child's development when he adopts a baby than when he adopts an older child whose previous unhappy experiences may have fixed his psychological patterns along undesirable lines.

Few adoptive parents ever wish to revoke the adoption. The overwhelming number of adoptions are happy for all concerned. Although in both of the cases cited the child had been placed by an adoption agency, and not by a black or gray market transaction, many authorities feel that such conflict between parent and child is less likely to occur in an agency placement because agency placements generally involve a full and careful investigation of both child and adoptive parents. Furthermore, if difficulties do arise, a good agency stands ready to continue helping the family after the formal adoption. This ready availability of expert help can often prevent any question of abrogating the adoption from arising by making it possible for parent and child to adjust to each other before the situation becomes hopeless.

While decline in the prosperity of the adopting family is not cause for revoking an adoption, some states decree revocation if the adoptive parents fail to give the child proper care or turn out to be financially irresponsible. Thus, the Catholic home which had placed two-year-old Stella with Mr. and Mrs. H., succeeded in abrogating the adoption by showing a New York court that Mr. H. could not properly support the child, that his family had on numerous occasions resorted to charity, and that Mrs. H. stayed in bed until noon every day and failed to tend her home properly and that the couple had incurred debts which they were unable and unwilling to pay. Usually there must be some element of wanton lack of regard for the welfare of the child or deliberate neglect in order for the courts to take the extreme step of removing the child from a home into which it has been adopted. Mere misfortune is no more a ground for breaking up an adoptive family than a natural one.

Occasionally an adoption is abrogated by the mutual consent of all parties involved if, in the opinion of the court, this course will be to the best interests of the child. In one case, for example, a mother permitted her father-in-law to adopt her child after her husband's death, feeling that she could not care for the child properly because she was in poor health and without means. Some years later the mother remarried and her father-in-law agreed that his adoption of the grandchild should be revoked and the mother's rights restored. The court revoked the adoption. An adoption may likewise be canceled by mutual consent where an agency has placed a child, has attempted and failed to help the parents and child adjust to each other and is willing to take the child back again.

In some states, there is no provision in the law at all for annulment or revocation of an adoption even if all the parties concerned wish it. The only solution in such cases is for the child to be re-adopted from the adoptive parents and the same factors would be considered by the court in passing on the petition for the second adoption as if it were the first adoption involving that child.

In the days when Charles Dickens wrote so pathetically of Oliver Twist there were far more destitute and unwanted children than there were parents who wanted to adopt them. Today the situation is precisely the opposite as is demonstrated by the high incidence in the daily press of stories about would-be parents paying enormous sums to doctors, lawyers, lying-in homes, and others who have access to adoptable children. By and large the law appears to have accomplished the about-face in this field demanded by changed conditions better than it has elsewhere—perhaps in part because the social service agencies have been and are increasingly pointing the way.

CHAPTER 10

Postscript

ABOUT ESTATES AND WILLS

ALL PERSONS die either "testate" or "intestate." To die testate means simply to die leaving a valid Will; to die intestate means to die without a valid Will. Every state has laws prescribing what is to happen to the property of a person—man or woman—who dies intestate. Thus, what happens in effect is that the deceased person having made no Will, the state makes one for him. The laws setting forth who shall inherit the property of an intestate are called intestacy laws. Usually, the spouse and the children in designated proportions are the sole or chief heirs. Depending in most cases on whether there is a spouse and/or children, parents, siblings and even more remote relatives are named as successive inheritors by the state laws governing intestacy.

If a person does not wish his property to be distributed in accordance with the intestacy laws, he can, within certain limitations, make a Will disposing of his property any way he wishes. These limitations generally have to do with the length of time during which property can be held in trust, the permissible proportion of an estate that can be given to charity and the rights of the surviving spouse. In almost every state a parent is free to disinherit any or all of his children (whether they are minors or not) if he so desires and clearly so provides. In Louisiana a child can be disinherited only if he has been guilty of one of several wrongs against the parent such as cruelty, willful failure to provide for the parent or marriage while a minor without the parent's consent.

In most states, however, a husband cannot wholly disinherit his wife or a wife her husband, if they are still legally
husband and wife at the time of death, unless the surviving
spouse has been guilty of abandonment, failure to support
or other serious misconduct. We have seen that during their
joint lifetimes, husbands and wives are today, for the most
part, distinct legal entities. The duty of the husband to support the wife and the corresponding duty of the wife to contribute to the husband's maintenance if he becomes ill or
otherwise disabled are the exceptions. On the death of one
spouse, on the other hand, quite generally the surviving spouse
automatically acquires an interest in the property of the
deceased partner.

At common law, the husband's surviving interest in his
wife's property was called "courtesy"; the wife's in her husband's holdings "dower." Even though most of the rest of the
common-law rules applicable to the property of husbands and
wives while they are alive have gone by the board, one form
or another of dower and courtesy interests persists in most
states. In some, for example, the spouse's rights in real property attach before death in the sense that the surviving spouse
will have a surviving interest in any real property owned by
his spouse or by them both, during their marriage; when this
is the case, a purchaser of property to which such a right
attaches must, to be protected, insist that the transfer to him
be by both husband and wife. In other jurisdictions, the surviving spouse's right attaches only to property owned by the
deceased spouse or by the couple at the time of his death
and is defined in terms of a minimum share of all such property owned. In still other states, like North and South Dakota,
there is no restriction whatever on the right of spouses to disinherit each other. A few states give this right to one spouse
but not to the other. Some permit a spouse to give away all of
his real property (land, buildings, etc.) or his personal property (money, stocks, cars, furniture, etc.) to people other
than the surviving spouse but insist that the surviving spouse

get at least part of the other type of property. In community property states, of course, the spouses acquire rights in each other's earned property during their lifetime. However it is put, what it comes to in most states is that on one theory or another, a surviving spouse, still married and not guilty of misconduct, is entitled at least to some part of the deceased spouse's holdings.

If a testator (a person who makes a Will) leaves the surviving spouse out entirely or wills the survivor a lesser share of the property than the statute provides for a surviving spouse, the survivor has what is called "a right of election" and may insist on the statutory share. Thus, Lawrence, a resident of state X, dies leaving stocks and bank accounts worth $50,000. In his Will, he leaves his wife, Margaret, $10,000. The law of the state says that since Lawrence had no children, Margaret is entitled to one-half of all of his property. Margaret can, if she wishes, decline to take only $10,000 and insist upon her statutory share of $25,000. She probably could not, however, make this election if she had agreed not to do so either by a prenuptial agreement or by a waiver signed after the marriage. Where Margaret has not waived her right of election she must usually exercise it within a short time after Lawrence's death. No one but she can exercise the right. Suppose, for example, that Lawrence had left the bulk of his estate to his aged, infirm mother and Margaret decides to leave matters as Lawrence wished them. Margaret dies soon after Lawrence, leaving her estate to her sister. The sister cannot claim, in Margaret's name, the share to which Margaret would have been entitled if she had exercised her right.

Except with respect to the type of restrictions previously mentioned, the law leaves people free to make whatever disposition of their property they please and most people prefer to make their own Wills rather than to let their property be divided in accordance with the intestacy laws.

Each state has a number of technical requirements with which a Will must conform to be valid. Except in cases of emergency when a lawyer is not available, it is advisable that a lawyer be consulted and draw the Will. It is hazardous for a layman to attempt to draw his own Will by filling in the blanks on a printed form or copying a friend's Will or one printed in a book. In addition to the technical requirements for the Will itself, the law of most states requires that a rather elaborate ritual be observed in connection with its signing. For example, witnesses must sign in the presence of the testator. A home-made document may give the testator a false sense of security that he has arranged his estate satisfactorily. After his death, the Will may be thrown out because it was not properly signed or witnessed or for many other technical reasons. Neither should any attempt ever be made to make changes in a Will without consulting a lawyer. Not only may the attempted amendment be of no force but the entire Will may be invalidated by an amateur attempt to change some detail. The amount saved in legal fees by trying to draft or change your own Will may be small by comparison with the amount wasted in litigation over an improperly drawn or executed Will.

In view of the hazards involved in "self-lawyering" no attempt will here be made to enumerate the requirements of the various states for drawing a Will. Lawyers will usually charge a very moderate fee for drafting a Will particularly where no trusts are to be set up and there is not a great deal of property involved. The failure of many people to have a Will drawn is due to the misconception that Wills are needed only by people who have a lot of money to dispose of. This is an especially injurious misconception for married people. Only a carefully drawn Will is apt to carry out your wishes.

Particularly is a Will important if you have a child or children in order to assure yourself of their proper upbringing and maintenance. The number of questions your Will should answer with reference to your children are legion. To mention only one—suppose you and your spouse are both killed in the same disaster or accident. The law of your state probably provides that each spouse shall be the children's guardian in the event of the death of the other. But if both are killed, or die within a short time of each other, the designation of the proper person to bring up the children may be a crucial factor to their entire future development. If the parents have not decided, a court will have to make the determination. Very frequently, couples presented with this question find to their horror that the relative most likely to be named as guardian if they don't leave a Will is the last person in the world whom they want to rear their children. One couple, for example, had been estranged from the wife's mother for years because of her intolerable efforts to run their lives for them. If both of them died, the domineering mother would probably have been quick to request the court to give her the guardianship of the children and the court might have appointed her. This couple had made no Wills because they had no substantial property. The fact that they had two children who were, of course, their most valuable possessions, had not seemed to them to necessitate their making a Will. They had attempted to solve the problem by asking their two closest friends, a couple whom they liked and trusted, to accept guardianship of their children in the event they both died. When it was explained to them that the mere fact of their friends' consent was not sufficient to safeguard the children's interests, they made Wills naming the couple as guardians of the children if they both died. While the law as to the appointment of guardians varies from state to state, the parents can usually make what arrangements seem best to them if they take the trouble to plan by Will in advance for the contingency.

The need for a Will, of course, increases when there are special circumstances affecting the children—where, for example, there are questions of legitimacy or where the child is adopted or is the result of artificial insemination. Even if there are no children, a person whose marriage has been terminated by a decree of annulment or divorce would do well to make his intentions clear in a Will, since there is always a chance of trouble from a former spouse. A former spouse, who is not estopped from doing so (see Chapter 21), may make trouble in any event by claiming still to be the spouse and therefore entitled to the statutory share. But this would be an ex-spouse's only reliance if a Will makes clear that he or she is to get nothing. In the absence of a Will there may be other complications as well. For example, the former spouse might claim to be entitled to the entire estate under the intestacy laws.

If the husband or wife dies intestate it may be to someone's advantage to try to prove that a child is not entitled to inherit because of some irregularity in his origin or that a spouse should not inherit because of the invalidity of a prior divorce. Such a possibility is materially lessened if both husband and wife take the trouble to make Wills which refer by name to the persons whom they wish to inherit their property.

It is probable, moreover, that the intestate succession law of your state does not provide for your estate to be distributed exactly as you would want it to be. These laws are generally designed to distribute property to the closest relatives of the deceased. Spouse, children, parents and siblings are usually preferred in that order. This may not, however, work out well for a particular family.

Assume that Bill Smith, a resident of New York, is married and the father of three children. He dies leaving an estate worth $10,000. He leaves no Will. By the law of New York his wife is entitled to one third of his estate and the children share the remainder equally. The children are young and Bill's wife will need every bit of the money to supplement her earnings for the next few years while the children are growing up. But she may not be able to touch their two-thirds of the estate without obtaining court permission every time she wants to use the children's money. Time and money would be expended in administering the children's share of the estate—far more time and money than it would have cost Bill to make a Will giving his entire estate to his wife whom he probably trusted to use his money wisely for herself and the children.

People who have made Wills before marriage should review them immediately after being married since in most states a Will made before marriage is at least in part revoked by the subsequent marriage of the testator. The birth of a child is another apt occasion for reviewing an old Will. Separation, divorce or any other drastic change of relationships or changes in the kind or amount of property owned also warrant reconsideration of an earlier Will. Changing tax laws sometimes call for remaking a Will which was satisfactory at the time it was made but because of increased taxes no longer does for the legatees what the testator intended.

Not all the property a person owns necessarily passes under his Will. For example, Charles Roe has an insurance policy naming his child, Edward, as beneficiary. He owns his house jointly with his wife, Mabel. He and Mabel have a joint bank account. He also has $500 worth of government bonds payable upon death to his brother, Nicholas. All of this property will go to the joint owner or the beneficiary as the case may be. Not only is a Will not needed to dispose of it, but Charles could not, by his Will, give it to persons other than those named, even if he so desired. For people of small means who have no minor children, such joint ownership of property obviates to a large extent the necessity of having a Will. By and large, however, a Will is a more certain way of insuring the desired disposition of *all* of the deceased's property and rights.

There is much resentment of the increasing extent to which government tells us during our lifetime what we may, must, and must not do. But except for the requirement that a spouse get his distributive share, there are few restrictions placed upon us with respect to whom we may leave our property after our death. If we may paraphrase: where there's a Will, there's a way to provide for what you conceive to be the best interests of your family and friends, hence—there ought to be a Will.

PART III

The Sex Side

CHAPTER 11

Birth Control

𝒴OU COMMIT a crime punishable by fine and imprisonment every time you use a contraceptive in the state of Connecticut. So does the doctor who tells you what contraceptive to use, the nurse who teaches you how to use it and the druggist who sells it to you. If, on the other hand, you live in Alabama, Florida, Georgia, Mississippi, North or South Carolina or Virginia, the state will pay public health workers to teach you how and when to use a contraceptive. Instruction in contraceptive techniques is part of the public health programs of those states. In the other forty states, many other kinds of official regulations govern—or attempt to govern—what is in essence the most intimate kind of personal choice.

Contraception was not always such a target for legislative action. Until 1873 what people chose to do about birth control was pretty much their own business. In that year, a man named Anthony Comstock descended upon Congress with a large supply of obscene post cards and good intentions. He succeeded in persuading the legislators that they had to do something to prevent the nation from sliding into the clutches of organized vice. Pursuant to his prodding, a bill was introduced which made it criminal to import, mail or transport in interstate commerce "obscene literature and articles of immoral use." The bill included in this category "any article or medicine for the prevention of conception or for causing abortion," but made an express exception for such articles when circulated "on the prescription of a physician in good standing given in good faith." For some reason which does not appear in the records of the Congressional debates, this exception was dropped in later versions of the bill and did not appear in the law as finally passed. Perhaps the omission was accidental; perhaps it was thought that the exemption of physicians was so obvious that there was no need to state it in so many words. The legislators who passed the bill were clearly not aware of its precise meaning and no doubt voted for it on the theory that it was "against sin." As one Senator (Conkling) put it:

> For one, although I have tried to acquaint myself with it (the bill), I have not been able to tell . . . and if I were questioned now as to what this bill concerns, I could not aver anything certain in regard to it. The indignation and disgust which everybody feels in reference to the acts which are here aimed at may possibly lead us to do something which, when we come to see it in print, will not be the thing we would have done if we had understood it and were more deliberate about it.

Notwithstanding the fact that many of the senators and congressmen must have been equally confused, the Comstock bill was passed with no further discussion.

Thus far in this book, we have been concerned almost exclusively with state law. That is because under our constitutional system, the control of marriage and the family rests in the separate states. The federal government is a government of delegated powers only and the Constitution did not delegate to it any right to legislate with respect to marriage and the family as such. However, the federal government does, under the Constitution, have the power to regulate and control interstate and foreign commerce and the mails. The Comstock Act was one of the first, and it remains one of the outstanding, examples of how Congress, through its commerce and post-office power, can by a federal act impinge directly on the fields of marriage and the family which are presumably the exclusive concern of the states. For the purposes of this chapter, we are concerned with that aspect of the Comstock Act which purported to make illegal the importation, carriage by mail and transportation in interstate commerce of articles for the prevention of conception. As we shall see in later chapters, the same Comstock law dealt with a number of other subjects, among them obscenity and abortion. Hence in these contexts, too, it has left its imprint on our marriage and family law.

The Comstock prohibitions did not only affect the states in terms of the effect on what could come into the state through the mails and the channels of interstate and foreign commerce. About half the states, playing a kind of legislative "follow the leader" quickly passed "little Comstock laws" of their own which applied directly to what went on inside their own borders. Unlike the federal law, most of the state laws specifically make exceptions for doctors and in many instances for druggists as well. This is the situation in Colorado, Delaware, Indiana, Iowa, Minnesota, Montana, Nevada, Ohio, Wisconsin, and Wyoming where doctors and druggists are exempted from flat prohibitions against the dissemination of either contraceptives or information about them. New Jersey does not specify any distinct class of exempt persons but makes the distribution of contraceptive devices or information about them a crime only if done "without just cause." It has always been assumed that a doctor's prescription for a contraceptive in that state is based on a "just cause." Mississippi has no express exception for doctors but the presence of public birth control services in the state is strong evidence that its statute prohibiting the distribution of contraceptives is not applicable to legitimate medical practice.

In New York, doctors may prescribe contraceptive devices "for the cure or prevention of disease." The word "disease" has been so liberally interpreted that it is assumed in that state that any physician acting pursuant to the dictates of his professional conscience is not violating the law. The statute does not specify that a doctor can prescribe contraceptives only to protect the health of married women, but in at least one case the court has read this limitation into the law. Fortunately, the law does not require the doctor to make a personal investigation as to whether the patient is married. If she says she is and if he has no reason to believe otherwise, the doctor will probably not be called to task. Incidentally, the Wisconsin statute specifically prohibits doctors from giving contraceptive advice to unmarried women.

Some states have directed their prohibition, not against the practice of contraception, but only against literature dealing with contraception. In Arizona and California, it is unlawful to advertise contraceptives or publish offers to give information about the prevention of conception. The Louisiana statute seems to prohibit only accounts or descriptions of "secret" drugs or nostrums for the prevention of conception; the statute is, however, by no means clear. Kansas, Missouri, and Nebraska prohibit printed descriptions of methods of contraception except in medical texts. Maine and Michigan have a similar law with no express exception for medical works. In Pennsylvania and Washington the only stricture is against the display or advertisement of contraceptive devices. Arkansas and North Carolina have in effect incorporated the federal law as far as contraceptive information is concerned. They make no specific mention of contraception at all but provide that within their borders the possession or sale of literature which has been barred from the United States mails is illegal.

An interesting approach to the legislative regulation of contraception is to be seen in the so-called Prophylactic Control Laws of such states as Idaho, Oregon, and Utah. These laws are designed not to suppress contraception but to channel the distribution of devices and information for contraception and the prevention of venereal disease through legitimate drug stores. They also involve state testing procedures intended to insure at least a minimum quality of product. A number of states prohibit the sale of contraceptives by slot machines. Maryland has an interesting exception to the rule; sale of contraceptives by slot machines is only permitted "in places where alcoholic beverages are sold for consumption on the premises . . ."

Many states have no laws at all aimed against contraception. Others (listed above), marking the swing of the pendulum away from the repressive intent of the original Comstock laws, have set up state subsidized child-spacing programs as part of their health services.

Notwithstanding the more than seventy years that have gone by with all the radical changes in mores and morals and the scientific development they have seen, the original federal Comstock laws have stayed on the books unmodified. However, in the past two decades, when it was sought to apply them unreasonably, federal courts have whittled away their absolute prohibitions and read into them exceptions for legitimate medical practice. In 1930 one of the Federal Circuit Courts of Appeal implied that the laws would be invoked only against the interstate transmission of contraceptives "for illegal contraception" and would not be construed to prevent their "proper medical use." A few years later another Federal Circuit Court of Appeals held that druggists who act as the source of supply for the medical profession were not intended to be included in the ban to the extent of this legitimate function on their part. These early cases reached their logical climax in 1936 when the late Dr. Hannah Stone, a pioneer in the field of medical contraception, attempted to import a number of vaginal diaphragms from Japan. The diaphragms were confiscated by the United States District Attorney in New York at the behest of the Customs Authorities. In the resultant case, the Circuit Court of Appeals sitting in New York read a clear exception into the federal statutes, holding that they could not be interpreted to forbid "the importation, sale or carriage by mail of things which might intelligently be employed by conscientious and competent physicians for the purpose of saving life and promoting the well-being of their patients."

Largely as a result of the decision in the Hannah Stone case, the Post Office Department, the Customs officials, and the various federal attorneys throughout the United States have freely permitted contraceptives and contraceptive information to travel through the mails and in interstate and foreign commerce, provided they are coming from or going to doctors or other qualified professional personnel or anyone acting at their direction or under their supervision.

The liberalization of the federal law, the development of prophylactic control laws and the establishment of state subsidized child-spacing programs did not take place in a vacuum. All are a reflection of increasing acceptance by the public and by the medical profession of the value of contraception in preventive medicine and the growing acceptance of the idea of voluntary, controlled child spacing.

In 1936, *Fortune* magazine polled a cross section of the adult population asking, "Do you believe in the teaching and practice of birth control?" Sixty-three per cent of all those polled answered "yes." Forty-two and eight-tenths per cent of the Catholics asked also answered "yes." Again in 1938, the *Ladies Home Journal* found that seventy-nine per cent of the cross section of women asked whether they "believe in birth control" responded "yes"—fifty-one per cent of the Catholic women asked responded in the affirmative. A Gallup poll in 1940 revealed that about seventy-seven per cent of the American people approved "having government health clinics furnish birth control information to married people who want it." In a further *Fortune* poll in 1943, eighty-four and nine-tenths per cent of the women questioned said that they thought "knowledge about birth control should be made available to all married women." The poll showed that women in these categories voted "yes" as follows: Catholic women, sixty-nine per cent; grammar school graduates, seventy and two-tenths

per cent; college graduates, ninety-two and six-tenths per cent.
During this same period, polls of physicians have indicated
that ninety-seven per cent of American physicians approve
contraception as a medical technique. As such it has been
endorsed by the American Medical Association and a number
of its specialized sections. Ads for contraceptives now circulate
freely in medical and pharmaceutical journals. Birth-control
clinics, many of them affiliated with the nation-wide Planned
Parenthood Federation of America, operate throughout the
country.

As against this background, the states of Connecticut and
Massachusetts stick out as sore thumbs. The Massachusetts statute, using substantially the same language as the federal laws, prohibits the distribution or display of contraceptives as well as the circulation of information about them. As
the federal laws were liberalized and more liberal laws were
adopted in other states, it had always been assumed that the
Massachusetts law, too, would not be so interpreted as to interfere with legitimate medical practice. However, in 1938, the
sovereign state of Massachusetts, its population forty per cent
Catholic, instituted a series of raids on one of its best known
birth-control clinics and arrested the doctor in charge, two social workers, and a nurse. The right of a physician to prescribe
in the best interests of his patient was forcefully pleaded. (It
was conceded that the social workers and the nurse were and
would be acting under physician's instructions.) The courts of
Massachusetts, disregarding the rationale of all the federal
cases, the legislative trend of the other states, and the predom-
inant public and medical attitude toward birth control as well
as virtually every relevant canon of statutory construction,
found that the Massachusetts statute permitted no exception—
not even for doctors. An attempt to have the United States Supreme Court reverse the decision was defeated on technical
grounds.

Having rejected the idea that the statute should be read
as exempting legitimate medical practice, the Massachusetts

judges have since been having much trouble in adapting their intransigent view to some of the facts of life. Many objects, capable of use as contraceptives, have a variety of other, perfectly legitimate noncontraceptive uses; various chemicals, syringe bags and condoms, for example. Even bottles of carbonated soft drinks or ordinary table salt are used by some people for attempted contraceptive purposes. Clearly the Massachusetts courts could not forbid the distribution of such articles entirely. When in 1940 a druggist was prosecuted for selling condoms to a plain clothes police detective, the Massachusetts court held that in order to convict the druggist, the prosecution must prove that the article was sold for use as a contraceptive and not for some other purpose—as, for example, the prevention of disease. Since the use is precisely the same, whatever the purpose, the sale of condoms is thus perfectly legal in Massachusetts except in the unlikely case where the purchaser says to the druggist, "Look here, I'm not at all concerned with preventing disease. I intend to use this solely to prevent conception."

The result of the Massachusetts rulings is that the sale of any kind of contraceptive which is capable of another use—the prevention of disease or the euphemistic "feminine hygiene" or anything else—is unlimited. The law operates mainly to prevent the prescription or distribution of the best and most reliable types of contraceptives such as vaginal diaphragms which entail the services of a physician for fitting purposes and which are solely designed for contraceptive purposes. Such devices, which are and must be channeled through the medical profession, are presumed to be illegal, although recently some doctors in Massachusetts have asserted that since they can also be used as menstrual cups, perhaps they too may be prescribed on this ground without violating the law. Less reliable articles can be bought anywhere by anyone with the price in his pocket.

So far the chief effect of the ban in Massachusetts has been the closing down of the maternal health centers whose purpose it was to give contraceptive advice to lower income groups in cases where medical considerations rendered pregnancy a real threat to life and health. Twice during the last decade, the proponents of medically supervised birth control in Massachusetts have succeeded in having the question put to popular referendum but both times the organized opposition of the Catholic Church defeated the measure. Further efforts in the form of test cases, legislation, and referenda are in contemplation.

Shortly after the Massachusetts clinic raids, Connecticut followed the lead of its older sister state and proceeded to indict doctors and nurses who had been working in a birth-control clinic. In Connecticut the statute, also derived from the old Comstock lode, forbade the *use* of contraceptives. As a practical matter, this statute is obviously unenforceable. Even if police officials spied on the most intimate bedroom scenes, they would have a hard job proving that a contraceptive was being or had been used. Practically speaking, however, the vice of the statute is that it can be invoked against doctors, nurses, druggists, social workers, and the like on the theory that they are accessories to the crime of use.

Acting on the accessory theory, the state of Connecticut forced the closing of all the birth-control clinics there. The usual results followed. While sales of less reliable, expensive and "capable of other use" contraceptives continued to flourish, the lower income women whose health urgently required the prescription of contraceptive devices were no longer able to obtain them at low prices or free from medically supervised clinics.

Three such women consulted Dr. Wilder Tileston, an eminent obstetrician and gynecologist connected with the Yale Medical School. The first of them (who subsequently became known as Jane Doe in the test case that eventuated) was forty-one years old. She had been married for sixteen years and had five children ranging in age from fifteen years to three months. She suffered from high blood pressure. During her last pregnancy she had had a toxemia which necessitated the premature induction of labor. Clinic records showed that her blood pressure had not improved since the birth of the child but was still abnormally high. Both the clinic physician and the specialist to whom he sent Mrs. Doe agreed that if she were to become pregnant again in the near future, her high blood pressure would tend to induce toxemia of pregnancy. Apoplexy, cerebral shock or heart failure were all strong possibilities under the circumstances. All the doctors felt that if Mrs. Doe became pregnant, it was quite possible her pregnancy would have to be terminated by abortion in order to save her life.

The second woman, Mary Roe, was twenty-two. She had spent most of the previous four years in a tuberculosis sanatorium. She had been dismissed as an arrested case but was still undergoing pneumothorax regularly every few weeks; both of her lungs were being kept in a partially collapsed condition. Her doctor had given her permission to marry but had warned her against becoming pregnant in the near future. It was feared that the strain of pregnancy would, at a minimum, induce a relapse—possibly cause her death. If, on the other hand, she could avoid becoming pregnant for two or three years until the condition of her lungs had improved, she could have a child without undue danger.

Sarah Hoe, the third woman, was twenty-five and had been married for three years. She had three children, twenty-seven months, fourteen months and six weeks old—three pregnancies in a period of two and a quarter years. Her physical condition was generally good except insofar as she had been weakened by the rapid succession of pregnancies. Medical opinion, backed up by cold statistics, indicated that a continuation of child-bearing at anything like this rate would involve as increased hazard both for Mrs. Hoe and the child in each successive pregnancy. Moreover, Mr. Hoe was a laborer who earned sixteen dollars a week—hardly enough to feed his family of five even at 1941 prices. Each successive child would decrease what the Hoes could provide by way of proper food and care for their children or themselves.

Doe, Roe and Hoe were not their real names, but these are the actual case histories of three women patients of Dr. Tileston. If they had happened to live in any state of the Union other than Connecticut or Massachusetts their doctor would, as a matter of course, have been in a position to say to each of them something of this sort, "Look here, Mrs. ——, your physical condition is such that it would be highly dangerous for you to have a child in the near future. I should like to fit you with a contraceptive device which will prevent conception during this danger period. Later on when your condition has improved, I will be in a position to advise you to discontinue use of the contraceptive and undertake a pregnancy with the assurance that the outlook for both you and your child is excellent." In Connecticut it was feared that such advice and its implementation would render the doctor liable to criminal prosecution and possibly permanent loss of his license to practice as well.

On the basis of the three cases described, Dr. Tileston, with the backing of the organized Planned Parenthood groups of the state of Connecticut, brought suit for a declaratory judgment. He contended: first, that the statute prohibiting the use of contraceptives must be construed to contain an implied exception for those women who used contraceptives on the advice or direction of their physician to preserve their lives or protect their health, and, second, that if the courts failed to find such an implied exception in the statute, then the statute was an unconstitutional deprivation of life and liberty. The three case histories were presented along with affidavits from other eminent doctors who had either examined the patients or studied their case histories and who concurred in the opinion that contraception was medically indicated. Even doctors called by the State agreed that it would be dangerous for any of the three women to have a child in the near future. Nonetheless, the highest court of Connecticut, taking its cue from the Massachusetts Supreme Court, refused to read any exception into the law and held it constitutional on the ground that the women had an alternative remedy which was "reasonable, efficacious and practicable"— namely, total abstention from sexual intercourse. "Reasonable" to ask a newly-wed couple to live together like brother and sister for two or three years? "Efficacious" and "practicable" to suggest to a couple happily married for sixteen years that they revert to a state of premarital abstinence for an indefinite period?

Ironically enough, Connecticut, like most states, has a statute prohibiting abortions. (See Chapter 12.) Yet the Connecticut courts have held that an abortion may lawfully be performed where it is necessary to save the mother's life. Had Jane Doe, Mary Roe, or even Sarah Hoe become pregnant, no doubt an abortion would have been legally permissible. The same doctor who could not tell them how to avoid becoming pregnant without exposing himself to a possible jail sentence could, after they became pregnant, abort them with the full blessing of the state.

The Connecticut case was also appealed to the United States Supreme Court which again dismissed on technical grounds. Many attorneys feel that if, as, and when the question is squarely presented to that Court in a manner that is free from technical infirmities, the Supreme Court may well, in line with relevant precedents, hold that a state which outlaws contraceptives in cases of medical necessity (such as those presented by Dr. Tileston) is guilty of abridging the rights of life and liberty guaranteed by the Federal Constitution.

Although Connecticut and Massachusetts are the only two states where birth control, regardless of the need and the circumstances, has been held illegal as such, sporadic attacks on the medical prescription of contraceptives have occurred from time to time. Many of these appear to have stemmed from the opposition of the Catholic Church to all so-called "unnatural" methods of conception control. By "unnatural" is meant mechanical and chemical methods of contraception. The Catholic Church does not oppose "natural" methods of family limitation, that is, total abstinence or the so-called "rhythm" method which means abstinence during that period of the woman's menstrual cycle when she is "fertile." The Catholic Church endorsement has given rise to an epidemic of rhythm books, slide rules, and calendars. Claims made for some of these have been so excessive that on occasion the Federal Trade Commission has stepped in and ordered the discontinuance of "false and misleading advertising."

Generally speaking, the medical profession finds much merit in the "rhythm" theory, especially when it is undertaken under medical supervision but the great majority of doctors have concluded that other methods are far more reliable and easier to use. Many of them have pointed out that since the fertility period for some women is their time of greatest sexual desire, the rhythm method which counsels abstinence at that time is most "unnatural" for them. Moreover, any climatic change, illness or emotional disturbance can affect a particular woman's menstrual cycle and is likely to render her rhythm calculations valueless. Generally speaking, reliance on the rhythm method often induces a sense of security which is not borne out by the facts.

On occasion Catholic pressure has forced or threatened to force the withdrawal from hospital staffs of physicians who would not agree to cease prescribing contraceptive measures in their own private nonhospital practice or to sever their connection with planned parenthood groups. Such pressures have not succeeded where they were strenuously resisted by the local medical profession and community.

Despite unremitting Catholic pressure, however, medically prescribed and controlled contraception continues to be legal in every state except Connecticut and Massachusetts. It is to be hoped that the future will see the evolution of an increasingly comprehensive definition of "medical" in those states and with respect to the federal government, where a medical indication for contraception is a prerequisite to legality.

What about the case, for example, of Mr. and Mrs. X. whose two-year-old marriage has not so far been a happy one. Their temperamental differences have led to quarrels, separations, and reconciliations in the classic pattern. With the help of a marriage counselor they are attempting to better their relationship and reinforce their marriage. They do not and should not want to conceive a child in the next few months. They feel that it would be unfair to have a child while they are not sure that their marriage will last. They are convinced that they will have a better chance of mending the marriage if they are not faced at this point with the possibly divisive presence of an infant. Most lawyers and marriage counselors would agree, incidentally, that the old adage about a child drawing people together is fallacious; at least in the crucial first year after its birth the readjustments made necessary by a child are often a tax on even a good marriage.

Or take the case of Mr. and Mrs. Y. Mr. Y. is in his last year of medical school. The couple live largely on Mrs. Y.'s earnings and will continue to have to do so during the husband's internship. They want to start a family in a few years when the husband has started practicing and his wife's earnings are no longer needed to support them. If they should have a child within the next year, Mr. Y. would have to leave medical school.

Or can a doctor give contraceptive information to a couple whose income is insufficient to support an additional child for that reason alone even if there is no other medical reason for his doing so?

Such questions as these are unanswered by the law in those states which have prohibitive laws on birth control but exempt doctors. As a practical matter, of course, many doctors feel that to have or not have a child is essentially a private decision to be made by the people involved and they do not restrict their teaching of contraceptive technique to cases where there is a medical indication for contraception in the orthodox sense. Moreover, statistical studies of child spacing as well as a growing awareness of the importance of psychological and economic components in physical well being, are influencing even conservative medical practice. It is interesting to notice that recent Papal statements recognize economic as well as health factors as justifying the use of "natural" methods of contraception.

It is estimated that despite the existence of restrictive laws in the federal sphere and about half of the states, probably over ninety per cent of the American people exercise what most of them consider their inherent right to limit their families if they want to and that they use whatever contraceptive techniques are available to them. As far back as 1930, one company alone admitted to the sale of 12,000 gross of condoms per month. It is, at the very least, unlikely that the bulk of their sales were for noncontraceptive purposes.

The law on the books has had slight effect on the widespread traffic in most contraceptives. It has, as is so starkly revealed in Massachusetts and Connecticut, interfered with the medical prescription and supplying of contraceptives to such ill and needy women as were involved in the Connecticut Tileston Case. Perhaps eventually the whole field of conception control will be recognized for what it is—a problem for doctors rather than theologians or moralists. The lawyers should be relegated to their proper function of devising regulations to insure ethical distribution of efficient, harmless, and reasonably priced contraceptives in place of the semibootleg methods and excessive profits which attend much of the distribution of birth-control devices and information in the United States today.

It is possible that to some extent at least the birth-control problem will be automatically solved by scientific discoveries rather than by public pressure or legal acumen. Recent experiments on mice have revealed that the birth rate at least among rodents can be controlled by a synthetic chemical introduced in their diet. Obviously, a chemical birth-control substance that can be taken orally will materially affect all our thinking on planned parenthood. Dr. James Bryant Conant, the president of Harvard University, itself in a state where birth control is completely barred, put the matter very well when he stated at the Diamond Jubilee Meeting of the American Chemical Society in September, 1951, that:

. . . by 1961 bio-chemists will have made available cheap and harmless anti-fertility compounds to be added as one saw fit to the diet . . . as the twentieth century draws to a close, the attitude of the religious leaders of the world will have been completely altered on this subject without any diminution of religious feeling.

CHAPTER 12

Abortion

ALL FORTY-EIGHT states have laws against abortion. They impose penalties ranging from moderately severe jail sentences to life imprisonment or death. Yet estimates as to the number of illegal abortions performed in the United States every year vary from a minimum figure of 700,000 to more than two million. Abortions are legal in a limited class of cases—the so-called "therapeutic abortions." But the law is in many situations so at odds with current medical knowledge and practice that even the most cautious physicians find themselves in the position of frequently not knowing whether they are violating it.

Abortion in the meaning in which it is used in the statutes means the intentional termination of pregnancy by detaching or expelling the embryo from the womb. (Spontaneous abortions—what laymen term "miscarriages"—present no legal problem.) Performed in a hospital by a competent surgeon or obstetrician in cases where there has been careful pre-operative examination and where post-operative care will be possible, abortion is a relatively safe procedure. But it is a very dangerous operation indeed when performed in the absence of these safeguards, by the woman herself, by midwives or even by doctors who are unskilled or operating under unsterile conditions. Several thousand deaths as a result of abortion are reported each year; there are probably several thousand more women who die as a direct result of abortion but whose death certificates list some other cause. A conservative estimate would be a total of about four to five thousand deaths a year. Moreover, while exact figures are not obtainable, doctors are generally agreed that abortions which do not seem to cause any immediate injury to a woman frequently have deleterious aftereffects. Sterility, invalidism, and complications in subsequent pregnancies are all possible results.

It is difficult to obtain precise figures about illegal abortions and their effect, for they are clandestine and performed in secret. Some abortions are brought to the attention of doctors and law-enforcement officers by complications which necessitate bringing in a doctor or by the fact that the patient dies. Birth-control clinics and private doctors have been able to get some picture of the situation from the case histories given by their patients. Women are often astonishingly willing to talk about abortions they have had once the danger of legal prosecution is past; there seems on the whole to be little feeling of guilt about having destroyed the foetus. On the basis of the available data, authorities have come to the conclusion that approximately one in every five pregnancies ends in an induced abortion. In some large industrial centers to which women from outlying areas tend to come in search of an abortionist, the number of abortions performed in a year has been estimated to equal the number of children born.

These figures include a shocking number of cases, probably reckoned in the tens of thousands, where abortions were performed (that is, the surgical procedure for abortion followed) but where no pregnancy in fact existed. One clinic reported that 40 per cent of the women who came there believing themselves to be pregnant were not. Most professional abortionists do not bother with a pregnancy test; they take the woman's word for it and no doubt "abort" many who are not pregnant at all. Technically speaking, of course, there can be no abortion without a pregnancy and partly to cover such a situation, many states make an attempted abortion criminal along with one that is actually performed.

Laymen are inclined to think of abortion as the last desperate resort of unwed mothers. Actually in only about 10 per cent of the cases is there any question of illegitimacy involved. Most illegal abortions are performed on married women between the ages of twenty-five and thirty-five who are pregnant by their own husbands and who already have other children. The New York Academy of Medicine report of a study made in the 1930's showed that the largest percentage of abortion deaths was found in the thirty-five to thirty-nine-year-old age group among women who had been pregnant six or seven times. The incidence of medical abortions in first pregnancies is low—it has been estimated to be about one in eighteen. In the fourth pregnancy, however, the estimated ratio is about one in four.

The present-day laws as to abortion must be viewed against this factual background. As with all other matters exclusively under state control, the federal law has no impact except with reference to importation and transportation through the mails and in interstate commerce of articles for performing abortion or information concerning it. It is interesting to note that while the federal law contains a flat prohibition against the carriage of contraceptives and contraceptive information, the same statute prohibits the distribution of information and materials, not for all, but only for "unlawful" abortions. As in the case of the contraception laws, the federal courts have liberally construed the abortion prohibition. It does not prevent the importation or shipment of medical books or periodicals containing information on abortion, nor the distribution of instruments to doctors, hospitals, pharmacies or medical supply houses. The primary effect of the federal ban is to slow down trade in instruments which women may buy to abort themselves. It has little effect in keeping out of drugstores a variety of pills, liquids, douches, and miscellaneous compounds euphemistically known as menstrual regulators. Despite medical insistence to the contrary, many women believe that a pregnancy can be safely terminated by a couple of pills or a few spoonsful of medicine. They are inclined to cite how so-and-so was "brought around" by pills prescribed by a kindly druggist. The chances are, of course, that in any case when pills bring on menstruation, there was no pregnancy in the first place.

One of the country's leading gynecologists, Dr. Alan Guttmacher, tells a typical story of a patient of his, an unmarried girl of good family and strict moral upbringing, who believed that she was pregnant after her first and only intercourse. After listening to her story, Dr. Guttmacher prescribed a perfectly innocuous medicine. Within forty-five minutes after taking the first dose, the patient called jubilantly to tell him that the "abortifacient" had worked, and that she had begun to menstruate. For such "pregnancies" anything in which the woman has faith is likely to prove effective.

Those preparations which actually are capable of killing the foetus are very likely to kill the mother as well. Preparations containing lead, for example, will often lead to abortion but they also have a toxic effect on the kidneys and intestines and can cause invalidism, blindness, and often death. The Federal Trade Commission has taken action against many preparations which falsely suggest to the buyer that they have the ability to terminate pregnancy, as well as those which are dangerous if taken in the dosages recommended. However, the Commission has not been able to do a thorough job because many abortifacients emanate from unknown manufacturers or reappear under different names after once being suppressed.

The state laws on abortion vary more in theory than in practice. In Florida, Massachusetts, New Jersey, and Pennsylvania, the statutes which make abortion a crime do not contain any specific exemption for doctors even where the mother's life or health is at stake. But they do use such words as "unlawfully" or "without lawful justification," and these have been interpreted to permit therapeutic abortion. A Massachusetts court, for example, said the statute would not apply to a doctor who, in good faith, performed an abortion to save the life of the mother or preserve her health providing his judgment corresponded to the general opinion of competent doctors in the community.

New Hampshire permits the destruction of the foetus after it has quickened if the life of the mother is endangered by reason of malformation or the prospect of difficult or prolonged labor. There is no specific authorization, however, for the performance of an abortion before quickening even to save the life of the mother. The Louisiana statute prohibits all abortions without exception. However, an exception for therapeutic abortions may be implied from the fact that elsewhere the law provides that a physician may lose his license for performing an abortion except where it was necessary to save the life of the mother.

All of the other states (with the exception of Colorado, the District of Columbia, Maryland, and New Mexico, which will be discussed later) specifically state that an abortion may be performed if it is necessary to save the life of the mother. They do not speak in terms of health considerations at all. Oddly enough, of the thirty-nine states having this kind of law, only nine—Arkansas, Georgia, Kansas, Mississippi, Missouri, Nebraska, Ohio, Texas, and Wisconsin, require that the decision as to the necessity for the abortion should be made by a doctor. As a practical matter, however, it would no doubt be risky, even in the other thirty states, for a midwife or any other person not a physician to attempt to take advantage of the exemption since if the legality of the abortion were challenged, the court would be likely to insist on medical testimony to prove that it was necessary. In any event, at the same time, there is considerable doubt under many of the state laws as to whether an abortion, to be legal, must be performed by a doctor. Typically the abortion statutes do not specify that only doctors may act—a curious omission that may stem from the tradition of midwifery.

In a few states, the fact that two doctors have agreed that an abortion is necessary to save the life of the mother will be accepted by the courts as proof of the necessity of the operation. Individual doctors in many more states, however, have adopted on their own the custom of having their conclusion that an abortion is indicated confirmed by one or more other doctors before they will perform the operation. Similarly, while no state requires that abortions be performed in a hospital, many doctors will not perform them elsewhere both for medical reasons and because hospitalization helps remove any aura of clandestine illegality. Many reputable hospitals insist that the head of the obstetrical department personally examine the case history and/or the patient before each operation to make sure that the hospital is not being used as a base for illegal practice.

Colorado, the District of Columbia, Maryland, and New Mexico permit abortions not only where necessary to save the life of the mother, but also where indicated to preserve her "health" or "safety," or to prevent "permanent bodily injury."

As a practical matter, doctors even in states whose abortion laws in terms seem to indicate that the operation is permissible only if the mother's life is at stake do often perform abortions to preserve her health as well. Their actions have been backed up by court decisions to the effect that the danger to the mother need not be as immediate or certain as a strict reading of the statutes would necessitate. In other states the boundaries of strict laws have been extended as a practical matter by the reluctance of law enforcement agencies to penalize doctors acting on their best medical judgment for the welfare of their patients. The net result is that in many more jurisdictions than the four just listed, the mother's physical and mental health, as well as her life, is a consideration in determining whether a therapeutic or "legal" abortion may be performed.

No definitive list of conditions warranting therapeutic abortion can be compiled because medical practice varies widely from state to state and because there is a wide diversity of opinion even among doctors in a particular area. Moreover, improved medical techniques constantly change the picture. Some diseases which meant grave danger in pregnancy some years ago can now be controlled sufficiently to eliminate much of the risk. Finally, nonhealth factors have a bearing so that two women suffering from the same physical ailment may not both require an abortion.

Consider, for example, the problems arising from tubercular pregnancies. At the beginning of the century a tubercular woman was pretty automatically aborted since the strain inherent in pregnancy and labor constituted a real danger to her life. Today, improved methods of treatment often make it possible for a tubercular woman to bear a child in relative safety. Naturally the stage and gravity of the disease in a particular patient determines in part the amount of risk for her. But many doctors feel that in deciding whether an abortion is indicated, they must look not only at the patient's X-rays and laboratory reports, but also at her bank account.

Mrs. A., who is fairly affluent so that she can afford to spend a good portion of her pregnancy in a hospital and can hire a nurse or housekeeper to help her after the baby is born, may have a good chance of bearing her child without undue danger to her health. Mrs. B., suffering from the same type of tuberculosis, who has other children and no help and who will have to continue to work hard during and immediately after her pregnancy, might well find the pregnancy fatal. The same type of consideration may be relevant where heart disease in some forms is concerned.

Contracted pelvis and similar conditions which might make normal delivery hazardous no longer necessarily call for abortion. The increased safety of the Caesarian section has made it possible for many women suffering from such conditions to bear children without undue danger.

Other factors which some doctors consider to warrant a therapeutic abortion are a very recent pregnancy, general debility with loss of weight, a prior Caesarian operation (sometimes), increasing prolapse of the pelvic organs, kidney disease, diabetes, pregnancy toxemias, and endocrine diseases.

Mental illness as an indication for abortion is a relatively new concept and doctors differ as to when a prospective mother's condition is sufficiently serious to warrant it. Often the problem arises where the mother-to-be threatens suicide. While undoubtedly women may make such threats in order to induce the doctor to abort, there can be a genuine risk of suicide where the woman's mental balance has been below par anyway and the pregnancy, for one reason or another, is deeply undesired. Where the mother suffers from dementia praecox or manic depressive psychosis the weight of opinion seems to be that abortion is indicated. Some doctors, however, are particularly wary of recommending an abortion for a psychotic woman because the abortion itself might result in a new or more confirmed psychosis centered around feelings of guilt for having permitted the unborn child to be destroyed. The extent to which mental health has been involved in the question of therapeutic abortion can be gauged from two cases known to the authors where reputable doctors said that in their opinions an abortion was indicated in order to preserve the mental health of the *father*. Whatever the psychiatric considerations, it is quite clear that an abortion for such a reason would probably run afoul of the present law in every state.

No state accepts abortion for eugenic reasons as such; that is, reasons having to do with the probably defective character of the offspring. Yet many such abortions are performed, theoretically because of some possible danger to the mother, but actually because of the fear of bringing forth a defective child. As one authority pointed out in recommending abortion and sterilization for insane or otherwise mentally deficient women, the chance of getting one normal child to three imbeciles just doesn't seem like a good enough percentage. Even if a normal child were born, its chance for proper development would be considerably handicapped by the fact that it had a mentally deranged mother.

In cases where the mother has, in the course of treatment for cancer or some other disease, been subjected to extensive pelvic radiation during early pregnancy, there is a danger that the child will be a microcephalic idiot or other monstrosity. Some doctors feel that the possibility of serious injury having been done to the foetus in this situation is strong enough to warrant the interruption of pregnancy. Recently some obstetricians have recommended abortion where the mother has had German measles in the early part of her pregnancy since this disease during the early months of gestation raises about a 60 to 70 per cent probability of a defective child.

In all of these situations, lip service is paid to the idea that the mother's life or health is the determining factor, but no doubt the doctor authorizing the abortion does so primarily because he feels that no mother should be forced to bear a child who is likely to be born defective.

The laws of some states still reflect the medieval viewpoint that there is a difference between aborting a child that has quickened and one that has not. Science no longer recognizes that there is any vegetative period in pregnancy. The foetus has life from the moment of conception. Yet some laws still impose different penalties depending on whether the child has quickened or not. Such difference can of course be more rationally justified in the light of present day knowledge: abortion is a much more dangerous operation if performed so late in pregnancy that the child has already become viable. In many states, permitting an abortion to be performed is not a crime for the mother unless the child has quickened. Even in those states, however, since the abortionist is guilty of a crime whether the child has quickened or not, the mother may be indicted for conspiracy to commit a crime with him. In Mississippi the wording of the statute seems to indicate that abortion is not a crime if performed before the child has quickened. Generally speaking, however, the viability of the child is not crucial today when his "rights" are generally given the same weight no matter what the state of gestation.

Not infrequently, situations arise where even in the absence of physiological, psychiatric and eugenic factors, abortion would seem to be indicated. Take, for example, the case of Mary, a respectable and intelligent young businesswoman of twenty-two who is attacked and raped. The man escapes and, despite the fact that Mary duly reports the attack to the police, they are unsuccessful in finding her attacker. Several weeks later, she discovers that she is pregnant. She is horrified at the idea of bearing a child conceived during the nightmare of rape. Under the circumstances she might not even be able to give the child out for adoption through ordinary channels since adoption agencies are very wary about taking a child of a father known to be a criminal who might also, considering the nature of his crime, be psychotic. Her only escape from being forced to have and to raise this child might be to place it with some unsuspecting adopting parents, a course which she is understandably reluctant to follow.

Then there is Jenny, a girl of sixteen found to be pregnant as the result of intercourse with her own father, and Betty, a girl of twelve, pregnant by a sixteen-year-old boy. According to the law of most states, any man who has intercourse with a child of Betty's age is guilty of statutory rape since she is legally incapable of consenting to intercourse. Yet she may be pregnant. Finally, there are many women like Louise, a woman of thirty-eight and the mother of three children. Her husband dies of pneumonia leaving no insurance. A few weeks after his death she finds that she is pregnant. She is without means of supporting the children she already has. Bearing a fourth will prevent her from working for many months and seriously handicap her efforts to support her family thereafter.

Rape, incest, minority and death are the less usual cases. A more typical situation is presented by Annie, who is married to a man who earns sixty dollars a week. They have five children, born within a period of ten years. As a result of her frequent pregnancies and her difficulty in raising her family on a small income, Annie is physically depleted, undernourished, and exhausted. While a new pregnancy will not present an immediate danger to her health, it will tend to worsen her general physical condition.

No matter what the reader's own reaction was to each of these hypothetical cases, a respectable body of medical men could undoubtedly be found to support the reader's viewpoint. Some doctors feel that the probable mental injury to the woman who has been raped and the sixteen-year-old girl who is pregnant by her own father warrants an abortion to preserve the mother's mental health. The case of the woman with five children is, of course, the type of situation most often met by doctors. Many physicians strongly feel that the ultimate damage to the mother's health and the probable disintegration of a family unit, called upon to shoulder greater burdens than it can carry, call for an abortion. Somewhat less support will be found in favor of permitting an abortion where the child is posthumous (as with Louise), where the mother has been deserted by the husband after conception and where the child is conceived out of wedlock. Abortion is not lawful in any of these situations unless supporting reasons having to do with the health of the mother are found. Where there are no such reasons, the fact that no lawful abortion is possible is usually no deterrent as a practical matter. These are the kinds of situations which lie behind the cold statistics on illegal abortion.

Although economic reasons—the inability of the family to support another child—realistically account for the majority of unlawful abortions, other factors also play their part. Sometimes occupational elements are involved. Frequently young women who had their first child aborted because they wanted to continue working outside the home, have a planned child a few years later, when the mother feels she can give up her job. Many abortions, of course, derive from unhappy marital situations, characterized by drunkenness, depravity, desertion or sometimes just plain incompatibility.

Interestingly enough, the mother's religious affiliations do not seem to have too much effect on her abortion history. A survey made by one Planned Parenthood clinic (to which Catholic women applied in about the same ratio as Catholics bear to the general population) found that somewhat fewer Catholic women had had abortions than Protestant or Jewish women. However, the number of abortions per woman was higher among the Catholics than among either of the other religious groups.

In most states women who submit to illegal abortions are subject to criminal prosecution along with those who perform the operations. The penalties imposed are less rigorous, but severe. Yet by comparison with even the minimum number of illegal abortions estimated, the number of prosecutions for abortion is astonishingly small. In a three year period in New York County only thirty people were indicted for the crime of abortion. Of the twenty-six indictments which have so far been disposed of, in almost half the cases the District Attorney permitted the abortion charge to be dropped when the defendant entered a plea of guilty to a comparatively trivial crime such as unlawful practice of medicine, failure to report a death properly, conspiracy or assault. A number of others pleaded guilty to crimes more serious than these but carrying lesser penalties than abortion. Of the twenty-six, only nine either pleaded guilty or were convicted of abortion. The willingness of the prosecutor to accept lesser pleas rather than to try to get a conviction of abortion is probably based on the fact that juries show a curious reluctance to convict the abortionist and will almost never convict the woman no matter what the state's statute says about her culpability.

There are many possible explanations for this small percentage of prosecutions and convictions. Probably the most likely is the understandable reluctance of people to report, to prosecute or to convict under a law with which they are not in sympathy. Women, moreover, have a curious loyalty toward the people who try to help them out of an unwanted pregnancy even where that attempted help has fatal results. In one hospital recently, eight women were brought in dying as the result of inexpert abortions. It was probable that all had been performed by the same person since examination showed that some instrument like a shoemaker's awl was used. Each of the women knew that she was dying and each refused to the end to reveal the name of the man who had performed the abortion.

Even those cases which do come to the attention of the respectable doctors who are called in when something goes wrong are not usually reported. Doctors cannot ordinarily reveal anything they learn in the course of treating their patients, least of all something that constitutes a criminal offense.

Although today in the United States, abortion looms large as a moral problem and one of criminal law enforcement, it was not until fairly recently in human history that it represented any problem at all. In primitive societies, it was (and in some places still is) a common and accepted method of population control. As man became more civilized, the views of a particular people on the subject were more apt to be conditioned by political and economic necessities than by abstract questions of right and wrong. In Greece and Rome, abortion along with homosexuality, onanism, sodomy, and the like were freely permitted. The Greeks' chief problem was to keep their population down to what their territory could afford to support. Homosexuality was accepted as a matter of course, infanticide was common and abortion was freely and openly practiced. In Rome, too, abortion was similarly widespread until so few children were being born to Roman women that the ratio between Romans and slaves was becoming dangerously low. Among the Jews, however, abortion was considered a crime and a sin. The Old Testament is replete with examples of the high regard in which the Jews held large families. The necessity for preserving and propagating Judaism was a strong motive. So, too, was the fact that the Jews were comparatively few in number and were surrounded by hostile peoples. Homosexuality, abortion and the like tended to keep down their birth rate and thus to diminish their ability to defend themselves; they developed strong sanctions against all such practices.

Christianity then came along and introduced new moral concepts which strengthened the already strong anti-abortion stand of the Jews. The early Christians also needed a population increase to defend and to propagate their faith. Moreover, the doctrine of the sinfulness of the flesh logically led to the justification of sexual relationship solely on the basis of its reproductive aspects. The theory of original sin made abortion a particularly serious crime because of the hurt to the unborn child. The foetus, as an inheritor of original sin, was certain of eternal damnation if it died without baptism. The story is told of a Queen of Portugal who was advised that she might die if she were not aborted and who promptly replied that she would not purchase her temporal life by sacrificing the eternal salvation of her child.

The ancient Talmudic law recognized an exemption to the prohibition against abortion where it was necessary to save the life of the mother. This exception is today recognized by almost all major religious groups except the Catholic Church, which forbids abortion or any other direct method of killing the foetus even when it is probable that both the foetus and the mother will die unless medical interference is undertaken. A recent Papal encyclical, reiterating that an abortion is permissible only when it incidentally results from some medical treatment but not when it is itself the aim of the treatment, has aroused much public controversy and strong opposition from other established churches.

When the Communists took over in Russia, they made a clean sweep of all the old laws against abortion. In 1920 they legalized all abortions provided they were performed in a hospital by a qualified doctor. Special hospitals were set up in some areas to handle nothing but abortion cases. The results of the experiment were enlightening. While the birth rate of

Russia declined during the next two decades, it is claimed
that it did not decline as heavily as did the birth rate of other
European nations with less liberal laws on the subject. Thousands of abortions were performed but it is impossible to know
how many more there were than there would have been if
women had continued to seek surreptitious, illegal abortions.

The estimates of the abortion rate for other European
countries during these years of economic distress indicate that
it was tremendously high even where the law prohibited the
interruption of pregnancy except in special cases. A few signi-
ficant conclusions can, however, be drawn from the Russian
experiment. For one, Russian doctors claimed that their mortality rate in abortions was about one in 20,000—substantially
less than the death rate for all abortions in the United States.
American doctors think this figure quite possible, since during
the period in question the operation was always performed in a
hospital by experienced doctors, never undertaken after the
third month of pregnancy and generally involved only women
who had previously given birth. The Russian figures seem to
bear out the proposition that illegitimacy plays a small part in
the abortion picture. Of 40,000 legal abortions performed in
Moscow in one year, 66 per cent were because of poverty;
twenty per cent for health reasons and only two per cent because the mother wished to conceal the origin of the pregnancy
either because she was unmarried or because the child was not
the child of her husband.

It is interesting to note that after some years of unlimited
abortion, the Russians substantially modified their permissive
attitude. While undoubtedly political reasons were the primary motivation for the change, there was medical evidence
as well that the experiment was not wholly successful. For
one thing, despite concentrated propaganda efforts to make
people rely on contraception, rather than abortion, the hospitals were full of "repeaters"—women who had had as many as
sixteen or seventeen abortions. One of the early modifications
which had to be made in the law was to prohibit women from

having an abortion less than six months after a prior one.

Despite the low mortality rate, as time went on it was found that the patient often paid a price for abortion even where it had been performed under the best possible circumstances. Some Russian doctors found that there was an increased percentage of spontaneous abortion ("miscarriage") as a result of earlier induced abortions. Later confinements tended to be more complicated, with a higher incidence of long labors, post-partum bleeding, adherent placenta, and so forth. Pelvic disturbances, menstrual disorders, functional neuroses, loss of libido, and sterility were all found to result in some cases.

Abortion has now been outlawed almost completely in Russia. Japan, however, is currently the arena of another experiment in widening the area of permissible abortions. A 1948 law permits abortion on the recommendation of a committee of doctors to preserve the mother's health or for other medical reasons, on the ground of economic hardship, and where the pregnancy is the result of rape.

Clearly the trend, in fact, in the United States today is in the direction of widening the scope of permissible abortions but the laws lag considerably behind the actual practice. Moreover, certain techniques are classed as abortion which actually have nothing to do with the termination of pregnancy. In four states—Alabama, Louisiana, South Carolina, and Texas —the induction of premature delivery is considered a criminal abortion. Yet this procedure is one which busy obstetricians utilize weekly, if not daily, to save the life of the foetus, not to destroy it. Of the four states named, only South Carolina permits such induction of labor if it is necessary to save the life of the mother or the child. In the other three, the induction of premature labor, like abortion, is permitted only to save the life of the mother. Yet in many cases it is necessary to save the life of the child.

Opinions as to what abortions the law should permit vary considerably among laymen and doctors both. Dr. Fred-

erick J. Taussig, in a book sponsored by The National Committee on Maternal Health, presents a proposal which seems to
balance the conflicting values rather well. Dr. Taussig proposes that all therapeutic abortions be performed by a physician in a hospital after consultation with two other doctors.
He suggests three grounds for permitting therapeutic abortion:

1. Where it is necessary to preserve the mother's life or
health.

2. In cases of "physical depletion"; that is, where the
mother is in a state of bodily exhaustion leading to disease
or where she is weakened by too frequent child-bearing, is
undernourished or has already excessive family responsibility.

3. Where the mother is morally irresponsible. In this category would be included all cases where the mental state of the
mother was such that she was incapable of giving free and
knowing consent to intercourse; for example, where the
mother was mentally defective, where she was raped, or
where she was under sixteen years of age at the time of conception.

Dr. Taussig's suggestion reflects the general opinion that
where a choice has to be made between a grown woman who,
in the majority of cases seeking abortion, has other children
dependent on her, and an unborn embryo, the welfare of the
woman and her family is the focal point of consideration. Only
the Catholic Church dissents.

It is today clear that the strongly worded laws on the
statute books against abortion are not operating. Laws according more nearly with the views of the medical profession
would probably not increase the number of abortions performed but would take them out of the hands of back street
abortion mills which yearly cause permanent sterility, invalidism, and death to uncounted thousands of women. There is
more integrity in a law which sets less exacting standards but
is enforced than in one which sets its sights so high that it
outstrips the ability and willingness of human beings to comply with it.

CHAPTER 13

Sterilization

$\mathcal{M}$RS. JOHN A. JONES is just twenty-four. She is married, lives in Massachusetts, and has just had her fourth child —all four of them were born within a three-year period and two of them were born dead. Mrs. Jones's doctor has advised her that she must not become pregnant again for at least two years. There's a history of tuberculosis in her family; she is herself anemic and underweight (weighs, in fact, only ninety-eight pounds although she is five foot five). However, to Mrs. Jones's anxious requests for advice as to how to avoid becoming pregnant, her doctor cannot easily respond.

He doesn't believe abstinence is the answer—he's seen too many broken homes, emotional disturbances, and mental illnesses result from that. He is precluded by the laws of Massachusetts from prescribing a birth-control device for Mrs. Jones, even from telling her to use one. So he has to tell her that in addition to abstinence, there are only two courses open to her. She can risk becoming pregnant again with a fair certainty that if she does, she will be legally entitled to a therapeutic abortion. Actually Mrs. Jones's doctor doesn't feel too enthusiastic about this prospect because he knows that an abortion is an operation which is apt to have adverse physiological and psychological effects on a woman like Mrs. Jones. Or, he advises her, she can be sterilized.

Massachusetts, the state which has prosecuted as criminal doctors, nurses, and social workers engaged in therapeutic and preventive contraception, has no such prejudice against voluntary sterilization. So that in that state at least, the more

200

extreme the remedy, the more easily available it appears to be. The fact that Mrs. Jones may perfectly well be capable of producing live healthy babies in a few years time if she has had no pregnancies or abortions in the meantime, is, of course, a factor that weighs with Mrs. Jones's doctor but it doesn't affect the legal situation in the state. Probably his best advice in the circumstances would be to advise Mrs. Jones, if she wants to avoid permanent sterility and still have a chance to regain her health, to go to some other state where either there is no law against contraception or where the law makes an exception for medical necessity.

Mrs. Smith, on the other hand, presents an entirely different picture. She is herself feeble-minded and she lives with her slightly less feeble-minded mother and her more feeble-minded sister. The house is a one-room shack—no plumbing, no doors or windows. Four small children, completely filthy and almost completely unclothed, are milling about on the floor. An unwashed baby cries fitfully on the bed; the sister rocks back and forth in the corner laughing and muttering unintelligibly from time to time. The mother says, "Hello" —Mrs. Smith just sits and stares out of the window.

A social worker's report shows that of the five children, two are illegitimate offspring of the idiot sister. The other three are Mrs. Smith's—two of them already show signs of feeble-mindedness. The family has for years been known to health and welfare agencies but the public institutions in the state are already so crowded with those who would be dangerous if not restrained that there is no room for imbeciles or feeble-minded people whose freedom at least does not threaten bodily harm to others.

To talk of contraception in a situation like the Smiths' is absurd. Neither of the sisters is capable of using a contraceptive or even of understanding what it is. Abortions, of course, may be theoretically available but neither Mrs. Smith nor her sister has the means to pay even a midwife and in all likelihood wouldn't bother since they themselves have no objection to going on propagating indefinitely. The Smiths, however, live in a state which makes provision for sterilization of the feeble-minded, which, in this case, would seem to be the only remedy that would make sense. As Justice Holmes once thundered for the United States Supreme Court in sustaining the validity of compulsory sterilization laws, "Three generations of imbeciles is enough."

Actually, sterilization has three distinct aspects. It can be eugenic in purpose; as with the Smiths, it can be utilized to prevent the further propagation of the unfit. It can be punitive; that is, invoked as a punishment for crime. And it can be resorted to voluntarily as a rather extreme form of contraception.

Whatever its purpose, sterilization, as the operation is currently practiced, merely prevents the sperm and the egg from meeting in the normal way so that fertilization cannot take place. It does not involve any loss of sexual powers or any diminution of sexual enjoyment. The operation on the male, known as vasectomy, consists of cutting and sealing a small portion of the vas deferens, the tiny tube through which the sperm passes. The entire operation can be performed under local anaesthetic in about fifteen to twenty minutes. No hospitalization is required. While there are a number of variations of the corresponding operation on a woman, probably the one most commonly used is salpingectomy, an abdominal operation involving cutting the Fallopian tubes between the ovaries and the womb. When done shortly after the delivery of a child, it usually adds nothing to the woman's hospital stay. Otherwise it involves not more than a two-week period of hospitalization. Neither the operation on the male nor that on the female involves the loss of sexual power or enjoyment. In one follow-up study of ninety-nine female patients who had voluntarily undergone sterilization, sixty reported no change whatever in their sexual patterns, three claimed that there had been some loss of libido, and thirty-six said that there had been an increase in their sexual satisfaction—probably due to freedom from the fear of a pregnancy which would have threatened the woman's health. In a survey of sixty-five male patients, who were likewise voluntarily sterilized, sixty-two were found to be satisfied with the results of the operation. Two claimed that there had been a decrease in virility, and one was belatedly indignant because he had undergone the operation under threat of divorce by his wife.

Eugenic sterilization, as in the case of the Smith family, is for the most part in the United States a compelled procedure; that is, one required by the state in certain circumstances. Arizona, California, Connecticut, Delaware, Georgia, Idaho, Indiana, Iowa, Kansas, Maine, Michigan, Minnesota, Mississippi, Montana, Nebraska, New Hampshire, North Carolina, North Dakota, Oklahoma, Oregon, South Carolina, South Dakota, Utah, Vermont, Virginia, West Virginia, and Wisconsin all have laws providing for the sterilization of certain classes of people. Many of the statutes (undoubtedly with an eye to the constitutional prohibition against "cruel and unusual punishments") specifically deny any punitive intent and are supposedly designed for eugenic purposes and for the protection of society. Yet a reading of them indicates that some are so far from having scientific support that they can only be explained as an additional punishment for people guilty of crime. A bill recently introduced in a Southern state, for example, would have compelled sterilization of people convicted of various crimes, chicken stealing among them. Whatever such a bill may reflect of the standards of the community, it can scarcely be supported on eugenic grounds; fortunately it failed of passage.

In the states which have eugenic sterilization laws, the feeble-minded, idiots, imbeciles and the insane may under certain conditions be sterilized. Epileptics are also subject to sterilization in all these states except California, Connecticut, Minnesota, Nebraska, South Dakota, and Vermont. In Minnesota and Vermont, sterilization is not compulsory but can only be done with the consent of the person involved or his next of kin or legal guardian. While the laws of the other states provide for compulsory sterilization if certain conditions are met, as a practical matter in many states the operation is not usually performed without consent. California, which accounts for more than one third of all the eugenic sterilizations in the nation, has followed this practice despite the fact that the law gives a clear right to sterilize without the concurrence of the patient.

While the procedure varies from state to state, the usual pattern of eugenic sterilization runs something like this: the superintendent of a state mental hospital submits to a special committee, usually composed of doctors, the names of patients whom the superintendent considers eligible for sterilization. The patient and his spouse, nearest relative or guardian are notified and are entitled to appear at the hearing. Evidence is submitted to the board as to the patient's personal history and his family history as far as it is known and, on this evidence, the board must decide whether the patient is likely to produce defective offspring. If the board decides that the patient is not incurable or that his deficiency is not hereditary or that his condition will be worsened by the operation, permission to perform it is refused. Otherwise the board orders it to be performed. Usually, the law provides that an appeal to the courts can be had if the board decrees sterilization over the patient's objections.

For the most part, the eugenic sterilization laws are applicable only to people confined in state institutions. A few statutes have been declared unconstitutional and wiped off the books on this ground by state courts. New York and New Jersey courts took this position, reasoning that the law was a denial of equal protection because, for example, Jane, a poor feeble-minded girl in a state asylum could be sterilized under the statute, while Jill, daughter of a wealthy family, in the same mental condition, would not be covered by the law simply because her family could afford to keep her in a private institution. Subsequently, however, when this question was presented to the Supreme Court of the United States, that court upheld the validity of such statutes, reasoning that a state has the power to pass a law which attempts a partial solution of a problem even though other aspects of that problem are left unaffected.

In the same case, the Supreme Court affirmed the constitutionality of sterilization statutes generally. The suit was brought on behalf of Carrie Buck, an eighteen-year-old feeble-minded girl, who was a patient in a Virginia asylum. Her mother, also feeble-minded, was a patient in the same institution. Carrie had already given birth to a feeble-minded child out of wedlock. It was in this case upholding the right of the state to sterilize the girl that Justice Holmes said, "Three generations of imbeciles are enough." The Court reasoned that the public welfare sometimes necessitates asking the nation's best citizens for their lives, as in war; concern for the welfare of the nation could require the lesser sacrifice of imposed sterility from people who were already sapping the country's strength. "It is better for all the world," said the Court, "if instead of waiting to execute degenerate offspring for crime, or to let them starve for their imbecility, society can prevent those who are manifestly unfit from continuing their kind."

It is difficult to estimate how much effect the eugenic sterilization laws will have in decreasing the mentally defective population. An estimated total of 52,000 people have been sterilized. This is, however, only a fractional part of our mentally defective population. In only eight states—Delaware, Idaho, Iowa, Michigan, North Carolina, Oregon, South Dakota, and Vermont—does the law cover people other than those confined in state asylums. In the other states having eugenic sterilization laws, such laws cannot reach any high degree of effectiveness so long as the overcrowding of mental hospitals prevents the admission of many people whose condition calls for confinement and probably sterilization as well. Even if the sterilization program were extended to more states and strengthened in the states which already have compulsory sterilization statutes, it is doubtful whether mental deficiency could be entirely eliminated. Many mental ailments are not hereditary but environmental. Some, while having an hereditary basis, appear among people whose parents showed no signs of mental aberration. The vast majority of feeble-minded children, for example, are born to normal parents. Even the most enthusiastic proponents of eugenic sterilization do not believe that the feeble-minded population of the next generation could be reduced by more than 36 per cent even if every feeble-minded man and woman were sterilized. It is clear, therefore, that whatever the merits of eugenic sterilization, it is nowhere near being the whole answer to the problem of the increasing number of mentally deficient in our midst.

Some of the so-called eugenic sterilization laws are, as indicated above, disguisedly punitive. In addition, there are sterilization laws which on their face appear to be punitive in intent.

Habitual criminals (sometimes defined as people convicted of three or more felonies) are subject to sterilization in Delaware, Idaho, Iowa, Nebraska, Oklahoma, and Oregon. In Wisconsin they do not even have to be "habitual" to come within the purview of the statute. It is extremely doubtful whether these statutes serve any eugenic purpose whatever in view of the increasing conviction of psychiatrists, psychologists, sociologists, and the like, that environmental factors rather than hereditary ones make criminals. Of course, it can be argued that even conceding the importance of environmental factors, criminals should be sterilized because they are incapable of giving their children a good environment. There is scant scientific support for such a conclusion. Moreover, criminals are not known for their fecundity. The Dillingers die childless and even lesser lights of the underworld are not usually eligible for membership in the PTA. It is, therefore, doubtful whether such statutes will materially lessen the criminal population in years to come.

Probably even less scientific justification can be found for those statutes authorizing the sterilization of so-called sex offenders and sex perverts. California, Idaho, Iowa, Michigan, Nebraska, Oregon, and Utah all have such provisions in their laws. The whole subject matter of sex offenses is only now beginning to be explored and understood. It is not even clear what crimes are sex crimes. On the one hand, many cases of shoplifting are known to be the result of sexual aberrations. On the other hand, even indecent exposure can reflect a temporary lack of control induced by one cocktail too many, for example, in a person who has always been and will thereafter be sexually normal.

Insofar as the sex offender laws have been tested in operation, it is doubtful whether many of the premises underlying them have any validity. Moreover, our mores are such that persons stigmatized as sex offenders are apt to be given scant consideration by police and prison authorities. It has even been suggested that the laws defining sex offenses represent in many instances more a means of trapping the unwary and blackmailing them than a thought-out system of evaluating and treating sex behavior. And it is well known that many sexual activities which are made the subject of criminal prosecution are in fact freely indulged in by the majority of the population that doesn't get caught.

The researches of Dr. Alfred C. Kinsey and his associates in The Institute for Sex Research, Inc., the efforts of such psychiatric bodies as the Group for The Advancement of Psychiatry will, it is hoped, eventually furnish a body of knowledge on which a more rational system of sex laws than we have now can be based. (See Chapter 14.) In the meantime, the laws as to sex offenses are so chaotic and many of them so without scientific foundation that it is very questionable whether violators of them should be made subject to such an extreme penalty as sterilization, particularly since it is not likely to prevent further offenses anyway.

In point of fact, an overt homosexual or a man addicted

to bestiality is not likely to have any children. If he did, it might be some indication that he had been cured of the very thing for which society has taken him to task. Nor is the sterilization of sex offenders likely to prove an effective deterrent to further offenses. While in some states, the kind of sterilization operation is left to the discretion of the institution's medical staff, most statutes specify that sterilization is to be performed by vasectomy or salpingectomy which do not affect sexuality. Sterilization of this kind does not, therefore, curb the desire of a degenerate to assault little girls. It may, however, give society a false sense of security in having "cured" the offender. The law of Nebraska which provides for castration for certain sex crimes, while less humane, is probably medically more realistic. A proposed new California statute would give sex offenders a choice between confinement for life or castration combined with a three-year program of psychiatric treatment. This seems a rather inconsistent and incongruous combination of solutions.

So much for sterilization in relation to crime and criminals. Far more people are apt to be concerned with it as a permanent and certain method of family limitation. The question that arises here is not whether the state compels sterilization but whether it will allow it.

A Minnesota case involved a wife who had had an extremely difficult delivery at the birth of her first child and who had been advised not to have any more. In view of the fact that sterilization of a woman is somewhat more complicated and hazardous than sterilization of a man, the husband in this case underwent vasectomy. The operation for some reason was unsuccessful so that the wife became pregnant and bore another child. The husband brought suit against the doctor who had performed the vasectomy claiming that he was entitled to damages from the doctor to cover the expenses incurred in connection with the pregnancy which the vasectomy was supposed to prevent. The court refused to hold the doctor liable, pointing out that the wife's health, which was the dominant consideration to begin with, had not been injured and that, on the husband's theory, the doctor might likewise be responsible for all the expenses of the child's up-bringing. In answer to the contention that the operation was illegal to begin with because the husband's physical condition did not warrant it, the court pointed out that there was no law prohibiting the operation even if it were not performed for therapeutic purposes so long as the patient had consented to it. The court went on to add that even if the law had prohibited the operation generally, it would be perfectly legal if performed for therapeutic reasons. The wife's physical condition, the court felt, would be considered sufficient justification for an operation on the husband provided he consented to it.

Indiana, Mississippi, Arizona, North Carolina, Oklahoma, South Carolina, Utah, Virginia, and West Virginia all have similar statutes rather oddly worded which indicate that sterilization is permissible if medical or surgical treatment for sound therapeutic reasons "incidentally" destroys the reproductive powers of the patient. Strict conformity to the language of the statute would seem to make illegal an operation deliberately undertaken to sterilize the patient for therapeutic reasons.

This would mean that if a woman had cancer of the womb and the womb were removed in order to prevent the spread of the cancerous growth, the fact that the operation sterilized her would not make it illegal. If, however, she were sterilized by an operation performed only for the purpose of sterilization, the operation might not be protected by the statute.

It is not likely that the statutes would be so interpreted. Actually they were probably intended to mean much the same thing as the Connecticut and Kansas statutes which prohibit sterilization unless it is "a medical necessity" or the New Hampshire one which permits it for "sound therapeutic reasons." The Vermont statute seems to imply that the operation is not permissible except for people who fall into the specified categories of mental defectives. While the Massachusetts law is silent on the subject, an operation to sterilize might come within the absolute prohibitions concerning conception but this seems doubtful. If, of course, the reproductive organs are diseased, it is unlikely that anything in the law of any state would prevent their removal.

As in the case of birth control and abortion, we find that the medical indications for therapeutic sterilization vary from state to state and even from doctor to doctor. Multiparity seems to be more commonly accepted as an indication for therapeutic sterilization than it is for therapeutic abortion. But there is no unanimity of medical opinion as to how many children a woman must have had before she is entitled to be sterilized if she so desires. A physician who had been a staff member of both hospitals, reported that a prominent southern hospital considered eight or nine pregnancies sufficient to warrant sterilization while an equally prominent New York hospital considered six pregnancies enough. The health and the economic circumstances of the individual patient are, of course, relevant in determining whether sterilization is indicated, but the same woman would be likely to receive a different answer to her request for sterilization depending on the place where and the particular doctor of whom she requested it.

Disagreement is likewise found as to how many Caesarian operations a woman can safely have. Some doctors automatically recommend sterilization at the time of the second Caesarian delivery. Others consider three the quota. Few will permit a patient to take the risk of more than three such deliveries. Heart, kidney, and lung diseases which are not likely to improve sufficiently to enable the patient to undertake pregnancy with relative safety are also considered reasons for sterilization. Mental deficiency is considered ground for sterilization, not only for eugenic reasons, but also for the protection of the patient. Mental disease, such as dementia praecox and manic depressive psychosis, likewise may present eugenic indications. Other milder mental derangements probably should not be considered to do so. Often there is a hope of cure and no clear reason to believe the disease is transmissible. In many cases the patient is capable of using other more temporary forms of contraception.

Sterilization as a means of conception control is more drastic than most people need or desire. Many doctors and social workers recommend it strongly where there is reason to believe the woman should never thereafter become pregnant and where ignorance or lack of co-operation on her part or on the part of the husband make other methods of contraception impractical. In some cases where the woman has borne many children and has had inadequate care at delivery, she may be so damaged internally that no ordinary contraceptive method is apt to be successful.

As in the therapeutic abortion situation, but without quite as intense a risk of illegality, the lack of clarity in the law on sterilization has put doctors in the position of operating with good intentions and crossed fingers. Many refuse to perform a sterilization operation without prior consultation with one or more other physicians. Some hospitals have set up committees to pass on all sterilizations which doctors propose to perform in the hospital. Clarification of the law as to voluntary sterilization is needed but there is always a danger that a definitive law will be less liberal than the standards by which doctors are now operating.

As far as compulsory sterilization is concerned, it is a pretty drastic penalty whether imposed with the idea of punishment in mind or not. We need only be reminded of the Nazi "experiments" along these lines to realize how dangerous a weapon compulsory sterilization can be when its invocation is dictated by prejudice, ignorance, and hatred. Compulsory sterilization should be resorted to only in those cases where substantial unanimity of medical opinion supports the conclusion that the particular illness or derangement—mental or physical—is both hereditary and incurable. Except in such cases, it may well be an unconstitutional deprivation of one important aspect of life and liberty, namely the right to have children.

CHAPTER 14

Sex and the Criminal Law

𝒯 HE CHANCES are nine out of ten that you are a sex criminal. Most of us think of people who violate the laws regarding sexual conduct in terms of men who attack little girls, of professional prostitutes, and the like. And without any question there must be laws—and enforcement of those laws —penalizing many forms of sexual behavior. Such crimes of violence as rape, such overreaching as is involved when a man of mature years persuades a girl of ten to have sex relations with him—these threaten the very fundamentals of any ordered or free society. But our statute books are replete with laws defining as sexual offenses conduct which does not involve any such threat and which is typically practiced by eminently respectable married couples. Dr. Alfred C. Kinsey and his associates in their monumental study of *Sexual Behavior in the Human Male* have suggested that more than 95 per cent of the total male population of the United States have in some way violated at least one criminal law governing sexual conduct. They estimate in fact that almost 60 per cent of all white American men are guilty of a particular type of sex crime—in many cases with their own wives. Both spouses in each such case were—theoretically at least—subject to criminal prosecution and substantial jail sentences in many states.

That our sex laws are a compound of necessary prohibi-

213

tions on the one hand and restrictive laws which no longer represent our contemporary sense of moral and social values on the other, rests on a set of unspoken major premises which underlie both sets of laws. If there is any one policy behind our laws governing sexual conduct, it seems to be that they are directed to channelling all sex relations into so-called normal intercourse in marriage. In this sense, "normal" intercourse has three characteristics: (1) it must be the type of sexual contact that can lead to the procreation of children; (2) it must be voluntarily undertaken by two relatively equal people who know what they're doing; and (3) the parties involved must be married to each other and to no one else. While the statutes dealing with sex behavior rarely state their purpose in any of these terms, almost every kind of prohibited sex behavior fails to fulfill one of these requirements.

As of today, most of us would agree that laws falling under requirement number (2) above should be enforced and possibly strengthened—sex contact to be legal should be voluntarily undertaken by equals who are in a position to know —and do know—what they're doing. We may feel less strongly about some phases of requirements numbers (1) and (3); in fact in many states, some kinds of sexual conduct which violate (1) or (3) are not even today always prohibited. In any event, the pattern is never perfectly clear. But a glance at some of the more typical laws dealing with sex in the forty-eight states may pose some of the issues which are today troubling those who, while recognizing the need for strong prohibitions in the sexual field, nonetheless feel that in some respects at least the enforcement of important and necessary laws may be prejudiced by the continued presence on the statute books of rules which no longer reflect our mores or our morals and which are honored more in the breach than in the observance.

In most states, it is a crime for unmarried people to have sexual intercourse. The crime is called fornication. The states differ as to how serious a crime it is; the penalties range, as far as imprisonment is concerned, from brief periods like thirty days to as much as five years. In some states, the penalty is higher if the intercourse is indulged in by two people who could not legally marry in that state by reason of their family relationship to each other or because one of the participants is an epileptic or is suffering from a venereal disease. If the woman has consented to the intercourse on the basis of a promise by the man to marry her, the man may be, in a number of jurisdictions, guilty not only of fornication but of the crime of seduction as well. If the intercourse is indiscriminate or for hire, that is, if the woman is paid, the crime of prostitution or one of its variants may also be involved.

When it comes to prostitution, many persons in addition to the participants themselves may be guilty of criminal behavior—the operator of the house where the prostitution takes place, the procurer who gets the girl, the pimp who gets the customer, and so forth. As a matter of fact, in some states the prostitute herself is guilty of a less serious offense than some of these others. If she has done nothing which involves a violation of the laws against loitering and solicitation, but rather has merely submitted to intercourse for money, her activity may be punishable only under a general prohibition of vagrancy or some similar minor offense. Only a handful of states have laws which specifically penalize the men who patronize houses of prostitution. In others, however, there are general statutes making it unlawful for any person to enter a building or place for the purpose of prostitution and such statutes might include the men involved.

Thus, the same act of intercourse between unmarried people might constitute three distinct crimes—fornication, seduction (if there was a promise to marry), and prostitution under other conditions. It might also ground a prosecution for a crime more serious than any of these if the female turned out to be under age. Every state has fixed an age below which no girl is considered capable of consenting to intercourse. Any man who copulates with a girl under that age is guilty of statutory rape. In some states the age of consent is as low as fourteen years; in at least one state it is twenty-one. In some places, the penalty will vary with the age of the female; for example, it will be more severe if the female is under fourteen than if she is between fourteen and eighteen. If a minor female is used as a prostitute, not only will the customer be guilty of statutory rape but other persons connected with the offense such as the procurer may be punished much more severely than they would be for an act of prostitution with a woman who is not a minor. In a few states, an adult female is guilty of statutory rape if she has intercourse with a male under the age of consent and the penalties imposed upon her can be extremely severe. Most states, however, confine their definition of the crime of statutory rape to intercourse with females who are under age and punish women who have intercourse with young boys for contributing to the delinquency of a minor, debauching the morals of a minor, indecent liberties with children, lewd behavior in the presence of children and so forth.

When one or both of the parties to an act of sexual intercourse is married to someone else, the further crime of adultery is involved. In some states, if either is married, both are guilty of adultery. In other states, if the woman is married and the man is not, both she and the man are guilty of adultery but where only the man is married, the woman is not considered an adulteress herself. In still others, only the one who is married to someone else has technically committed adultery. At common law, adultery was not considered a crime against the state at all; it was punishable by the ecclesiastical courts. Today, a number of states evince a tendency to require as the basis of a criminal prosecution for adultery something more than an act of sexual intercourse between two people one or both of whom is married to someone else. Some statutes penalize only "habitual" adultery. Others specify that the adultery is criminal only when it is open and notorious; adultery committed in secret is not punishable under such statutes. A few states permit a prosecution for adultery only on the complaint of the spouse of one of the parties to the adultery or (in at least one state) of the parent of a girl less than twenty years of age. The premise in such states appears to be that no sufficient wrong is done the community as a whole to warrant prosecution unless the person who is directly injured complains. There may be behind such laws, too, a realization that a prosecution for adultery with its attendant publicity and the discredit it casts on both the innocent and the guilty parties to a marriage is hardly calculated to keep the marriage alive—a result which might otherwise follow. It is not impossible that a husband who discovers, for example, that his wife has had a single adulterous relationship in the course of a "wild party" will find it possible to forgive her and re-establish their relationship. Not so, of course, if they have been paraded before their fellows in a court proceeding, she with a figurative, if not a literal, scarlet letter, he with the proverbial horns.

If the couple having sexual intercourse outside marriage pretend to be married to each other, they may find that they have committed still additional crimes. Some states particularly proscribe the crime of "Hotel Marriage" which occurs when a couple falsely register themselves as husband and wife at a hotel. The hotel keeper who "knowingly allows and permits such false registration" and "thereby extends the privileges ordinarily afforded to *bona fide* married couples" can also be guilty. Some states enumerate a separate crime of "lewd cohabitation" which may apply to situations where a man and woman who are not legally married to each other live together as husband and wife in one dwelling. Proof of actual intercourse is not usually essential to a conviction for this crime.

Should our erring couple go further and, despite the fact that one or both of them is married to someone else, attempt to marry each other, the further crime of bigamy may be committed. Bigamy is the willful contracting of a second marriage when the contracting party knows that a first marriage still exists. If more than one marriage already exists, still another is, of course, polygamy rather than bigamy but most states do not draw any distinction along these lines. The person marrying a bigamist is ordinarily punishable too, usually by a less stringent penalty, occasionally by a heavier one. At least one state statute imposes a heavier penalty in the unlikely event that the defendant marries more than one person on the same day. Some states have for many years had on their statute books laws apparently aimed primarily against the Mormons who during the nineteenth century were thought in many quarters to represent a serious threat to American monogamy. A typical statute provides that any person "who shall solicit to a polygamous life or teach polygamy as a correct form of family life" is guilty of a felony entailing a maximum punishment of $4000 and four years.

Thus far we have been talking about a voluntary act of sexual intercourse between two members of opposite sexes not married to each other. We have seen the great variety of infractions of the criminal law which such an act can entail. Serious, however, as these infractions may be, they are for the most part considered far less socially menacing than either sexual contacts which are not voluntary (those which are the result of force, or taking undue advantage), or sexual contacts which are not "normal." Included in the latter group, of course, are all sex relationships with persons of the same sex or with animals.

The crimes we have thus far discussed, though they deviate from the norm of voluntary "normal" intercourse between a husband and wife, are voluntary, do involve "normal" intercourse and are, for the most part, between two persons who, but for their external circumstances, would be free to marry. Where, however, one or more of these elements is lacking, the law tends to go all out in the strength of its prohibitions.

The crime of rape, for example, having sexual intercourse

with a female by force or the threat of force, is one of the most serious crimes in American jurisprudence. About a third of the states impose a death sentence for rape and in many of these the only alternative sentence is life imprisonment. The penalties in the states that have no death sentence are also very severe: many impose prison sentences for life, or ninety-nine or some lesser but nonetheless lengthy period of years—the average maximum sentence being twenty years or more. In a few situations, a defendant may be guilty of rape although no force is threatened but where there is nevertheless a lack of free consent—for example where the female is overcome by drugs or an anesthetic administered for the purpose of making her unable to protest. Generally speaking, a husband cannot be guilty of raping his own wife by forcing her to have sexual intercourse with him. By definition, the crime is ordinarily that of forcing intercourse on someone other than the wife of the person accused. However, a husband might be guilty of rape if he procured or assisted someone else to overpower his wife. A female's previous lack of chastity is no defense to a rape charge, although in some states the penalty will be less if it can be proved that the woman raped was a prostitute.

We have referred above to the lesser crime of statutory rape. Although, unlike rape itself, statutory rape does not involve the use of force, it nonetheless presents an important social problem since it involves the having of intercourse with minors who cannot be expected fully to appreciate the nature and consequences of what they are doing and whom, therefore, the laws seek to protect.

Less serious than rape but also involving heavy penalties is the crime of forced marriage. Although like rape this crime negates the "voluntary" element which appears to be a fundamental in our sex law, it does not involve an equal affront to our conception of legally blessed monogamy. Hence, while three quarters or more of the states mention a crime of forced marriage, such a crime never entails the death penalty although it can on occasion call for a maximum term of life imprisonment.

Likewise greatly frowned upon by the law although less strenuously than rape are any "abnormal" sexual contacts; that is, sexual contacts of a type that cannot lead to offspring. In this category, fall mutual masturbation and all mouth-genital and anal-genital contacts between members of opposite sexes or between members of the same sex and sexual activities with dead bodies, animals, or birds. Such contacts are collectively or individually characterized as sodomy, bestiality, buggery, crime against nature, and the like, and for the most part they call for the imposition of heavy penalties.

Sexual contacts outside marriage involve in almost every instance one or more violations of the criminal law. It does not follow that sexual contacts inside the marriage relationship are not also suspect. We have suggested that a prime aim of our criminal laws on sex is to prevent any form of sexual contact other than intercourse voluntarily undertaken by the parties to a monogamous union, and of a type that can lead to the procreation of children. If the parties have each voluntarily entered into a monogamous marriage and if they engage in "normal" intercourse without using contraceptives, they have probably not involved themselves in any violation of the criminal law. But if they permit themselves any one of a number of deviations in their sex relations from what the law regards as the norm, they may find themselves guilty of anything ranging from a civil ground for divorce to a violation of the criminal law that puts them in the same class as homosexuals and grave desecraters. Masturbation, for example, is not a crime but in several states one spouse may make it a basis for divorcing the other for "unnatural behavior." Divorces have been handed down on the ground of extreme cruelty where a wife complained that her husband forced her to watch him masturbate. Other types of sexual behavior such as mouth-genital or genital-anal contacts are heavily punished in most states, even when both parties to a monogamous union voluntarily choose to indulge in them.

In some states no distinction is made in law between such contacts and having intercourse with birds, animals, and dead bodies. In New York, for example, until recently, the maximum penalty for such contacts was twenty years; at the time, it was fifteen for second-degree robbery and manslaughter, ten for grand larceny and statutory rape. The divergence in penalty indicates the official view of the gravity of so-called "crimes against nature" or sodomy. Today the New York statute is milder and it now considers mouth-genital and anal-genital contacts as serious a crime as intercourse with dead bodies and animals only when such contacts are involuntary—that is where force is used or where one party lacks capacity to consent to the act. A person over twenty-one who indulges in such contacts with a minor is guilty of second-degree sodomy, though consent is given and no force is used; the maximum penalty is ten years. The new statute concludes with a general interdict that "a person who carnally knows any male or female person by the anus or by or with the mouth under circumstances not amounting to sodomy in the 1st degree (force, etc.) or sodomy in the 2nd degree (minority) is guilty of a misdemeanor." The New York statute thus remains stringent, though less so than it once was. Few other states have yet followed suit. In some, "crimes against nature" can be punished by a maximum sentence of life imprisonment at hard labor. Yet, as stated above, Dr. Kinsey's studies indicate that about 59 per cent of American males commit at least one of the acts usually included in the strict prohibitions of "crimes against nature" and such acts are accepted as part of normal love play by most physicians and sexologists.

We have elsewhere in this book discussed other phases of the criminal laws which impinge on the subject matter of sex: the laws against contraception, abortion and miscegenation, to mention only a few. In addition to all of these, there are a miscellany of laws which forbid such particularized forms of sexual activity that they are not often invoked. There is a statute, for example, declaring that any sleeping-car passenger who remains in a compartment other than the one to which he is assigned is guilty of a misdemeanor; another law makes sexual intercourse between a male teacher and his female pupil a separate and distinct crime.

Superimposed on the network of interlocking specific laws defining distinct sexual offenses, there are in all states general catchall statutes which serve to cover where none of the specific shoes fit. Reference has already been made to the general laws impinging on sex and minors—contributing to the delinquency of a minor, and the like. In addition, the law books are replete with prohibitions of Vagrancy, Loitering, Disorderly Conduct, Indecent Exposure, Committing a Nuisance, Lewd Behavior, Lascivious Acts, and similar statutes which can be and are invoked to punish various forms of sexual conduct.

Not only do our laws prohibit what is regarded as aberrant sexual behavior, they attempt also to remove wherever possible any provocation that might lead to such behavior. The states and the federal government have obscenity statutes which forbid in general terms the selling, lending, giving away, possessing in order to sell, lend or give away, the exhibition, etc., of any obscene, lewd, lascivious, filthy or disgusting book, play, paper, story, picture, or other object. In addition, there are a great many specific prohibitions aimed at special kinds of obscenity—obscenity over the phone, obscenity on walls and fences, obscenity in the presence of women or of children under ten. Almost a quarter of the states have legislated with reference to the public mating of animals. Nudity is proscribed in a number of different ways. The New York statute, which is fairly recent, reveals a careful effort not to interfere either with "normal" married life or with ordinary procedures in doctors' offices and clinics. Apparently it was feared both might be included if there was a general prohibition of nudity. The New York statute, therefore, punishes only "a person who in any place exposes his private parts in the presence of two or more persons of the opposite sex whose private parts are similarly exposed." Notwithstanding the cautious wording of the New York law, it would seem to make criminal the behavior of a mother, father, son, and daughter all of whom undress in the same room at the same time preparatory to going for a swim.

Virtually every form of human expression is subject to censorship on obscenity grounds to a greater or lesser degree. The forms vary all the way from the motion picture field where official state censorship bodies decide what the public may and may not see on film (how long a kiss may last, etc.) to the realm of books, newspapers and magazines where such advance censorship is acknowledged to be unconstitutional but where prosecutions for obscenity are always a threat. The Post Office Department claims and exercises a life and death power to determine what may go through the mails. Anything which in the opinion of the Department is obscene is simply declared nonmailable by an administrative official and refused carriage. It is very difficult indeed to get a court reversal of his decision.

The federal law further imposes heavy criminal penalties for importing obscene material into the country and for transporting such material in interstate commerce even though the mails are not involved. The Federal Communications Act prohibits the transmission of obscenity by radio or television. Various state laws and city ordinances heavily penalize obscene shows. In New York, the capital of show business, a theater may lose its license to operate even though in reality the owners of the brick and mortar may have had nothing whatever to do with the particular performance adjudged obscene, beyond renting their facilities for a price.

In addition to the official censorship bodies, a host of unofficial but perhaps equally potent censors work night and day to prevent the spread of "sexually impure" thoughts among our population. The Motion Picture Association— MPA—has a very elaborate code of morals administered by a special office (formerly the Hays, now the Breen office). It is almost impossible to secure general exhibition of a picture which does not have the MPA seal of approval. Backing up the MPA code in effect is the Catholic Legion of Decency, which rates films and urges the public to stay away from those found undesirable. And today the television people are working on their own moral code. Throughout the country, various private groups struggle to keep our culture and entertainment free from the incitement to "impure" sexual thought and action which it is thought obscenity creates.

Exactly what constitutes obscenity remains in the realm of speculation. We don't have enough facts in the first place. We know relatively little about what types of stimuli provoke sexual conduct nor have we really decided what types of sexual conduct we don't want provoked. In the second place, perhaps the nature of the concept of obscenity is such that it can never be delineated more specifically than it was by Judge Learned Hand of the United States Circuit Court of Appeals when he said that it must be viewed as "the present critical point in the compromise between candor and shame at which the community may have arrived here and now."

Until recently the courts said the test of obscenity was whether the tendency of the matter charged as obscene was calculated to deprave or corrupt those whose minds were open to such immoral influence or who might come into contact with it. If this test were literally applied, the lowest common denominator of the community, that is, the most easily corruptible, would be the criterion of what books, plays, and movies might circulate. A more workable test has emerged in terms of whether the material challenged "has a substantial tendency to deprave or corrupt" the average reader "by exciting lascivious thoughts or arousing lustful desire." At least today the average man rather than the man "whose mind" is "open to said immoral influence" is the gauge. Nonetheless, it is within the past few years that serious works like Edmond Wilson's *Memoirs of Hecate County* have been suppressed while "girlie" shows and very explicit brassiere, stocking, and other ads are accepted as part of our everyday life.

Much of the research done thus far seems to indicate that only the more highly educated and cultured are sexually aroused by pornographic literature as opposed to pictures. Yet this group probably yields the fewest number of accused and prosecuted sex offenders. In other words, our ignorance about what type of sexual behavior is dangerous to our society is abysmal and our elaborate interlocking system of laws defining sex crimes bears but slight relation to our sex mores.

Within the past few years, there has come to be an increasing awareness, fostered by many thoughtful studies in the field, that notwithstanding our stringent laws, we do not seem as a society to be achieving the purpose that apparently animates those laws confining sexual contact to "normal" intercourse voluntarily undertaken by the parties to a monogamous union. At the same time, students of sexology and the criminal law have to some extent sorted out the wheat from the chaff of the present laws now in being and have concluded that at least in two realms there should be both laws *and* enforcement. What these two realms are is suggested by the new New York statute on "crimes against nature" discussed above: prevention of the use of force and undue advantage in the sexual sphere and protection of youth. Whatever our individual morals may be, society has a vital interest in the accomplishment of these two purposes. Many laws devised to cover "sexual psychopaths" reflect this concern with the need to protect our young people and to prevent sexual assaults and the taking of undue advantage in sexual matters.

For the rest, the criminal laws applicable to many forms of sexual activity bear little more relation to the incidence of that type of activity in the community than the "grounds" for divorce bear to the actual reasons for divorces. Even if we grant that much of the conduct penalized should be discouraged, considerable doubt exists as to whether enacting unenforced and probably unenforceable criminal laws is the best way of discouraging it. The indications are that the next decade or so will see a great increase in the sum total of our knowledge about sex. As sex moves out of the realm of a taboo and is accepted as a legitimate subject for scientific investigation, we may begin to ascertain on the basis of something other than prejudice what is "good" or "bad" sexual behavior from the social point of view. Until our criminal laws on the subject of sex are redrafted in the light not only of what we think ought to be but in terms as well of what is and what can be, we shall no doubt remain what we are now—a nation the overwhelming majority of whose citizens are at least technically sex criminals.

PART IV

Termination of Marriages

CHAPTER 15

The Beginning
of the end

$\mathscr{T}$HERE PROBABLY never has been a marriage in which the husband and wife lived in unbroken harmony from the wedding to the grave. Even Adam and Eve had their differences as to whose will should prevail about the apple. Whether a particular couple can weather the difficulties of adjustment and readjustment which marriage demands depends on many factors ranging from the calibre of their pre-marital education (if any) and their relative maturity to such questions as the interaction of the particular neuroses of the spouses.

Many couples remain permanently in the no man's land of separation without formal agreement or technical termination of their marriage. Many others agree to disagree, enter into formal separation agreements determining their rights and duties toward each other and their children. They then proceed, usually in concert (though the law requires them to assume the appearance of controversy) to get decrees of annulment or divorce.

Assuming that one or both spouses come to the conclusion that the marriage is untenable, there are a number of alternative methods by which they can terminate or attempt to terminate the relationship.

Very frequently, couples in effect end their own marriage without recourse to the courts at all. Thus, Jim and

Frances have been married for two years and have no children. Both work. After a series of quarrels, they decide that they cannot go on living together. They give up their apartment. Frances moves home and Jim moves to a boarding house. Frances does not want or need money from Jim and both are so disgusted with the whole idea of marriage that neither wants to marry again. This state of affairs can continue permanently or until one of them wants to remarry and therefore wants to make the divorce official. In the interim, they have, for practical purposes, divorced themselves. Their lack of recourse to the courts may not injure either of them or anyone else.

On the other hand, such an unofficial divorce may have results which are not desired or contemplated by the parties. For example, years after the couple have ceased living together, Jim dies leaving money or property. No matter what his wishes may have been, Frances is in most states entitled to a substantial share of his estate since the law still regards her as his wife. Or Jim may take a job in another city or state and they may lose contact entirely. Frances eventually meets another man whom she wants to marry. She has no way of knowing whether she is free to marry; Jim may be dead or may have divorced her, but it may cost Frances huge sums of money in order to determine her status. If she cannot find him, she may have to wait some time before the law will presume he is dead so she can remarry. If she lives in New York, she must wait for five years after she last heard of him before she is free to marry. Other states may permit her to get a so-called Enoch Arden divorce after a shorter period but the chances are that she would not be free to marry for at least two years unless she succeeded in tracing Jim. And if she did, she might find at that point that Jim was unwilling to give her a divorce; he might prefer, for example, a continuation of his technical status as a married man to help him stay free of further tangling alliances.

The unofficial "divorce" has worse repercussions when

children are involved. Frequently a husband who finds his marriage intolerable and who lacks either the grounds or the funds for a divorce will simply walk out one morning and not show up again. Theoretically, he is still obliged to support his wife and children but as a practical matter it may be difficult or impossible to force him to do so unless the wife has recourse to the courts and where the husband has disappeared, such recourse is not infrequently futile.

A couple who have separated or who are about to do so may have a variety of reasons for not rushing into court to have their marriage legally dissolved. Sometimes one or both may hope that the separation will be temporary and that they will resume life together at some later date. One or both may have religious objections to divorce, and no grounds may exist for annulment. The Catholic Church, for example, does not recognize divorce and holds that a valid marriage can be dissolved only by the death of one of the spouses. As pointed out below, however, that church does accept the theory of an annulment which is simply a declaration that no valid marriage ever existed between the parties.

In many cases, the law of the state may not recognize whatever is a particular couple's trouble as "grounds" for either annulment or a divorce. As will become evident in later chapters, if both parties want to terminate their marriage, the lack of "grounds" provides merely a technical obstacle which is easily overcome if the parties don't mind perjuring themselves and have sufficient funds to hire attorneys or if they are willing and able to travel several thousand miles to set up temporary residence elsewhere. The fact that no provable "grounds" exist may, however, prevent the divorce of a couple, one of whom does not want a divorce or does not want it on the terms proposed by the other, as well as of people without money or with scruples about perjury and collusion.

If for any reason a formal end to the marriage like annulment or divorce is not immediately contemplated, there are several intermediate steps which the couple may take. Where there is no financial dependence, no children and no substantial property involved, as in the hypothetical case of Jim and Frances, the couple may simply separate without further ado. If there are questions of support, property or custody which must be settled before they can go their separate ways, they may decide informally what will be done about these questions or enter into a formal separation agreement. (See Chapter 16.) If they can come to no agreement, they can in some states go to court and get a kind of semi-divorce which will still leave them man and wife but which redefines some of their rights and duties toward each other. This is sometimes called a legal separation or a judicial separation or a bed and board divorce or a limited divorce. For purposes of convenience, we shall refer to all of these actions as a "limited divorce." Whatever the title, the practical results are usually the same in most states. The court fixes the amount which the husband must pay for the support of the wife and the children, if any, decides who is to have custody of the children and what rights of visitation and control the parent not having their custody shall enjoy.

In many states a limited divorce can be obtained on all the same grounds which the state recognizes as grounds for an absolute divorce. (See Chapter 18.) Other states, particularly where there are few grounds for total divorce, specify additional grounds as well on the basis of which the courts can give some relief to people caught in an intolerable matrimonial situation by permitting them at least to live separately and decreeing some adjustment as to finances and custody. In New York, for example, a total divorce can be secured only for adultery or in the relatively unlikely event that one spouse has totally disappeared. A decree of legal separation can be had, however, for adultery, cruelty, desertion, nonsupport, or any conduct which makes it unsafe or improper for the spouses to live together. A limited divorce is sometimes granted for a fixed period of time and sometimes for an indefinite span, depending not only on the statutes of the particular state but also on the wishes of the party seeking the limited divorce and the opinion of the court as to the gravity or hopelessness of the family situation.

A limited divorce cuts off some but not all of the marital rights discussed in Chapters 4 and 5. It terminates the right and duty to live together, to have sexual intercourse and to have the services and society of the marital partner. The wife is entitled to establish a separate residence. The duty of the husband to support the wife is restricted to the amount which the court orders him to pay for her support. She is no longer entitled to use his credit for necessaries. Generally even if a husband and wife later change their minds and want to resume living together they are not entitled to do so without court permission. Indiana, for example, makes it a misdemeanor for a couple to whom a bed and board divorce has been granted to resume cohabitation while the decree is in force.

A limited divorce does not terminate or diminish other marital rights or duties at all. Husband and wife are generally still entitled to share in each other's estates at death. The spouses still cannot testify against each other. Neither party can remarry. While they have no right to have sexual intercourse with each other, they may not have sex relations with anyone else either; if they do they are as guilty of adultery as if they were still living together. A vindictive spouse may be able to prevent the other even from seeking companionship with members of the opposite sex by the threat of a suit for alienation of affections since, as we have previously seen, a preexisting lack of affection between spouses—even the fact that they were not living together—is in many states no defense to an alienation-of-affections suit.

The limited divorce leaves a couple in the anomalous position of being neither married nor unmarried. For this reason, many states have eliminated it—among them, Arizona, Florida, Idaho, Kansas, Massachusetts, Missouri, Nevada, Ohio, and Wyoming. Instead they permit the wife to bring suit for "separate maintenance." Usually she has the right to bring such a suit only if the separation is not the result of her "fault." Sometimes in order to maintain such an action, she must be able to prove that her husband has been "guilty" of something which constitutes grounds for divorce in the state. In these states the husband, however, has only the alternatives of either continuing the marriage or of suing for absolute divorce but nothing in between, probably on the theory that being conventionally the economically independent partner, there is nothing intermediate that a court can give him. He is in most instances not entitled to support from the wife and he is capable of just walking out if his marriage displeases him. His only problem in this regard would be that he may by so doing be guilty of desertion unless his wife's conduct somehow justified his taking such a step. If, on the other hand, the wife is the aggrieved party, she may need the help of the court to keep her from destitution even if she neither seeks nor is entitled to a formal divorce. A decree of separate maintenance differs from a limited divorce in that it puts no impediment in the way of a couple who wish to resume cohabitation. Where the state's laws make no provision for a limited divorce, a suit to determine the custody of the children of a couple who have separated may be possible in addition to a suit for separate maintenance.

Suits for separate maintenance or for limited divorce are sometimes brought by people who have religious objections to divorce or in cases where one spouse for some reason is genuinely unwilling or unable to seek a total divorce. Very frequently, however, such suits are used only as a skirmishing ground preliminary to the real business of getting a divorce.

Harold and his wife Florence, for example, are unhappily married. After years of disagreement, they finally find a point on which they are in harmony; they both want a divorce. They live in New York where adultery is the only ground on which they can get one. Neither has been guilty of adultery and they do not want to set up the kind of fake hotel-room "adultery" on which so many divorces are granted in that state. Florence is willing to go to Reno and Harold is willing to pay the expenses of her getting a Nevada decree. Here, however, their area of agreement ends. Florence wants Harold to agree to give her seventy dollars a week alimony and Harold is unwilling to give her more than forty-five. Florence thereupon refuses to sue for a divorce or to "co-operate" if Harold sues for one. She proceeds to bring a suit for legal separation instead, charging Harold with cruelty and asking for one hundred dollars a week. She hopes that the threat of an unpleasant trial and the fear that the court may award her more than the seventy dollars a week she was willing to accept will make Harold more amenable to compromise.

Many suits for legal separation are thus started in the hope and expectation that they will never come to trial. If Harold and Florence, with the aid of their lawyers, do not succeed in settling their differences out of court, they may use the court's judgment only as a bargaining point in their further negotiations looking toward a total divorce. If, for example, the court awards Florence alimony of sixty-five dollars a week, Harold is apt to agree to continue paying her at least that much if she then gets a Reno divorce. If, on the other hand, Harold brings a counter suit for separation and the court finds that he is the aggrieved party and awards Florence little or no alimony, Florence is quite likely to accept Harold's offer of forty-five dollars a week (if it is still open) if she will get a Nevada decree.

In this way the suit for separate maintenance or limited divorce is frequently used, not as an end in itself, but as part of the process of reaching a separation agreement where more amicable methods of settling differences have failed.

CHAPTER 16

Separation Agreements

*T*HE LAWYER rose from his desk to greet the couple entering his office. He remembered the last time he had seen them, some three months earlier. They had come to him with the announcement that they wanted a divorce. After much persuasion he had convinced them that they owed it to themselves and to their children to try every possible avenue of assistance to salvage their marriage. They had agreed to consult a marriage counselor whom the lawyer had recommended and to try to find out whether their relationship could be improved before taking any steps to dissolve it. It was obvious from their attitude toward one another as they came into the room that the efforts at reconciliation had not been successful. The man and woman seated themselves in the chairs on either side of the lawyer's desk. The man spoke first.

"First of all, Mr. Jones, Mary and I want to tell you that we both appreciate everything that you've tried to do to save our marriage. But it just hasn't worked. We've tried our best but we've come to the conclusion that we just can't live together happily."

The woman broke in. "And that's about the only thing we *are* agreed on. I just hate the idea of having to go to court and have some strange judge tell us what we have to do about our children and our money and everything, but I don't know what else we can do now."

"Well," said the lawyer, "I'm sorry that you haven't been able to work things out. But I don't think the picture is quite as dark as you paint it, Mrs. Parker. For one thing, if you peo-

236

ple can agree on what you want to do about the children and alimony and your property and so forth, you can enter into a separation agreement as to those things."

"But supposing we get a divorce later on," said Mr. Parker. "What good will it do us to make an agreement about all those things if the court is going to decide these questions all over again?"

"A court won't," said the lawyer, "except where there's been fraud or overreaching or somebody is left destitute by the agreement. For the most part, courts are willing to incorporate in the divorce decree an agreement made by the parties so that in effect it becomes part of the decree. Courts quite correctly feel that a husband and wife who are fully familiar with the facts and problems involved can make better arrangements for themselves than the court could."

"That sounds sensible to me," said Mr. Parker. "I'm perfectly willing to have you draw a separation agreement for us if we can get together on the terms."

The lawyer shook his head. "I won't represent both of you in this matter, Mr. Parker. One of you will have to get yourself another lawyer."

"But why?" asked Mrs. Parker. "We both have confidence in you, Mr. Jones. You've been very helpful and understanding up to now and I'm sure you can help us come to a reasonable agreement."

The lawyer smiled. "Thank you, Mrs. Parker. I'm willing to draw the agreement if you want me to, but I should prefer you to bring in a lawyer to represent you. I'm suggesting that you, rather than your husband, get another attorney because, as you know, I've previously represented your husband on some business matters and I wouldn't like you ever to wonder whether the agreement wouldn't have been more favorable to you if you had had a lawyer whose only job was to see things from your point of view." He turned to the husband. "I'm making this suggestion for your protection, too, Mr. Parker. One of the few situations in which courts throw out separation agreements is where it is shown that the wife was inexperienced in business matters and was imposed upon in fixing the terms of the agreement. But if it can be shown that the wife was represented by a lawyer of her own choosing, the courts are apt to conclude that she knew what she was doing."

"All right," said Mrs. Parker. "I'll get Bill Brown to represent me before I sign anything. He's a friend of my sister and I like him. But first let's see whether we can agree on anything. Every time we've tried to make some arrangement about the children, we've ended up fighting."

"Mary thinks the children ought to stay with her all the time," the husband said belligerently. "They're my kids, too, and I want them to be with me half the time. That's only fair."

The lawyer shook his head. "Fair to you, maybe, Mr. Parker. Not fair to the children, though. We find that splitting custody like that is very hard on children. Two homes boil down to no home at all. Every six months the poor kid has to move himself bag and baggage to another place and has to get readjusted to a different household, new playmates, even a new school in many cases."

Mr. Parker thought this over for a moment. "Well, even assuming that's true, why should Mary be the one to get full custody. After all, a father has some rights too. Why shouldn't the children live with me? They're not babies. Marjorie is ten and Jimmy is seven. I can take care of them."

"Can you really?" asked the lawyer. Then he added, "It's true that in some few states, the courts give preference to the father when the matter of custody is contested in court. But the trend is the other way. Research that's been done in child study indicates that young children particularly are better off with their mother and that's where most people leave them. In most cases the decision is influenced somewhat by the fact that the father has to work all day and after going through the unhappy period while their home was breaking up, children are better off living with their mother who's apt to be home more and for whom the home is the real center of gravity. Even where the mother works too, the children are usually better off in her custody."

"Well," said Mr. Parker, "I suppose that a girl needs her mother more. But don't you honestly think it would be better for Jimmy to live with me? A boy needs his father. Mary'll make a sissy out of him if I'm not around."

"Even if Mrs. Parker has custody of the children, that doesn't mean that you won't have any influence on them at all," replied the lawyer. "But we'll discuss that angle in a minute. First I want to dispose of your suggestion about splitting the children up. Before even considering such a possibility, if I were you I'd discuss it very carefully with your doctor, or with the school psychologist (if your school has one), or with some other professional person who knows your children well. Experience has frequently demonstrated that just because their parents are no longer a unit, children of parents who are separating derive supplemental security from each other which they badly need at this point in their lives."

"How about letting the children make up their own minds?" asked Mr. Parker.

"Well, with older children than yours, that's sometimes the best way. A youngster in his teens often has a very strong preference as to the parent with whom he wants to live. But it's not wise to force children as young as yours to make a choice. The child may decide to go with the parent who has had the least to do with his upbringing simply because one parent is associated in his mind with discipline and routine, and the other parent is not. Then too, I should venture a guess that during these past months when you could see the break-up ahead, each of you has, unconsciously perhaps, been wooing the children over to your side—extra little presents, trips to the zoo, that sort of thing."

The suddenly sheepish expressions on the parents' faces indicated that he had accurately guessed the pattern of their relationship with the children over the past months. He smiled and continued. "Now if you tell the children that they're going to have to choose between you, the winner may be not the parent best qualified to have custody but the one who's given or can promise the largest bribes. Besides, the burden of making such a decision is far too heavy for a young child to bear. He simply hasn't the equipment to make the choice. And if he is compelled to, he may never get over a feeling of guilt toward the parent he didn't choose—a feeling incidentally which is apt to boomerang, when the child gets older, against the parent selected."

"But suppose as things work out the children aren't happy with their mother and want to come live with me?" argued Mr. Parker. "What happens then?"

"Well," responded the lawyer. "It does sometimes happen when children get older that they want to move in with the parent with whom they haven't been living. That doesn't mean that the original decision as to custody was wrong, however. I drew a separation agreement for a couple a few years ago in which they gave custody of the daughter to the mother. The other day the father came in and told me that his daughter Grace, who's now fourteen, wants to come and live with him and his new wife because her mother doesn't understand her and she thinks they would. Now actually Grace may be just reflecting the traditional revolt of the adolescent; if her parents still lived together she would doubtless be complaining that neither of them understood her. But where the parents are separated, she, unlike the child of an unbroken home, thinks she has some place to go where people would be more sympathetic to her. It's difficult, if not impossible, to force her to stay with her mother against her will. You can't anticipate in your separation agreement every possible problem that may arise, but you can make the terms flexible and set up machinery, now, when the agreement is being made, to solve any difficulty that may develop in the future."

"If I do agree that Mary should have custody of the children, I want it clearly understood that I'm to have the right to see them," said Mr. Parker.

"There are two ways in which the problem of what we call 'visitation' is usually handled," said the lawyer. "Some people like to fix definite times when the father can visit the children or have them visit him. This has its advantages particularly where the couple are very bitter toward each other and would probably have a row each time if they had, each week or month, to decide questions of time and place. It also helps the parent who has custody to plan ahead for the child without having plans disrupted at the last minute by an unexpected demand from the other parent that the child be allowed to visit him. Sometimes these agreements provide that the father can see the child three evenings a week from five to seven (if, for example, the child is very young) or can have the child every Saturday (or every weekend, or every other weekend) and for the entire Christmas or Easter vacation and for one month of the summer vacation or some combination of all of these. If you do decide on a plan of this kind, you will find that things will work out best if neither of you is too rigid about sticking to the formula where the child's best interests make it desirable that you waive it every once in a while— some summer Jimmy may want to go to camp for the whole summer, for example, or Marjorie may have been invited to visit a friend for Christmas when the schedule says she's supposed to be with her father."

"I'm not sure how well that kind of fixed arrangement would work for us," said Mr. Parker. "My business takes me out of town a lot. I might not be able to take advantage of the time with the kids I'm supposed to have. I'd like to see more of them while I'm here."

"Well, then," said the lawyer, "You might consider the advisability of a more flexible arrangement. We could put in a clause like this one that I've just used in another separation agreement." He picked up a sheaf of papers from his desk and flipped through the pages. "Here it is: 'The Wife shall have sole custody of the Child and sole control and supervision of its upbringing. The Husband shall have the right to visit the Child and to have the Child visit him at reasonable times, and such visits shall be arranged on terms mutually satisfactory to the parties.' Doing it this way has a number of advantages. Sometimes this business of having the father show up at specified hours on specified days like two o'clock every Saturday or between five and six every other day creates a very artificial situation and a period of high tension for the children. Some people find that not having fixed visitation times helps for a more spontaneous relationship for all concerned. The choice between the two methods depends on what kind of people you are and whether you think you can co-operate fairly well together. I suggest that you both think it over for a while."

"If Mary has custody don't I have anything to say about how the children are brought up?" asked Mr. Parker.

"You can have as much say as you and Mrs. Parker decide you should have. There is no fixed formula for a separation agreement. I do suggest, though, that you leave ultimate decisions in the hands of one person rather than trying to maintain equal authority for both of you. I remember one case where the couple had agreed that major decisions as to the child's education and upbringing were to be made by joint agreement. When their boy was fourteen years old, the father wanted him to go to the prep school which he had attended. The mother wanted to send the boy to a different school. They squabbled over it for six months and succeeded in so completely upsetting the boy in the process that he failed to get into either school. It didn't really matter which school the boy went to. What did matter was that no machinery had been devised in advance to resolve the conflict without tearing the boy apart. If you like, you could agree that Mrs. Parker is to consult you on major decisions affecting the children—schooling, camps, illnesses, the need for surgery or orthodonture and so forth. Then you should further provide that in the case of disagreement, some one has the power to make a decision. This can be the parent having custody or some third party whom you both respect—a family friend, perhaps, your family doctor or minister, a child psychiatrist or some such person. Furthermore, the parent in whose custody the child is at the time clearly must have the right to make both routine and emergency decisions. It would be silly to require consultation before calling in a physician either when the child only has cold symptoms or requires an immediate appendectomy."

Mr. Parker shook his head. "This is too complicated for me to absorb all at once. Suppose you let us think over some of the things you've said."

"Surely," responded the lawyer. "Today I'm just trying to give you the general picture. And while you're thinking it over, there are a few more things to which I'd like both of you to give very serious consideration. Whatever you do, don't either of you try to influence the children against the other. Sometimes a wife, for example, who feels bitter and rejected tries to make her children feel the same way toward their father. Aside from the fact that this hurts the child, it usually ends in defeating the mother too. The child will come to prefer his father. If either of you tries to make your children judge whose fault the break-up was, you may find that when they grow older they'll decide against you. Even if one or both of you remarries, Marjorie and Jimmy still need to maintain close contact with the two of you. When a marriage breaks up, both husband and wife are likely to feel a sense of failure and it's a great temptation to bolster up your self-confidence by getting your child to agree that it was all the other parent's fault. But don't do it. Someone told me the other day about the young son of divorced parents who announced happily that his mother was going to get married again and that they were going to have a new car and, best of all, he was going to have *two* fathers. Your children will never be that well adjusted if you use them as a weapon against each other."

Mr. Parker sighed. "I came in here resolved that I was going to fight for at least partial custody of the children. But I've got to admit that what you've said makes sense. I'm willing to let Mrs. Parker have full custody provided I can see the children regularly. And I would like to be consulted about all major problems as you suggested."

The lawyer turned to Mrs. Parker. "I presume that's agreeable to you?"

Mrs. Parker nodded. "Of course. But I do think I ought to have the final say where the children are concerned."

Mr. Parker interrupted. "No, I'd like to have Dr. Williams act as judge if we can't agree on something important. He's known the children all their lives."

Mrs. Parker made a protesting motion, then stopped herself. "All right, but I do hate to go to a stranger to decide things."

"You may never have to utilize Dr. Williams's services," the lawyer said reassuringly. "We lawyers find that one of the advantages of having an arbitration clause in a contract is that it often induces the parties to adjust the matter themselves rather than leave it to a third party who knows less about it than they do. Actually there's some doubt about the enforceability of promises to arbitrate anything other than questions which can be answered in dollars and cents but in most cases both parties usually find it to their interest not to challenge such a method of settling all kinds of disputes."

"Now what kind of arrangements do we make about money?" asked the husband.

"I think it would be helpful if you could prepare a memorandum for me, listing your earnings, your investments, your insurance, the amount of the mortgage on your house if you have one, and so on. With these facts I think probably Mr. Brown and I can help you to work out some satisfactory arrangement."

"All right," said Mr. Parker. "But could you give me some idea of what's customary in this kind of case? I want to do what's right but do I have to support Mary for the rest of her life no matter what happens? Suppose we get a divorce and she remarries, or suppose she never does remarry but the children grow up and get married? Or suppose my earnings decrease? Then, too, Mary may go back to work? Frankly, I'm scared to tie myself down not knowing what will happen."

"Let me give you an idea of some of the factors which we consider in fixing an arrangement for support. Very wide variations are possible. Frequently, for example, a wife who has no children and who works or a mother with independent means of her own waives all her rights to be supported by her husband. An agreement which bars alimony altogether is not acceptable in some states and is freely permitted in others. Some states permit the wife to waive her right to support only if an examination of the financial position and earning capacity of both parties indicates that no undue hardship is likely to result. Many women, particularly older women who have never worked, continue to be completely financially dependent on the husband. Now, Mrs. Parker, you may be somewhere in between these two extremes. I gather that you did work before your marriage. What kind of work did you do?"

"I used to teach art at a private school up until the time Marjorie was born. I've been thinking of trying to get a job mornings while the children are at school. I'd like to support myself if I can."

"Fine," said the lawyer. "We'll keep that in mind as a possibility when we come to fix terms."

"But I certainly won't be able to support both myself and the children."

"I don't expect you to," said Mr. Parker quickly. Turning to the lawyer, he asked, "Leaving the question of support for the children aside for the moment, could you give me some idea of what proportion of their income men usually contribute to their wives' support in this kind of situation?"

"Where children aren't involved, the wife usually gets somewhere around a third or less. In the case of many childless marriages, a lump sum settlement is sometimes made. This means that the husband gives the wife so many thousands or tens of thousands of dollars (depending on the parties' circumstances) and the wife renounces all further claims for support. This has the advantage of settling the husband's liability, for the time being at least, without the running sore that weekly or monthly alimony payments are apt to be. On the other hand, weekly or monthly payments cease in the event of the wife's remarriage while a lump sum once paid stays paid even if the wife remarries six months later. The other catch in this kind of arrangement is that the courts will not in any event permit a wife to remain in need or become a public charge if her husband has any means, no matter what the provisions of the separation agreement are. While they are apt to be guided by whatever regular payments the parties have agreed upon, the courts are not likely to pay much attention to a lump sum paid years before when confronted with a wife who is threatened with destitution."

Mr. Parker shook his head ruefully. "I don't have enough capital to make a large enough lump sum settlement anyway. I think we'd better figure on some kind of regular monthly payments."

"It seems to me I should have some kind of lump sum settlement too," said Mrs. Parker. "Otherwise what would happen to me if Jim dies before I do?"

"There are a number of ways that can be handled," replied the lawyer. "Part of Jim's capital can be put into a trust fund for that purpose. If you predecease him or remarry, the fund will revert to him. If he dies first, either the whole trust fund would be paid over to you or monthly payments could be made to you by a trustee. Most people in moderate circumstances don't have enough money, however, to make this kind of trust arrangement. Instead the wife is covered by insurance. The separation agreement can require the husband to maintain sufficient insurance so that if he dies before the wife she will be taken care of, at least to some extent.

Of course, if she dies or remarries during his lifetime, she has
no further rights in the insurance which the husband can then
make payable as he sees fit—to the children, for example, or his
new wife if he has one."

"Well, what about supporting the children?" asked Mr.
Parker. "About how much of a man's income is he expected
to give for them?"

"The percentage varies depending on how large his income is. Obviously a man who earns $5000 a year will have to
contribute a higher percentage but a smaller sum than a man
whose income is $75,000. In the $15,000 to $20,000 bracket
the usual agreement probably gives to wife and children
about a half except where there are special circumstances."

"Such as what?" inquired Mrs. Parker.

"Oh, where the wife has independent means or an earned
income as great as her husband's, for example. Or where
'there is money' on one or both sides of the family—grandparents or the like. I remember one case where the parties
couldn't agree on the amount of support and went to court to
have a sum fixed. The court awarded the wife and three children $7500 a year out of the husband's total income of $9000.
The evidence had shown that the husband's parents were very
wealthy and that he was their only child."

"Suppose I marry again," said Mrs. Parker, "I gather that
payments for my support would stop but does that mean that
Jim wouldn't have to contribute to the children's support any
longer?"

"Not at all. The usual arrangement is to make the wife's
support terminate at her remarriage but the payments for the
children ordinarily continue until they reach a fixed age—
eighteen, twenty-one or twenty-five are probably the three
most commonly used. Sometimes the payments go on until the
children have completed their education or have reached
twenty-one, whichever happens sooner.

"What worries me," said Mr. Parker, "is what happens
if my income decreases. I earn about $10,000 a year. Suppose

we agreed that I'm to pay $100 a week for Mary and the children and then we hit a year when business is bad and I only earn $7000. That would leave me less than $2000 a year to live on."

Mrs. Parker broke in before the lawyer had a chance to answer. "Well, suppose, on the other hand, that you earn $20,000 next year. It seems to me that we're both taking a gamble on your future earnings."

The lawyer went on to explain. "We can take some of the gambling element out of it if you like. We can provide that in the event of a substantial change in circumstances for either of you, the amount of support can be adjusted up or down from time to time. If you people can't agree on what the adjustment should be, the question can be submitted to arbitration in the same manner as questions affecting custody of the children, although you might want to name a different arbitrator for this purpose—some one more knowledgeable in business affairs than the doctor or clergyman you might want to consult about the children."

"I'm afraid I don't exactly understand about arbitration anyway," admitted Mrs. Parker. "You sound as if anyone can do the arbitrating."

"Anyone you choose," answered the lawyer. "If you two can agree on someone in whom you both have confidence, any disagreement that arises can be submitted to him for decision. If you can't agree on a person or if the person you agree on now is not available at the time, you can agree that disputes are to be arbitrated by a board of three, one arbitrator to be chosen by each of you and the third arbitrator to be chosen by the two you've designated. Arbitration is still relatively new in our legal system, so there's some variation from state to state regarding the legal status of arbitration agreements. But for the most part, if you have agreed to submit disputes to arbitration, the courts will make every effort to enforce the agreement and to make both parties abide by the decisions of the arbitrator."

"Is there anything else beside custody and support that we should include in the agreement?" asked Mr. Parker.

"Yes. Usually an agreement specifically states that the parties shall henceforth have the right to live separate and apart and to be free from control or interference by each other as fully as if they were unmarried."

"How about putting in something about agreeing to get a divorce if either of us decides we want one?" interrupted Mr. Parker.

"Definitely not," answered the lawyer. "The courts consider that an agreement to get a divorce or to agree to consent to a divorce is against public policy. You can, however, provide that if you do subsequently get a divorce, the separation agreement will be incorporated in the divorce decree."

"I see. Is there anything else that we ought to agree about?" asked Mr. Parker.

"Yes. Your agreement should set forth whatever you decide about the division of your personal possessions—clothing, jewelry and other personal effects, your car, furniture and household furnishings, stocks and bonds, and so forth. Generally speaking, both parties tend to keep what was originally theirs; the one who has custody of the children gets most of the household effects, and securities acquired during marriage are divided or put in the children's names."

"How about our house?" asked Mrs. Parker. "We can't very well divide that."

"Not unless you want to sell it and divide the proceeds," concurred the lawyer.

"I'd rather let Mary go on living in the house," said the husband. "I think it would be better for the children not to uproot them at this point."

"I think that's wise," agreed the lawyer. "However, if you have a mortgage on the house, you're going to have to figure out how the payments are to be made. Incidentally, if either of you owns any other real property, we'll have to make arrangements about that, too. In this state a husband and wife have an interest in each other's real estate even if it is not owned jointly."

"We probably ought to change our Wills, too, shouldn't we?" queried the husband.

"Probably. You may also want to make some provision in the separation agreement about testamentary disposition. Often where the husband hasn't custody of the children, we guard against the possibility of their suffering too much financially from his losing interest in them by requiring him to take out a certain amount of life insurance of which the children will be the irrevocable beneficiaries. Sometimes the husband also agrees to make a Will, leaving the children not less than a fixed percentage of his estate."

Mr. Parker looked offended. "I'm hardly likely to 'lose interest' in my own children, Mr. Jones."

"I wasn't implying that you would, Mr. Parker. It sometimes does happen, though. I had a woman client once ask me in complete exasperation whether there wasn't any way in which a separation agreement could force her husband to take an interest in their child. But even where both husband and wife are devoted to the children of their marriage, this kind of provision is often made to protect the children in the event that either parent remarries and has children by the second marriage who may have a more immediate claim on his or her affections. However, all these details can be worked out later. I've just been trying to give you a general picture of what a separation agreement can include. As you can see, we can cover a number of things in addition to the two questions of custody and support to which the court ordinarily restricts itself in a suit for separation or in a divorce or annulment action. Now, if you will prepare a list of your earnings, your securities, bank accounts, real-estate holdings and other property, Mr. Brown and I will go over it and see if we can advise you as to what would be a fair agreement in the circumstances."

The following day, Mr. Parker sent Mr. Jones a memorandum of his financial position. It showed that Mr. Parker, a vice-president of a small building supply company, earned a salary of $10,000 a year. He owned securities with a listed value of $15,000 and a $25,000 home on which there was a mortgage of $10,000. He carried $20,000 of life insurance which was payable to Mrs. Parker. During the next few weeks there were numerous conferences between the lawyers and their respective clients and between the two lawyers. After some dickering, it was agreed that Mr. Parker was to pay a total of $5700 a year for the support of his wife and the two children, $2600 to be considered as Mrs. Parker's share.

It was explained that so long as the parties were not divorced, the income tax on the entire $5700 going to Mrs. Parker was payable by Mr. Parker. If they did get divorced and the separation agreement was made part of the divorce decree, then that part of the payment which represented support for Mrs. Parker would be taxable to her. In this connection, Mrs. Parker again mentioned that she might decide to go back to work, part time anyway, and there was some disagreement as to what should be done in the event she did. Mr. Parker at first took the position that his obligation to support her should be diminished by whatever amount she earned. Mrs. Parker claimed that her working would necessarily involve her in additional expenses—hiring someone to help her in the house, clothes, lunches, and carfares *and* taxes. Under the conditions proposed by Mr. Parker, she would have less money if she worked. A compromise was eventually reached whereby Mrs. Parker's alimony was to be decreased by one third of whatever amount she managed to earn herself. It was further provided that if, in general, the financial circumstances of either party changed drastically, the amount of support could be renegotiated and arbitrated if necessary.

Title to the house was transferred to Mrs. Parker and it was agreed that she would carry the mortgage alone. In view of the fact that she got the house, the parties agreed that Mr. Parker was to retain all but $3000 worth of the securities. Mr.

Parker's insurance policy was to be made irrevocably payable
to the children and he also agreed to make a Will leaving
at least 25 per cent of his estate to Marjorie and Jimmy. In
addition, Mr. Parker agreed to take out a $10,000 insurance
policy payable to Mrs. Parker to tide her over for a while in the
event he predeceased her and her alimony payments stopped.
In the event that Mrs. Parker remarried, all payments to her
for her support would stop; the payments for the children
were to continue until each reached the age of twenty-one or
was graduated from college, whichever event happened first.

The enforceability of separation agreements such as the
Parkers' varies somewhat from state to state. If the agreement
is incorporated into a subsequent court decree it, in effect, becomes the decree. If the husband fails to live up to his promises
to pay alimony, he can be required to do so by court order
and may be subject to imprisonment for contempt of court in
many states if he does not do so. This is not true for the most
part if the court which dissolves the marriage merely *approves* the terms of the separation agreement or makes no ruling at all on the questions of support and custody and merely
lets the existing separation agreement stand. In these cases,
the wife can only sue on the contract and get a judgment but
disregard of the judgment does not involve a contempt
penalty. In some states, however, where the husband has
failed to live up to his agreement the wife is permitted to
rescind the contract and sue for alimony as if no agreement
had ever been made.

In some jurisdictions, the question of whether or not the
agreement is incorporated in a divorce decree is also signifi-
cant in determining the power of the court to alter the
amount of alimony. In one case, for example, the separation
agreement provided that the wife was to receive $200 per
month. Subsequently the wife secured a divorce and the separation agreement was incorporated in the decree. Seven years
later the husband obtained a court order reducing the
alimony to $100 a month because of drastically changed eco-

nomic circumstances. A few years later when the husband was once again prosperous, the wife sued for the difference between $100 and $200 a month for the period during which she had received the lesser amount. The court rendered a verdict for the husband on the theory that when the separation agreement was incorporated in the decree, it lost its identity and could no longer be enforced as a separate contract. If, on the other hand, the agreement is not incorporated in the decree or if under the law of that state it remains in effect as an agreement as well, a court can no more change its terms than it can arbitrarily alter the terms of any other kind of contract unless the separation agreement involved fraud, duress or resulted in acute financial need.

All of this is, of course, subject to the over-all proviso that the courts will not allow any agreement between the parties to deprive them of the power to protect a wife or children from want or destitution. Nor will they permit themselves to be foreclosed by agreement of the parties from changing the custody of a child if it can be shown that the child is living in an undesirable environment. But courts rarely touch the other provisions of separation agreements and, even where custody and support provisions are involved, accord great weight to the terms upon which the parties themselves have agreed. Moreover, the mere fact that they have agreed, especially if the agreement has worked out or is working out well, makes it unlikely that the parties will resort to the uncertainties of litigation to redefine their status.

If and when the family court becomes a reality in more states (see Chapter 19), it may represent a more desirable way of doing things. In the meantime, a separation agreement, carefully worked out between the parties and their lawyers, represents in most cases the best available way to chart the future course of a disintegrating family group.

CHAPTER 17

Annulment

"THOSE WHOM God hath joined together, let no man put asunder." These traditional words of the marriage ceremonial represent the classical and the current Catholic view as to the dissolution of marriages.

During the years before the Protestant Reformation, while the Catholic Church was the dominant influence in Europe, Church law was the only law as far as most all marriages and the family were concerned. Then, as now, the Catholic Church took the position that marriage once entered into was indissoluble except by death. However, this doctrine does not apply to annulment and never has. For the theory of an annulment is that no valid marriage has ever taken place and therefore God hath not joined the particular couple together. Here lies the basic difference between annulment and divorce. An annulment proceeds on the premise that no marriage ever existed and that all the court does is to declare this fact, namely, the *nullity* of the purported marriage. A divorce, on the other hand, presupposes that a valid marriage did exist but declares it terminated by reason of so-called "grounds" which arose subsequent to the marriage.

In the United States today, all forty-eight states grant divorces on one or more grounds. At the same time, decrees of nullity or annulment continue to represent an important way of getting out of an unsatisfactory marriage. Actually the number of annulments and the grounds on which they are granted are in inverse ratio to the liberality of the divorce laws. Where the law of the state specifies a large number of grounds for divorce, annulments are rare. Where divorces are hard to get, annulments are numerous. About one-third of all the annulments granted in the country are granted in New York where (except in cases of the total disappearance of one spouse) the only ground for divorce is adultery. At the other end of the scale is New Mexico, the only state permitting divorce for incompatibility, where annulment actions are virtually unknown.

Despite the difference in theoretical origin, the distinction between the grounds for annulment and the grounds for divorce have in many states become foggy. What is cause for annulment in one state may be cause for divorce in another and vice versa. In one state, Georgia, the grounds for both have become so synonomous that the courts for the most part refuse to entertain suits for annulment at all, preferring that people get a divorce on the same grounds so that no question will arise as to the legitimacy of children.

There are two general classes of marriages which are subject to annulment. First, there are those marriages which society has a prime interest in preventing. These are marriages which may not be valid no matter how much the parties want them to be (see Chapter 2). Incestuous and bigamous marriages are void in all states and so-called miscegenetic marriages are void in those states which prohibit marriages between white people and people of other races. It is often said that all of such marriages are void from their inception. In some states it is not necessary even to obtain a court decree annulling the marriage. The marriage is void on its face. Then there is a second class of marriages which in and of themselves are not considered an affront to society but which the parties are given an option to avoid because some element in the contracting of the marriage prevented one or the other from entering into the relationship with full understanding of its implications or ability to fulfil its duties and obligations. Such marriages are voidable—that is, they can be declared a nullity at the suit of one or both of the parties.

As we have seen in Chapters 2 and 3, each state has laid down some requirements for marriage—minimum ages, pre-marital tests, requirements of mental capacity, etc. For the most part the responsibility for enforcing the state's rules is in the hands of the people authorized to issue licenses and, in a few states, the people who perform the ceremony. Noncompliance with such formal requirements, in most instances, is not sufficient reason to annul the marriage. While the states try to enforce their regulations by penalizing licensing officers who do not observe them, failure to meet these requirements does not so violate public policy or individual rights as to warrant nullifying the marriage status completely.

Where, however, the noncompliance with law has to do not with what the parties did or did not do in accomplishing their marriage ceremony, but with who they are, what they are or what they said or did prior to the ceremony, their marriage, although technically correct, may in the eyes of the state be no marriage at all if a question is raised as to its validity.

In a majority of states, for example, the marriage is subject to annulment if the state's minimum age requirement is not met. As we have seen, most states set a minimum age of consent under which people are incapable of marrying at all and a somewhat higher age bracket in which they may marry only with the consent of their parents. In Arkansas, California, Idaho, Minnesota, and New Mexico the marriage can be annulled if the parties were either under the age of consent or if they married without the consent of their parents before reaching majority. However, in Pennsylvania, Rhode Island, Georgia, and Louisiana the only way of enforcing any of the state's age requirements is by refusing to grant the license or marry the parties; if the marriage has been performed it cannot be annulled no matter what the ages of the parties. In virtually all of the other states the marriage can be annulled if the parties were under the legal age of consent. The marriage is however not void; it is only voidable. In other words, it will stand unless a court decree annulling it is secured. In most states, such a decree can be obtained either by the party who was under age or by his parents. The statutes governing age requirements are for the protection of youngsters. The other party to the marriage who was not under age has no right to claim an annulment on the ground of the minority of his spouse.

In most states, moreover, annulments on the ground that one or both of the parties were under age, are discretionary with the court. Such annulments may be denied where, for example, the couple has had a child or the wife is pregnant. Sometimes the determining factor where annulment is sought on the ground of minority is whether or not the marriage has been consummated; if it has not, the courts are more apt to annul the marriage because the parties really can be put back in the same positions they occupied before the ceremony.

If the parties were over the age of consent, their marriage is usually not subject to annulment even though parental approval has not been obtained and should have been according to the state law.

The importance of sexual intercourse to a valid marriage entirely apart from its reproductive function is recognized by the fact that in most states, impotence is a ground for annulment though sterility is not. In order to be the basis for annulment the physical incapacity must have existed at the time of the marriage and (in some states) must be continuing and incurable. The statutes make no distinction between impotence in the husband and the wife, although for obvious reasons the cases almost always involve the alleged impotence of the husband.

In one New York case, however, a husband sought an annulment on the ground of physical incapacity, claiming that the dimensions of his wife's sexual organs were such that no satisfactory intercourse was possible. The court refused the annulment on the basis of medical testimony which indicated that while the wife's vagina was short, sexual intercourse was possible even though it might not be completely satisfactory to the husband.

Sexual incapacity in order to be a ground for annulment must be a complete inability to have intercourse at all. Many states (including Arkansas, California, Delaware, the District of Columbia, Georgia, Idaho, Iowa, Michigan, Montana, Nebraska, New Jersey, New York, North Carolina, North Dakota, Texas, Vermont, Virginia, West Virginia, and Wisconsin) permit annulment on this ground. In a few other states, the courts have held that a marriage can be annulled for physical incapacity even in the absence of specific statutory authorization. In other states, impotence, while not a ground for annulment, is cause for divorce.

Despite the fact that the desire to have children has been recognized by the courts as one of the paramount aims of marriage, the fact that the husband or wife is sterile is, of itself, not sufficient to warrant annulling the marriage in any state. In all likelihood, cause for annulment would be shown if one of the parties knew that he or she was sterile at the time of the marriage and either withheld this fact from the other or falsely represented to the other that he was capable of having children. But it is the fraud, not the sterility itself, which would be the moving factor here.

In order to enter into a valid marriage contract, both parties must be capable of understanding what they are doing and the nature and effect of marriage. The idiocy, insanity or feeble-mindedness of one of the parties makes the marriage completely void in some states and subject to annulment in practically all. This virtual unanimity is no doubt due in part to the state's desire to prevent the propagation of the mentally defective. (See Chapter 13.) Where the state considers the marriage void from the beginning either party can usually ask for a judicial declaration to that effect. Other states, however, which apparently consider their laws on this subject as being designed more for the protection of the subnormal individual than for the protection of society in general, will only allow the validity of the marriage to be challenged by the mentally defective person or by someone acting in his behalf. It is not necessary in order to secure an annulment that there must have been an adjudication of insanity. Nor is it conclusive, on the other hand, that there was, prior to the marriage, an official finding of insanity. The important question is the mental state of the party at the time of the marriage ceremony. Some jurisdictions have made special efforts to prevent the marriage of people who are temporarily incapable of understanding what they are doing, even though they may generally be mentally normal. These states, for example, prohibit the issuance of a license to anyone who, at the time of application, is under the influence of drugs or alcohol. For the most part, however, such a temporary lack of mental capacity is not a ground for annulment unless it was induced by the other party and amounts to fraud or duress.

In New York a dissolution of the marriage, which is called an annulment, can be obtained if one of the parties has been incurably insane for five years or more. It is not necessary that the insanity have existed at the time of the marriage; an annulment will be granted even if the spouse was perfectly normal when married and became insane afterward. Strictly speaking, of course, this is not really an annulment proceeding. Other annulments are based on a fact or condition which existed when the parties were married and which therefore justify a judgment that no valid marriage between them has ever taken place. The New York annulment for insanity is actually a divorce. It was called an annulment so as to avoid the violent opposition that has always attended any effort to liberalize the New York divorce law.

A marriage can be annulled in many states if the parties went through the ceremony with no intention of conducting themselves as married people afterward. Mock marriages, which happily are not a very popular form of amusement, are generally invalid for lack of genuine consent and can be voided. Getting married for a lark has been viewed differently in various climates of opinion. In a Connecticut case two youngsters on a date finished off the evening in high style by driving to a neighboring state to get married for no better reason than that the girl dared the boy to do it. After the ceremony, they drove back to their respective homes and, in the cold light of morning, promptly tried to get the marriage annulled. The Court granted the annulment on the ground that neither party had given real consent to the marriage. In a Maine case, however, where the girl and boy had also married on a dare, the court refused to grant an annulment because the judge felt that this kind of thing was becoming too common and that young people should not be permitted to make a mockery of marriage. Fortunately, this kind of situation is rapidly becoming extinct as more and more states have imposed waiting periods between the time of application for the license and the time when the marriage can be celebrated.

A decision against annulment is apt to be reached where the husband and wife have had intercourse before their marriage, even though they may not have intended their marriage to stick. In one such case the parties had agreed to be married in order to legitimize their unborn child. They had further agreed that they would not live together after the marriage and that the wife would sue for an annulment six weeks after the marriage. Subsequently the wife refused to bring the annulment suit as she had promised. The husband brought suit himself, alleging that there had been no consent to a genuine marriage. The court ruled in favor of the wife on the theory that the parties did intend to create the marriage status even if only for a short time. The decision was undoubtedly influenced by the fact that an annulment in this case would have bastardized the child.

The free consent of both parties is necessary in order to create a marriage. In all but a few states a marriage can be annulled if the consent of one of the parties was secured by force, duress or coercion. The "shotgun wedding" is the typical example of this kind of forced consent. The threat need not, however, be of a physical nature, particularly where the party coerced was young, or for some other reason subject to the domination of the person or people applying the threats. The threat of arrest or prosecution for seduction or rape is not generally regarded as the type of coercion warranting an annulment. Thus, when the husband seeking the annulment had argued duress on the ground that he had been arrested on a rape charge and had entered the marriage because the officers told him he would be released if he married the prosecutrix, he was refused an annulment on the ground that there had been nothing illegal about the form or substance of his confinement. The court considered that he had had a free choice between marrying the girl or refusing to marry her and defending himself against the charge by regular legal processes. The verdict would probably have been different if the husband could have proven that he had been subjected to third degree methods by the police or threats of imminent physical harm by the girl's family.

Perhaps the most common ground for annulment and one which covers a great variety of factual situations, is annulment for fraud. In all states except Kansas, Louisiana, Mississippi, New Mexico, North Carolina, Oklahoma, and Rhode Island, an annulment can be had by the party deceived if the spouse, prior to the marriage, made some deliberate misrepresentation of an important fact in order to induce the other party to consent to the marriage. But the states have widely different ideas as to what constitutes an important enough fact. In most states, the misrepresentation must go to the heart of the marriage. That is, it must involve some matter which makes it impossible or improper for the parties to live together as man and wife. New York, the state with the strictest divorce laws, leads the nation in the liberality of what its courts will consider fraud, thus accounting for the fact previously referred to that one third of all the annulments in the United States are granted in New York. There, any misrepresentation of a material fact without which the deceived party claims he would not have entered the marriage is sufficient to warrant an annulment.

No state, not even the most liberal in this field will grant an annulment on such complaints as, "He told me he loved me, but he was lying. He didn't care for me a bit," or "She married me for my money." Where, however, it can be shown that the party who made the misrepresentation of love did not intend to fulfill any of the obligations of marriage or to live with the spouse, an annulment may be granted.

In a Massachusetts case, William, a widower, engaged Elsie as a housekeeper to take care of his house and children. After she had worked for him for a while, he reluctantly told her that he could no longer afford to pay for her services and would have to send his children to live with relatives. Apparently operating on the theory that a wife is cheaper to maintain than a domestic servant, the unromantic gentleman followed up the dismissal with a proposal of marriage. Elsie declined and left his employ. Shortly thereafter she decided to return to her mother's home in Germany. She was a little perturbed by the problem of how to present to her mother the illegitimate child whom she had borne some time before her employment as William's housekeeper. Moreover, a friend had told her that the passport authorities might be narrow-minded about the matter and advised her that matters would be considerably eased if she could travel as a married woman. Elsie thereupon informed William that she had reconsidered his proposal and was willing to marry him and make a home for him and his children. The couple were married a few days later. Immediately after the ceremony, Elsie told William she had some errands to do and would meet him at home later in the afternoon. William and the friends and relatives whom he had assembled to greet the bride waited in vain. Some weeks later, he got a letter from Elsie, now safely established in her mother's home in Germany, telling him that she had no intention of returning. The court granted the indignant widower an annulment.

The crux of cases such as this obviously is not whether or not the deceiving party loved the other but whether he or she intended ever to be married to the other in any meaningful respect.

Misrepresentation of financial status has been held to be a ground for annulment in some states, but not in others. In New York a court granted a husband an annulment where he said that his wife had falsely told him that she had $6,000 in the bank which she would give him to set himself up in business after they were married. Contrast this with a California case in which the husband had told the wife before their marriage that he owned a shoe store and could support her in the style to which she was accustomed. After the marriage the wife discovered that he was only a clerk and earned a very small salary. The court refused to grant an annulment, holding that the misrepresentation was not "material." A New Jersey court offered a slightly different reason for refusing to grant an annulment in a similar situation. In the New Jersey case the wife claimed that the husband had told her that he had $2,000 in the bank, earned seventy-five dollars a week and had two cars, one of which he would give to her. The bride discovered shortly after the wedding, but before the marriage was consummated, that none of these things was true. She promptly went home to her mother and sued for annulment. The court denied her petition on the ground that if the financial angles of the marriage were important to her, she should have investigated her prospective husband's financial standing before she married him.

The courts are generally cynical about premarital puffing. They have taken the position that a certain amount of exaggeration is common to courtship and that not every lie is a fraudulent misrepresentation. No one is—according to the law, anyway—entitled to take too literally statements made before marriage as to social position, character, personal traits or undying affection.

Misrepresentations as to health have likewise been

treated differently in various jurisdictions but are apt to be taken more seriously by the courts. In some states an annulment can only be obtained if one of the parties fraudulently concealed the fact that he suffered from a disease which affected his sexual powers, such as a venereal disease. Elsewhere it is sufficient if the disease is one which would make it dangerous or even just unpleasant for the parties to live together as man and wife. Drug addiction, tuberculosis, epilepsy and the fact that the husband had concealed a prior commitment for insanity have all been held to warrant an annulment.

What is considered fraud sufficient to warrant annulment changes with our general mores. Consider, for example, a case where May and Arnold have an affair. After a few months, May announces that she is pregnant. Arnold promptly proposes that they marry immediately. Shortly after the marriage he discovers that the child is not his but was the result of another affair which May had been carrying on simultaneously with another man. Arnold sues for an annulment on the ground that he had been tricked into marrying May by her fraudulent misrepresentation that the child was his.

At one time the courts' reaction to this type of situation was apt to be against the husband on high moral grounds: "He had intercourse with this woman without being married to her. He's no better than she is. If he hadn't acted like a bounder in the first place he could not have been tricked in this fashion and the court will not give any relief to a man whose own conduct is not above reproach." Some courts have in the past, therefore, taken the position that if a man had pre- or extramarital relations with a woman, he knew that she was unchaste and was therefore bound to suspect her moral character generally. It is up to him, they said, to make a careful investigation before accepting the truth of any statement she made. In one case, the court held that the husband was guilty of "negligent credulity" in believing that he was the only man with whom his wife had had intercourse.

More recent decisions in cases of this sort have reflected the shifting moral and ethical standards of this century. The current view tends to be that a man should not be penalized for having tried to do the honorable thing in marrying a woman whom he believed he had impregnated. As one court put it, the husband was not required to subject his intended wife to "the unspeakable humiliation of an inquisition." The courts today will generally grant an annulment in the Arnold-May situation described. If, however, May had not been pregnant but had told Arnold she was, the courts are much less likely to grant him an annulment.

There is no absolute right to expect the marital partner to have been chaste before marriage. West Virginia permits annulment where it is discovered after marriage that the wife was a notorious prostitute or the husband was a "licentious male," but even here unchastity in any lesser degree is not cause for annulment. This is true even if the spouse claiming fraud had specifically asked the other before marriage whether he or she had been chaste and received an affirmative answer. In one case the wife sued for annulment because she discovered that her husband had had a paramour and two children in Cuba. She claimed that she had been tricked into marrying him by his representations that he was a man of good character. The court denied the annulment, saying that, "Marriage covers with oblivion antenuptial incontinence and lapses from virtue."

There are three situations in which lack of chastity may possibly make the marriage voidable. If a woman tells her fiancé that she is a stenographer and he finds after marriage that she was a call girl there is more of a deception involved than there is in a case where a woman merely withheld information that she had had a premarital affair. The latter situation would not entitle the husband to an annulment; the former might in some states. A second situation in which annulment would probably be granted is where the wife never had intercourse with the husband before marriage but is pregnant by another at the time of marriage. Some courts have distinguished this from the nonpregnant unchastity situation on the theory that her pregnancy made the wife temporarily incapable—whether of copulation or reproduction is not clear. Others have more frankly based their decisions on the ground that no man should against his will be burdened with the responsibility of a child who is not his. The third situation likewise involves children; a New York court granted an annulment, for example, to a husband whose wife had several illegitimate children before the marriage.

While sterility as such is not a ground for annulment, in some states a misrepresentation as to willingness and intention to have children has been held to constitute fraud. New York has gone so far as to permit an annulment on this ground even in the absence of an express premarital statement of intention to have children. Since children are one of the normal purposes and results of marriage, a spouse's silence on the subject is deemed sufficient to imply willingness to have children. The determining factor is what he or she really intended at the time of the marriage but this can be proved by showing the course of conduct after the marriage. For example, if it can be shown that the husband from the very first day of the marriage consistently refused to have intercourse without the use of contraceptives, the court will infer that he never had any real intention to have a child. The fact that one spouse started using contraceptives some time after the marriage will not, however, support a case of annulment for fraud. An annulment was refused, for example, where the wife claimed that although the husband had expressly promised her before marriage that they would have five children, after the birth of their first and only child he admitted that he had never had any intention of having more than one.

Although the theory of an annulment is that no marriage ever existed, as a practical matter, the realities of two people having lived together as man and wife cannot be erased by a court decree. Children, joint property, debts and obligations which were acquired before the annulment of the marriage do not quietly disappear in deference to the court's dictum that there never was a marriage in the first place.

In the absence of statute, the children of an annulled marriage are generally considered illegitimate. In Alabama, Arkansas, California, Georgia, Indiana, Minnesota, Nevada, New Jersey (with one minor exception), New Mexico, New York, North Dakota, Oregon (with one possible exception), Rhode Island, Texas, Vermont, West Virginia, and Wisconsin the children of all annulled marriages are, by statute, legitimate. Other states have distinguished between the issue of void marriages; that is, those which are against public policy and invalid from the beginning, and voidable marriages which are not considered invalid unless challenged in an annulment suit. In Iowa, for example, the child of a marriage between relatives is illegitimate; in Florida, the child of a miscegenetic marriage; in Tennessee the child of a bigamous marriage. Some states reserve the distinction of legitimacy in the case of a bigamous marriage to the offspring of parents who married in the honest but mistaken belief that there was no prior existing marriage. In a few states, the children are considered the legitimate offspring only of the parent who was "capable of contracting" where the other parent was under age, insane or barred from contracting a new marriage by the existence of a prior one. In a few states, all children are considered the legitimate offspring of their natural parents and this would be as true of the issue of an annulled marriage as it would be of the children of people who had never made any attempt at all to marry.

Where the law of the state makes the child legitimate only as to one parent, that parent will ordinarily be awarded custody. Where the child is legitimate as to both or neither, custody will usually be awarded in deference to the same considerations which govern custody decrees in divorce suits (see Chapter 20). However, California, Idaho, Montana, Nebraska, South Dakota, and Wyoming have a special rule to the effect that where an annulment is granted because of the fraud or force of one party, custody must be awarded to the innocent spouse although the court may make the other spouse pay for the support and maintenance of the child.

Again, in dealing with problems of property and obligations which arose before the annulment, the courts have tended to distinguish between void and voidable marriages. In a Massachusetts case, the wife sued for annulment on the ground of fraud. After the annulment was granted, she proceeded to bring suit against her former husband for the injuries she had suffered in an automobile accident caused by her husband's negligence. The accident occurred before the annulment and the law in Massachusetts did not permit husbands and wives to sue each other. The woman claimed that this law had no applicability to her situation because the annulment decree had wiped her marriage off the books and she, therefore, had not been married at the time of the accident. The court rejected her claim, saying that where a marriage was merely voidable at the option of one of the parties, the parties are bound by the laws applicable to husbands and wives for the period prior to the annulment. The court indicated, however, that its ruling would have been different if this had been an incestuous or bigamous marriage which is considered void from the beginning and which the state will not recognize as valid even if neither party seeks to set it aside.

Similarly, the rights of third parties which arise during the marriage cannot be defeated by an annulment. Storekeepers who have given the wife credit for "necessaries" for which the husband is liable (see Chapter 5) can enforce their claims notwithstanding the annulment.

Even where a marriage is void, the courts do not ordinarily try to readjust the financial relationship of the couple as if no marriage whatsoever had existed. In an Illinois case, a wife was granted an annulment on the ground that, unknown to her, her husband was insane at the time of the marriage. The husband's guardian who had been appointed to care for his property tried to make the ex-wife repay money belonging to her husband which she had used to support herself during the period between the marriage ceremony and the annulment. The court ruled that even though by the law of Illinois the marriage of an insane person was void from the beginning, the woman did not have to reimburse her husband's estate for the money spent on her support before the annulment.

Insofar as it is possible without doing either party an injustice, courts do, however, seek to return to each spouse the property which he owned at the time of the marriage. Property acquired during the marriage is sometimes divided between them, regardless of who holds legal title, on the theory that it was acquired by both of them acting as a kind of partnership.

In many states no permanent alimony will be awarded after an annulment on the theory that alimony is something to which a spouse becomes entitled only by virtue of a valid marriage having existed. Occasionally, the courts will get around this rule by awarding damages for fraud or deceit to the innocent party.

In some states (like New York, for example) statutes expressly confer upon the courts the right to grant permanent alimony in annulment cases. The states are divided as to whether the wife is entitled to temporary alimony and an allowance with which to pay her lawyer while the annulment suit is pending such as she would ordinarily get in a divorce suit. Some courts will award temporary alimony and counsel fees only if it can be shown that the wife needs it; she is not entitled to it as a matter of course. In many states such awards will only be made to the wife if the husband is the one who is seeking to annul the marriage. In such states, the courts do not permit the wife to claim at one and the same time that the mar-

riage is invalid and that she is entitled to such financial benefits of a valid marriage as temporary alimony and counsel fees
in connection with her efforts to have the marriage annulled.
Realistically this view might prevent an impecunious wife
from ever being able to challenge an invalid marriage.

In considering the question as to who may bring suit to
annul, the distinction between void and voidable marriages
often has significance. Where the purpose of the law is protection of society rather than of the individual spouses
(bigamy, incest, and miscegenation in some states) the marriage is ordinarily void and either party may bring suit to
annul. In some jurisdictions, the suit may also be brought by
the District Attorney or the validity of the marriage may be
collaterally challenged by anyone who has an interest in so
doing—for example, a relative of the husband who would
inherit his property in the absence of a valid marriage. In
those cases, on the other hand, where the annulment is predicated primarily on a grievance of one of the parties to the
marriage (rather than of the state as a whole) the marriage
can usually be challenged only by the injured party or someone acting in his behalf as, for example, the parents of a
minor or the lunacy commission or guardian appointed for an
insane person. In only about a quarter of the states can the
sane party also sue for annulment.

The rules as to *when* an annulment suit may or must be
brought vary widely from state to state. South Carolina only
permits suit to be brought before the marriage has been "consummated by cohabitation." In some other states, definite time
limits have been set after which no annulment suit will be entertained.

The California law is typical of this group. A suit for annulment on the ground of nonage must be brought within four
years after the minor reaches the age of consent or, if the suit
is brought by a parent, before the minor reaches the age of
consent. An annulment because one party was of unsound

mind must be brought during the lifetime of both spouses. Suit for fraud must be brought within four years after the discovery of the fraud. Force or duress in the inducement of the marriage, and impotence are waived if suit is not brought within four years after the marriage. The specification of such a fixed term of years often gives more leeway than when no term is specified.

In New York, for example, the party who claims fraud cannot bring suit if he continues to live with the spouse after he discovers the fraud or reasonably should have discovered it. In one case where the husband claimed that the wife defrauded him into marriage by pretending that she was willing to have children, the court refused to grant him an annulment, reasoning that the wife's insistence on using contraceptives over a period of many months after the marriage should have given him warning of the fraud in time to have brought the action sooner. The fact that he delayed bringing the suit was interpreted as acquiescence.

Of the approximately 150 cases a week which are brought in New York on the ground of misrepresentation as to intent to have children, comparatively few are reported. It is difficult, therefore, to try to estimate how long a period is considered evidence of acquiescence and waiver in that state. We do know, however, that in some cases annulments on this ground have been granted even after the couple has been married for several years where the plaintiff can show that the circumstances were such that he or she was really fooled into thinking that the defendant meant to have children eventually. In one such case the wife claimed that she did not discover that her husband had no intention to raise a family until after they had been married for ten years because each year he gave her such a plausible reason for delaying having a child for another year—wanting to continue his education, having to contribute to his mother's support, the possibility of his being drafted, etc. The willingness of the courts to accept this kind of proof of fraud is less dependent on fixed standards of law than on the individual attitudes of referees and judges, the climate of the state at a given moment in regard to "easy" annulments and the relative availability of divorce as an alternate remedy.

In some states a suit for annulment on the ground of force in the inducement to marriage must be brought at the earliest moment after the threat of force is removed. Otherwise the party claiming that force was used is deemed to have given free consent to the marriage. Likewise, if one who was under age at the time of the marriage continues to live with the spouse after reaching the age of consent the right to an annulment is waived. In some states no annulment for mental incapacity is allowed if the couple continued to cohabit after the handicapped person had regained his reason.

Some courts have evinced a tendency to grant annulments more freely in cases where the marriage has not been consummated. In effect, they regard consummation as a waiver even of something which the parties might have made a condition to the marriage. There was at one time a rash of suits in New York for fraud on the ground that the defendant spouse had deceived the plaintiff by promising to follow up a civil marriage ceremony with a religious one. Where the marriage has been consummated, the courts are not cordial to this kind of claim. They apparently take the position that if the party claiming fraud really considered the religious ceremony important, he would not have agreed to consummate the marriage before the religious ceremony had taken place. In other cases, courts have ruled that initial consummation is not important; the vital question is whether or not the parties lived together *after* the discovery of the fraud or other fact which is now being asserted as the basis for annulment.

The existence of children is another factor which often influences the court. Where the husband and wife had been married for seventeen years and had two children, one court refused to grant an annulment on grounds which it indicated might have been sufficient if they had not so long constituted a family unit. Where the law of the state is such that children of annulled marriages are bastardized by the annulment, the courts are particularly reluctant to permit annulments. This is true in Georgia, as pointed out above, with the result that even though elaborate laws as to annulment still stand on the statute books, annulment as a method of dissolving a marriage has in practice been abolished in that state and the same grounds used as the basis for divorce.

Thus, to a considerable extent the laws as to annulment continue to perform their traditional function of dissolving marriages defective in their inception because of (1) who the parties are (incest, bigamy or miscegenation), (2) some lack of capacity in one of them to enter into a permanent marital relationship (impotence, insanity, imbecility or mental deficiency) or (3) because one party was wrongfully induced into the marriage. Increasingly, however, annulment has been used as a legal weapon for people whose real complaint is not that the marriage was defective in its inception but that it has proved to be an unhappy alliance. Simultaneously the trend of the law has been to treat the children, financial relations, and other common interests of the couple exactly the same where the marriage is declared null as where there is a valid marriage which has been terminated by divorce. Thus, the distinction between annulment and divorce is becoming shadowy.

Insofar as the state takes the position that some marriages are so socially undesirable that they should not be permitted to stand no matter what the desires of the parties, as in (1) above, the concept of annulment will probably persist. The vast majority of annulments, however—those in (2) and (3)—serve primarily to ameliorate the rigidity of the divorce laws in strict divorce states. It may well be that such grounds

for annulment as well as formal grounds for divorce will give
way to the more constructive approach of the family court
with its stress not on who is lacking what or who is at fault,
but rather on the question: Is this marriage one which is sick
and if so how, if at all, can it best be cured?

CHAPTER 18

Divorce:

THE LAW ON THE BOOKS

*T*HE NURSE stepped briskly into the surgeon's office. "There's a man outside who says he's got a ruptured appendix," she said.

The doctor looked up briefly from the scalpels he was polishing. "How does he know?" he asked.

"He says he's got a pain in his right side."

"Can he prove it?" asked the doctor.

"Yup. He's got two witnesses with him who testify that he's swooned, holding his side, a couple of times."

"Okay," said the doctor, picking up his scalpel, "I guess it *is* his appendix. Get him on the operating table and I'll take it out."

Half an hour later, after having removed the appendix, the doctor returned to his office to work on a monograph which he was preparing for presentation at the state medical convention on "Peritonitis; a Threat to the American Way of Life." Since his schedule was rather tight, he never saw the patient for a check-up after the surgery. In fact, there was no reason why he should have; he considered his job finished when he had taken the last stitch in the wound.

The foregoing, of course, is completely hypothetical, bearing no relation to anything likely to happen to you in your doctor's office. Unfortunately, it's a pretty accurate picture of how our divorce courts operate in performing what should be the most delicate kind of emotional and social surgery. No doctor will rely on a patient's self-diagnosis, backed up by the enthusiastic agreement of the patient's friends. He will examine the patient and look for other possible physical and psychological factors which might explain the patient's pain. He may prescribe medication, diet, exercise or other appropriate remedies short of surgery. If an operation is necessary, he will prepare the patient for it and see the patient after it is over so that he may gauge the effects of his treatment, prescribe aftercare and know better whether he should treat the next patient with a similar ailment by the same or different methods.

Divorce courts should function with respect to ailing marriages in much the same way that a doctor functions in regard to an ailing patient. For the most part they don't. They are not equipped so to function. Chiefly they exist to put the rubber stamp of state approval on arrangements made by the parties. At least 85 per cent of the divorces granted by the courts of this country are uncontested. This means, in effect, that the parties decide what "grounds" they will use for dissolving their marriage and what the setup will be after the divorce—financially and with respect to the custody of the children. All the court has to do—actually all it has the power to do in most states—is say okay.

In terms of legal theory, of course, the state is an actively interested third party in every marriage. For this reason, a marriage, while it is a contract, differs in one vital respect from all other contracts. If Tom Adams contracts to work for Bob White for five years, and Adams and White decide one afternoon over a friendly drink that the arrangement isn't working out as they had hoped, they are perfectly free to tear up the contract, shake hands and go their separate ways. Not so with the marriage contract, at least as far as legal forms are concerned. Society asserts an interest in every marriage and must approve its dissolution. This interest results, as the lawmen put it, in marriage being a *status* as well as a contract.

There are good reasons for society interesting itself actively in the marriage relation and its termination. On the practical side, property titles and inheritance rights, tax liabilities, and many other tangible consequences depend on who is married to whom and who their legitimate children are. Moreover, the modern state has become paternalistic to the extent of accepting the responsibility for seeing to it that no one starves. In ancient Rome, alimony was unknown although divorce was common. If a man chose to make a settlement on his ex-wife, that was his business. If he did not, the fact that she might become destitute did not concern the community as such; she was free to join the company of the other beggars who were also none of Rome's official concern.

Today the state assumes a continuing responsibility for the welfare of wives and children. In many respects, all children are considered wards of the state. The state is not likely to assert any special interest in the ordinary situation, assuming that parents will do the necessary. But where parents mistreat or fail to support children, where there are no parents, and where the marriage which produced the children is about to be dissolved, the state, at least on paper, steps in to see that proper arrangements are made for their upbringing and maintenance.

These are the practical, material reasons why the state is an interested third party in every divorce action.

A less tangible but probably more important reason for the state's concern with the dissolution of marriages is the belief generally held in democracies that society is a chain and that each family constitutes one of the links that together make up the chain. If the links are not individually strong—if marriages are not holding together—then the very foundations of the state itself are threatened. This belief became entrenched at a time when the family was, far more than it is today, the basic unit of society—economically as well as socially and psychologically. Great-grandpa and great-grandma may have hated each other violently after a few years of marriage, but the chances are that they stayed married anyway. A far larger percentage of our population lived on farms then than do now, and on farms particularly the wife was an essential part of her husband's ability to earn a living. If she did not churn butter, milk the cows, look after the chickens, and do a hundred other jobs, the money which her husband would have had to spend to hire some one to do her work would probably have eaten up the profits of the crop.

Even in urban communities the wife was an integral part of a functioning economic entity. Present-day labor-saving devices like washing machines and vacuum cleaners, and day nurseries to care for children, were equally unknown. Moreover, in great-grandma's time, the wife's economic dependence on the husband was almost complete. Strengthening the economic reality was a strong moral code which strenuously disapproved of divorce. The mere fact that a woman was a divorcée made her something of an outcast in her community. Most religious creeds, although they did not go as far as the Catholic Church and ban divorce entirely, sanctioned it in only the most extreme circumstances.

As against this background, it is not surprising that the states passed laws which made the "badness" of the defendant the sole test of whether a divorce could be obtained. The one value which had to be preserved above all others, except in the most extreme cases, was the unity of the family.

All of this may have made a great deal of sense in great-grandma's day. As the industrial revolution went into full swing, the family became less and less important as the basic unit of our society. The forces at work today seem to pull the family apart rather than force it together as in the "old days." Something like 50 per cent of our population live in cities; more than one third of our women work outside their homes; two world wars and a variety of other factors have violently shaken all the "do's" and "don'ts" that great-grandma believed in. Moreover, a host of experts have come into being—psychiatrists, psychologists, marriage counselors, sociologists, and the like—who mirror the times and question the hypothesis that at all costs the home must be held together. They agree with A. P. Herbert that in some situations holy wedlock becomes holy deadlock and that its consequences may be disastrous to all concerned including society itself. As a result of all these contemporary developments, divorce today, far from being an anomaly, is what happens to one out of every four or five marriages.

But while a real social revolution has been going on affecting in a thousand ways the importance and relative permanence of marriage, the divorce laws have remained the same with only a few minor exceptions. True, South Carolina, which formerly permitted no divorces whatsoever, a few years ago acknowledged the failure of its effort to keep marriages together forcibly and now permits divorce. Beyond this, however, a survey of the changes in the divorce laws in the last fifteen years indicates that outside of the fact that several states now permit the spouse of an incurably insane person to get a divorce (or an "annulment," as it is called in New York), there has been little liberalization of the grounds for divorce. A few states have lowered their residence requirements (see Chapter 21) but for the most part the tendency has been, if anything, to toughen up the procedural requirements for divorce. The fact that though the number of divorces has vastly increased, the divorce laws themselves have not changed, is a clear indication that the divorce rate has little to do with whether the law makes divorce "hard" or "easy" to obtain.

The divorce laws today still proceed on the old assumption that a divorce defendant is "bad," that the divorce is in fact a punishment for his sins. The law in most states is based on the "good" spouse being able to prove that the "bad" spouse is "guilty" of something, this despite the fact already stated that at least 85 per cent of all divorces are uncontested; that is, the result of mutual agreement in fact though not in law. The "guilt" theory continues to permeate our law in this field to such an extent that in most states if the court is shown that both parties are "guilty" then neither can get a divorce. A status of continuing matrimony is presumably their punishment. The welfare of the family as such, the desirability of continuing a marriage which may be wrecking father, mother, and children alike, are concepts which for the most part under our divorce laws have, like the flowers that bloom in the spring, nothing to do with the case.

In line with the theory that a divorce should be granted only if the plaintiff can prove the defendant to have been "guilty" of a specified "offense," the various state laws set forth "grounds" for divorce.* Prime among these is adultery which is a ground for divorce in every state of the union. Subject to certain minor exceptions, the law generally assumes that no marriage can or should be expected to survive after one party has engaged in even one act of extramarital intercourse. In point of fact, of course, many marriages do survive adultery but the law says they needn't. The law, for the most part, acknowledges no distinction either in terms of the circumstances surrounding the adultery or its actual or probable effect on the marriage. Consider, for example, three hypothetical cases.

John Jones, an otherwise satisfactory husband, goes to a convention in Chicago. In the irresponsible (and slightly intoxicated) state which conventions are apt to induce, he takes a young lady to his hotel room for the night. After an embarrassed farewell the following morning, he dashes for his train home. He can't remember her name and he never knew where she lived. He feels a little guilty, a little sheepish, and perhaps, secretly, a little proud of his adventure. He never again sees and rarely even remembers the young lady involved.

Tom Smith, our second case, has been having an affair with another woman for several months. He frequently meets

* See chart on page 356.

her for lunch and cocktails and spends many evenings with her when he is theoretically "tied up at the office."

George Brown, a third wandering husband, goes further than either of the other two. His extramarital affair develops to the point where he leaves his wife and goes to live with the other woman.

Realistically, there is probably a great difference in the effect of the adultery of these three hypothetical Romeos on their respective marriages. Experience indicates that unless Mrs. Jones finds out about the lady in Chicago, her husband's rather casual adultery will probably have no real effect on their relationship. Assuming that Mrs. Smith doesn't know the nature of the business which is keeping her husband tied up nights, their relationship may or may not suffer because of the diversion of his time, attention, and affection. In the case of the Browns, the adultery, while probably itself the result of an unsatisfactory marriage, has precipitated a breach in the marriage.

The divorce laws generally recognize no difference among these three cases. All three wives are automatically entitled to a divorce if they can prove the facts stated. No investigation is made as to the extent to which the adultery actually has damaged the marriage nor would the results of such an investigation be relevant. In only two states is any distinction made between casual and continuing adultery and these, unfortunately, are rather too reminiscent of the double standard to warrant enthusiastic support. In Kentucky, a wife can get a divorce if her husband is "living in adultery" which would not include our first case and possibly not the second. A husband, however, can sue his wife for divorce for any act of adultery or even for "lascivious behaviour" without any actual proof of adultery. Texas, similarly, permits Justice to lift her blindfold to see which is the adulterer. A husband is entitled to divorce if his wife is "taken in adultery." A wife can only complain if her husband actually abandons her and lives in adultery with another woman.

Adultery is defined in many state statutes as "voluntary sexual intercourse" with one other than the spouse. Even where the statute does not use these words, there must be an element of consent involved. A husband cannot divorce his wife for committing adultery if she was attacked and raped. Courts in several states have held that no divorce will be granted for adultery if the accused spouse was insane or otherwise mentally irresponsible at the time of the act or acts. While we know of no case where the offending spouse's drunkenness was held to be the kind of irresponsibility which would free him from the consequences of his conduct, such an extension of the theory of the insanity cases seems possible.

Adultery can rarely be proven by direct evidence. People ordinarily do not have sexual intercourse in front of witnesses. The courts over a long period of years have come to take judicial notice of the ways of man with woman and will accept circumstantial evidence which indicates that adultery was committed. If, for instance, it can be shown that, at eleven in the evening, Mr. Jones entered the apartment where Miss Smith resides alone and that he emerged at nine the next morning, the court will assume that they were not playing checkers. (For some reason, the courts are not quite so ready to assume that adultery is committed during daylight hours.) Similarly, if the two occupy a suite at a hotel for a weekend registered as Mr. and Mrs. Jones, the court will assume the relationship between them was not platonic.

The standard hotel room scene staged for the purpose of getting a divorce in New York, where adultery is the only stated ground for divorce other than complete and total disappearance, takes advantage of this kind of presumption. When the wife's two friends—or a detective hired by her—testify that they saw Mr. Jones and an unnamed blonde in their nightclothes, occupying a single room containing a rumpled bed, the court presumes, as one judge put it, that they did not pass the time saying their "Pater Nosters." As a practical matter, the lady may have been hired for the occasion and Mr. Jones probably never gets to a stage of intimacy where they hold hands or know each other's first names, but the presumption operates nonetheless.

The "evidence" in adultery cases in New York has come to follow such a standardized pattern, that a printed card is given out in court by a clerk, telling lawyers for the plaintiff what questions they should ask. The entire procedure rarely consumes as much as ten minutes. Many lawyers complain that if circumstances differing from the routine hotel room set-up are offered in evidence, the referees who hear divorce suits are apt to be less willing to grant the divorce than if the standard situation is presented. They find the truth harder to believe. The classic story is told of the wife who was refused a divorce after having proven that her husband and another woman had for many months been living together as Mr. and Mrs. So-and-so in the same house. The house, said the court, had more than one bedroom and the wife had not proven that her husband and his "friend" had been sharing the same one.

Next to adultery, cruelty is the ground for divorce recognized by the largest number of states. Originally, cruelty was confined to extreme physical abuse; later it was defined as action which was likely to impair the physical health of the spouse; still later the concept was enlarged to include danger to mental health. While only a few statutes specifically give a right to divorce for mental and emotional indignities inflicted on the plaintiff, the courts in many more states view nonphysical cruelty as well as physical violence as being within the terms of their statutes.

It is difficult to generalize about what the courts will consider cruelty warranting a divorce because the standards differ so from state to state and even from case to case. In two cases decided at about the same time, a wife whose husband had spanked her was denied a divorce and another whose husband had merely threatened to hit her was granted one. The distinguishing factor between the two cases may have been that the wife in the second case was pregnant and the court found that the husband's action was a threat to her health.

Many courts have indicated that what might constitute cruelty to one kind of person in one setting might not be so regarded with respect to a person of differing culture and background and in different circumstances. In one Texas case, for example, the wife sued for a divorce after twenty years of marriage, alleging cruelty. She proved that although her husband was a wealthy man, he forced her to do menial work—run a large household unassisted, irrigate the ranch, help with the haying and raise a garden. The wife claimed that as a result of this arduous labor she was "just about to break down." The court granted the divorce on the ground that her husband's actions constituted a danger to the wife's health. Obviously the court would not have granted the divorce on this set of facts no matter what the danger to the wife's health if it had been shown that the husband was a poor farmer who did not earn enough money to have any of these services performed by hired help. The fact that married life proves harder than the hopeful bride expects does not constitute cruelty on the husband's part unless there is something which he can within his means reasonably do to make it easier but which he deliberately refrains from doing.

Somewhere midway between the physical and mental cruelty cases are the cases also coming under the head of "cruelty" in which the cruelty consists of some aberration from the normal in the sexual relations. Forcing a wife to submit to "abnormal" sexual intercourse was declared an "indignity" in one case and grounds for divorce. So was a husband's refusal to have intercourse with his wife and his indulging in "abnormal" sex practice in her presence. In some states any deviation from the sex norm is an independent ground for divorce, usually designated as commission of a "loathsome crime." Forcing the wife to undergo an abortion has also been held to be cruelty. Refusal to have intercourse altogether is more frequently termed desertion than cruelty.

Often there is a correlation between the mental and physical effects of nonphysical cruelty. One example can be seen in the case of the husband who brought another woman home to live in the house he occupied with his wife. He showed the other woman marked attention both in private and in public and frequently assured his wife that he loved the other woman and did not love the wife at all. The wife claimed that as a result of this treatment she had become nervous and anaemic. In this type of situation, courts do not require very convincing proof that the wife is in actual danger of becoming sick or dying; they are glad to accept the claim that the wife's physical health is being impaired even though obviously it is her mental health and happiness which is directly affected.

In many states, the courts have given up all pretense of needing a physical health peg on which to hang their verdict and have said flatly that cruelty includes the infliction of mental suffering. Occasional nagging, fits of anger or complaining are not usually considered sufficient to constitute cruelty. Where, however, there is a consistent enough pattern of this kind, mere verbalizing can be sufficient.

In one Florida case, for example, the husband proved that his wife constantly upbraided him, accused him of having relations with other women and of engaging in homosexuality and cursed and chided him for having only one leg. To make matters worse, she publicly charged him with being a bootlegger and in the pay of criminals; the embarrassed husband happened to be the county sheriff. These accusations were made by the wife, not only at home but at her husband's office and in public places in the presence of friends and relatives—and presumably voters. The court granted the husband a divorce.

Accusations of unchastity have frequently been held to constitute extreme cruelty. In one case the court found the wife guilty of extreme cruelty because she had brought (and lost) a divorce suit against her husband in which she charged that he had infected her with a venereal disease. Another husband's accusations in front of friends and relatives that his wife had set fire to their house won a divorce for her.

Ordinarily being unpleasant or having unpleasant habits is not sufficient to constitute cruelty. The cases of which we read frequently in the papers where divorces are granted because the wife ate crackers in bed or the husband kept his false teeth on the breakfast table are apt to be cases in which the defendant has agreed to the divorce and does not put in any defense. There is usually an understanding between the parties that the plaintiff will ask for the divorce on as innocuous a ground as possible and the defendant will let the divorce be obtained by default. If the divorce is contested, however, it is necessary in most states to show a pattern of much more serious misconduct.

On the other hand (as in the adultery situation), no matter how extreme the cruelty alleged, it will not ground an action for divorce if the spouse complained of was not mentally responsible at the time the acts were committed. In one case, for example, the husband proved that his wife had attacked him with a knife and had made various other attempts to kill him. Divorce was refused on the ground that the wife (who was subsequently incarcerated in an asylum) was insane at the time she attacked him. In most of the cases of this sort, we find that the mental illness which was pleaded was sufficiently grave to force commitment of the insane spouse. It is dubious whether any court would give the same immunity to a spouse who could only prove that his or her cruelty arose from a neurotic or even a borderline psychotic condition. However, as pointed out below, insanity itself grounds an action for divorce in many states.

Habitual drunkenness is a recognized ground for divorce in about three quarters of the states. In many, the condition must be one which has arisen since the marriage though others permit a divorce on this ground if the spouse complained of was an habitual drunkard before the marriage if it can be proven that the other spouse did not know it. In order to obtain a divorce on this ground, it is necessary to prove something more than the fact that the spouse occasionally gets drunk. It is not, however, necessary to show that he is continuously drunk. One authority defines habitual drunkenness as "the fixed habit of frequently getting drunk." This means something more than a regular habit of getting lit every Saturday night. A few states have by their statutes defined habitual drunkenness as that which "disqualifies the person a great portion of the time from properly attending to business." This seems to be the chief test used even by those states whose laws have not so specifically worded it.

Perhaps because it is a relatively newer problem in our social scene, drug addiction is a ground for divorce in only a few states. In other states the actions of a drug addict may entitle his spouse to a divorce for cruelty, but it is his conduct, not his addiction, which is the test.

Desertion or abandonment are grounds for divorce in all states except New York and North Carolina. The term covers many more situations than the obvious one where one spouse packs his bags and leaves. Ordinarily the husband has the right to choose the place where the couple shall make their home and if his wife refuses to accompany him, her refusal constitutes desertion on her part even though he is the one who does the actual leaving. In one case, the eighty-five-year-old husband sued his sixty-five-year-old wife for desertion. The couple had lived all through their married life in a city house in which the wife had a life interest. As the husband grew older he found it impossible to earn any money in the city with which to supplement the sixty-five dollars a month pension which he received from the government. The couple had, however, managed to live on this plus what the wife was able to earn by renting rooms in the house. The husband, against her wishes, bought some land in the country where he hoped to be able to make a modest living by farming. The wife refused to accompany him and the court granted the husband a divorce, holding that she had deserted him.

The husband's right to choose the residence is not, however, an unlimited one. If he insists that the wife live in a place which is an unfit residence considering all the economic, social, and health factors of the parties, the wife's refusal does not constitute desertion on her part. On the contrary, the courts construe such insistence as desertion by the husband.

One spouse cannot sue the other for desertion if he has, by his own actions, made it dangerous for the other party to live with him. A husband who beats his wife, for example, cannot claim that she has deserted him if she leaves the house. Nor will the courts allow one spouse to goad the other into leaving and then take advantage of the departure to sue for desertion.

In a Wisconsin case the court found that the husband had done just that. Immediately after their marriage the couple had moved into a very small house. The bride soon found that her husband was an unusually hospitable soul. He invited a few members of his family to come share the cottage. The guests included his mother, his sister and her five young children, and an adolescent niece and nephew. The young wife became pregnant. A few weeks before her baby was due, she apparently decided that the house was not big enough for still another person and returned to her mother's home, saying that she would return when her husband had cleared the house of all their guests except his mother. The husband sued for divorce on the ground of desertion several months later. The court refused to grant the divorce, pointing out that the husband's conduct seemed deliberately calculated to drive his wife away. Moreover, the court placed emphasis on the wife's state of mind at the time of her departure, finding that she did not intend to abandon her husband permanently but probably intended to come back either when the guests had left or after her baby had been delivered.

The state of mind of the departing spouse is of importance and is usually gauged by the whole pattern of behavior. A husband whose work necessitated his going abroad for an extended period without his family might be deemed to have deserted them if it could be shown that he did not write or send money or that he had told friends that he had no intention of returning to his wife or having her join him. If, however, his conduct was consistent with that of a man who intended to reunite the family as soon as circumstances permitted, his departure would not constitute desertion.

As has been previously mentioned, the refusal of one spouse to have intercourse has been judged to be desertion. The right to a normal sexual relationship is an essential part of marriage and either party usually has the right to terminate the marriage if the other is either incapable or unwilling to have intercourse. While annulment or divorce for impotence is deeply rooted in the law, there is usually no specific provision in the statutes for granting either where there is a refusal to have intercourse although both parties are capable. Such a situation has been judicially viewed as a kind of desertion probably for lack of any better peg on which to hang it. In order to constitute desertion, the refusal must be a total or nearly total one; the fact that one spouse does not desire to have intercourse as frequently as the other is not sufficient. Nor would a divorce be granted if it were shown that the refusing partner had some sound health reason for insisting on abstention.

In some states, the total disappearance of one spouse, as distinguished from desertion, is ground for divorce. In addition to the physical absence which also characterizes desertion, the plaintiff must prove that the other spouse has been absent from home for some time and that there is reason to believe that he is dead or at least no reason to believe that he is alive. Some states require that the plaintiff prove that reasonable efforts have been made to locate the missing spouse, such as contacting relatives, advertising, and so forth. The statute

usually specifies how long a period of absence is required before a divorce may be granted for this cause. Such a divorce is
popularly known as an Enoch Arden divorce. If the missing spouse does turn up years later, he cannot claim the right
to resume the marital relation if the other party has gotten a
divorce on the assumption that he was dead despite the fact
that his presence would appear to prove that the assumption was erroneous.

There is another special category of cases in which a
party is entitled to divorce because of the absence of the
spouse despite the fact that the desertion is not voluntary
and even though there is no doubt as to his whereabouts and
the fact that he is alive. In some states, the law provides that
where a spouse is convicted or imprisoned for certain offenses
or for a certain length of time, the other is either entitled to a
divorce or the marriage is automatically terminated. Even if
the convicted spouse should subsequently be pardoned, a
marriage so dissolved would remain dissolved and a marital
status would exist between the parties only if they remarried.

The fact that the parties have been separated for a specified number of years is ground for divorce in some states. This
is one of the rare examples in our law where the realities of
the marriage, not the guilt or innocence of the parties, are the
test for divorce. In some states, however, the divorce can only
be secured if the separation has been the result of a court order decreeing the separation of the parties, a so-called bed
and board divorce or legal separation. In these cases one
party has had to prove the other guilty of something in order
to get the separation decree. Hence, here too the guilt element
is present.

In many states the insanity of one party is ground for
divorce; in New York we have seen that it is a ground for
annulment even though the statute does not insist that the insanity have existed at the time of the marriage—the usual
characteristic of an annulment ground. While there are variations in the requirements from state to state, the statutes nam-

ing insanity as a ground for divorce have a fairly common pattern. They ordinarily require that in order for the sane spouse to secure his freedom, it must be proven that the other spouse has been insane for a specified period of years and that in the opinion of a committee of psychiatrists (at least one of whom must usually be a state appointee) the insanity is incurable. Unless the mental illness of the spouse achieves these proportions, the law usually offers no relief to the other party.

All states offer the wife some help in forcing a reluctant husband to fulfill his obligation to support her and their children. But in many states, a woman who has married a man who refuses to provide for her and their children, if any, is not doomed to chasing him in and out of courtrooms for the rest of their natural lives. If the husband has the means to support his family or if he is physically and mentally capable of earning money and refuses to do so, the wife can in some jurisdictions get a divorce. Some states require that the neglect to provide must have lasted for a specified period, usually a year. A wife is not entitled to a divorce merely because her husband does not earn as much as she might wish; if he is doing his best and if he is allotting a reasonable amount of his income to the support of his family, the fact that the family is forced to live on a low subsistence level does not entitle the wife to terminate the marriage. If, however, the amount which the husband allocates to the support of the family is grossly out of proportion to his income, he may come within the provisions of the statute permitting divorce for failure to provide. If, for example, it were shown that the husband's income was eighty-five dollars a week and he refused to give the wife more than thirty dollars a week, out of which she was expected to feed, clothe, and pay medical bills for herself and three children and pay the rent as well, the token payment made by the husband would probably not be considered adequate fulfillment of his duty to provide.

Where there is a total failure to provide despite ability to do so, a divorce will usually follow. Short of a total failure,

every case will be judged in the light of relevant facts. In the
example just given, for instance, the court would probably refuse to give the wife a divorce if the husband proved that he
had not been dissipating the rest of his earnings but had been
using them to pay off pressing debts or to invest in a farm
or business which he had reason to believe would ultimately
earn more money for the entire family.

In some states, there are a number of grounds for divorce
which are, by strict reasoning, properly annulment grounds
because they relate to a condition which existed at the time
of the marriage, not to conditions which arose afterward. The
recognition of these as grounds for divorce rather than annulment can probably be explained by the fact that the legislatures were seeking to avoid the questions of illegitimacy of
children which frequently arise where marriages are annulled. Fraud or force in inducing the marriage, bigamy,
marriage of close relatives, unchastity before marriage, impotence, and the fact that, unknown to the other spouse, one
spouse was convicted of a felony prior to the marriage, are
all grounds for divorce in some states and for annulment in
others.

There are a number of defenses which a spouse who is
being sued for divorce may offer beside, of course, having the
right to challenge the truth of the accusations made against
him. One of these is known as "connivance." What a defendant does in pleading connivance is to say to the court in effect,
"Yes, I committed this offense of which I am accused. But it
happened because my spouse deliberately induced me to do it
so that he could use it as a ground for bringing a divorce
suit." This is a complete defense in practically all states. In
the case previously discussed where the husband sued his
wife for desertion for leaving his guest-filled house, the court
obviously suspected that he had been deliberately making life
as unbearable as possible for his wife in the hope that she
would leave so he could sue for desertion. In a nineteenth
century case, a court refused to grant a husband a divorce for

his wife's adultery because she proved that he had deliberately left her stranded without money in a strange city. The court felt that under the circumstances, the husband knew and probably hoped that she might be driven to prostitution in order to keep from starvation and would not permit him to benefit from a cruel situation which he himself had created.

Connivance as a legal defense is found most commonly today in situations where husband or wife has hired a detective agency to watch the other in the hope of finding proof of adultery with which a divorce suit may be brought. If the detective tries to hurry up the process of getting evidence by hiring a beautiful blonde to pick up the husband and take him to her apartment, no divorce will be granted even though adultery was committed and can be proved. It is not enough to show that the husband is susceptible; it must be shown that he committed adultery without any help or inducement from his wife. Even if the wife did not specifically authorize the detective to hire a woman to lure her husband, the participation of the wife's agent in arranging the adultery is sufficient to prevent her from using the evidence so gathered against her husband. Some courts have gone so far as to say that if a spouse has once connived at the adultery of the other, the conniver is forever prohibited from suing for divorce for any subsequent act of adultery on the part of his spouse. Such rulings would appear to rest on one, two or all of three possible grounds. It may be intended as an additional punishment of the conniving spouse. It may signify the court's view that once a spouse has in effect condoned a violation of the marriage bed, he has no right to complain if it is again violated without his co-operation. Or perhaps the courts felt that if a spouse had once connived to provoke adultery, he might do it again and the court could never be sure in a subsequent case whether the adultery was spontaneous on the part of the defendant or induced by the plaintiff.

Another defense available in divorce actions is "condonation." This is, in effect, pleading, "Yes, it's true that I committed adultery with X. But my wife found out about it six months ago and I promised her I'd never do it again. She said she'd forgive me and we lived together for two months after that before she left me and started this divorce suit." This, if proven, wipes out the wife's cause of action in most states. In order to give some protection to the forgiving spouse, some states say that two conditions must be met in order for the offense to be completely condoned. First, the offending spouse must not thereafter be guilty of the same offense or any other affording ground for divorce. If he is, the original grievance is revived and the other can use it as the basis for a divorce action. Second, if the forgiven spouse acts so badly after he has been forgiven that doubt is cast on his good faith in asking forgiveness, the court may ignore the condonation. In some states, the defense of condonation has been limited by statute to cases in which the divorce is sought on the grounds of adultery. This is true in Alabama, Arizona, Kentucky, Minnesota, Mississippi, New Jersey, Pennsylvania, Texas, Washington, and Wyoming.

The standards of what constitutes condonation vary somewhat from state to state. In a few, there must be a specific agreement by which one party agrees to forgive and the other promises to reform. In other states, living together after one spouse finds out about the other's dereliction is conclusive proof of condonation even if the parties never put it into words. In some states, a single act of intercourse is sufficient to wipe out previously existing grounds for divorce.

The doctrine of condonation appears sound enough in theory. It seems reasonable that if one party, with full knowledge of the fact that he has grounds for divorce, agrees to forgive the other, he should not be permitted to hold the threat of divorce over the other's head for the rest of their natural lives. In practice, however, the doctrine works out so badly that students of our divorce laws are practically unanimous in their condemnation of it.

For example, a husband comes to his lawyer, much disturbed, and tells the lawyer he has discovered that while he was overseas in the army, his wife had an affair with another man. The husband, hurt and angry at his discovery, asks the lawyer to sue for divorce. The lawyer may, if he knows the couple, feel in his heart that the wife's infidelity need not necessarily break up the marriage and that, given time, the couple might work things out and save themselves and their children the anguish of a divorce. But, whatever his feelings, he is duty bound to tell his client what his legal rights are. He must, therefore, in all conscience, advise the husband to move out of the house immediately and not to have anything to do with his wife. Otherwise, a court might find that he had condoned the adultery and he would lose his chance to get a divorce if it turns out that the marriage is in fact untenable. Thus, condonation acts as a deterrent to possible reconciliation by making people concentrate on protecting their legal rights instead of encouraging them to wait and see whether the offense complained of actually will have any lasting deleterious effect on their relationship.

The same theory that underlies the defense of condonation works out somewhat better in statutes which provide that a divorce action can be brought on the basis of a given state of facts only if the action is started within a named period after the facts occur. If the action is not started within the specified number of years, it cannot be brought thereafter. These laws wipe out old grounds; they do not prevent bringing a divorce suit on new grounds. California, Idaho, Indiana, Kentucky, Minnesota, New York, Oregon, Virginia, West Virginia, and Wyoming are among the states having such statutes of limitations which apply to some grounds for divorce. New Jersey has introduced a slight reverse twist by prohibiting anyone from bringing suit for divorce based on cruelty until six months after the commission of the last act complained of. This does not mean that one must continue living with a cruel spouse indefinitely; a legal separation can be obtained in the meantime. But it is apparently New Jersey's theory that many of the things labeled cruelty might be forgiven or adjusted if the husband and wife had time to think things over.

Nowhere is the enthusiasm of the law in fixing guilt for broken marriages more evident than in the defense of "recrimination." This is the rule that if one party breaks his marriage vows, there should be a divorce but if both are guilty, they must stay married. In some states, in order to plead recrimination, the defendant must show that the plaintiff was guilty of the same offense with which the defendant is charged; that is, only proof of the plaintiff's adultery can vitiate the defendant's adultery. In other states, no divorce will be granted if the defendant can prove that the plaintiff was guilty of any other kind of misconduct which is grounds for divorce in the state. Some courts have taken a middle position and limited the doctrine of recrimination by applying it only where there is a direct relationship between the offenses committed by the two parties. Thus, if the wife asks for a divorce on the ground of cruelty, alleging that on several occasions her husband slapped her, no divorce will be granted if he can prove that on each occasion he was provoked by the wife's throwing things at him. If, however, the retaliation was excessive (for example, if the husband chased the wife down the road firing a shotgun at her) his misconduct would not be deemed to have been provoked by hers even if she had been throwing things at him, and she might well be entitled to a divorce. Some states have adopted a standard of comparative rectitude. This means that where both parties are at fault, the court may grant a divorce to the one who is least blameworthy.

So much for the law-on-the-books: the "grounds" for divorce, the misdeeds of which the plaintiff must prove the defendant to have been "guilty" in order to "punish" him with a divorce. An examination of the facts behind our divorce proceedings reveals that the divorce laws actually have little to do with the whys and the hows of the dissolution of marriage.

CHAPTER 19

Divorce:

THE LAW IN FACT

EACH YEAR in the United States 400,000 divorces and annulments are granted—9,000 people come to Nevada alone every year to get a divorce. There are about 7,000,000 divorced spouses in the United States at any one time. On the basis of the present trends, almost one out of every three marriages entered into in this country during the past ten years will end in divorce. Every year, the divorce of their parents affects the lives of 300,000 children.

If the law-in-fact were the same as the law-on-the-books, the "grounds" set forth in the preceding chapter would represent the reasons behind these hundreds of thousands of dissolved marriages. But, as we shall see and as is well known, the "grounds" ascribed for a divorce are almost never the true basis for it.

A few states provide that divorce may be obtained on the basis of the parties having lived separate and apart for a given period of years. Here the divorce is actually and in terms granted because the parties have resolved by deeds and probably words as well, not to live together any more. For the rest—in the overwhelming majority of cases—the theory is that the divorce action is an adversary proceeding based on the guilt of one spouse. John sues Mary (or vice versa) and proves something against her which she vigorously denies—

adultery, cruelty, desertion or any of the other grounds we have discussed. From the contest between them as to the facts, the court is supposed to ascertain the truth. The assumption is that, subject to the limited exception noted, husbands and wives cannot get a divorce in the United States by simply agreeing that a divorce shall be obtained. Such an agreement is against public policy. Moreover, "rigging" a divorce case is collusion, and in almost all states a divorce will be denied if it can be proven that there has been collusion between the parties.

What the law calls collusion arises in a number of different ways. The parties may agree that the plaintiff will plead a completely false ground for the divorce and the defendant will not attempt to defend himself. The typical hotel room adultery setup is an example of this kind of collusion. The wife knows perfectly well that her husband did not commit adultery with the woman with whom he was found. In fact, she has been informed as to time and place to make sure that her detective or other witnesses are around to get the evidence. Collusion is also present where the wife pleads a completely fictitious case of cruelty and it is understood that as long as she keeps it as innocuous as possible, her husband will admit it by his silence. Another type of collusion is the tacit agreement of the defendant not to put in a perfectly valid defense which is available to him. For example, he might be able to prove condonation. But because both want the divorce, the husband agrees not to mention the fact that his wife really did not discover his adultery last week, but last year and that they lived together for several months thereafter. Or the defendant might himself have a cause of action for divorce, such as crueltry. But, knowing that if he proves it, the court will grant neither spouse a divorce, he refrains from mentioning it.

Notwithstanding the theory underlying our divorce laws, however, the fact is that the overwhelming number of divorces granted by the courts in the United States today are, in fact, the result of nothing more or less than agreement between the husband and wife to get a divorce. Because the divorce laws do not reflect realities or contemporary moral attitudes, few people today take divorce grounds literally or seriously. A man does not lose his place in the community because his wife has divorced him for "extreme cruelty" or "adultery." People understand that these are convenient catchalls which the law insists the parties use if they want to terminate their marriage.

A poll taken a few years ago in New York City was very revealing. Five clerks to official referees were asked what percentage of the divorce cases which they heard they thought were the result of collusion. Four said 75 per cent. One guessed at 60 per cent. An official referee said that he thought fully half of the 6,000 divorces he had granted were collusive. Lawyers who were similarly questioned estimated between 75 per cent and 90 per cent. Judge Paul W. Alexander of the Toledo Family Court, of whom more anon, has estimated that in less than one per cent of all divorce cases is there any quarrel between the parties as to whether or not there should be a divorce. Their contest, if any, has to do with the custody of children, the amount to be paid by the husband for the support of the wife or the like. The defendant puts in a defense either to expedite the case or because the plaintiff wife is asking for more alimony than he wants to give.

We have come to see that the offenses which the law lists as causes for divorce are not the actual causes at all, but merely labels under which the victims of already broken homes obediently group themselves like steamship passengers going through customs. We have seen that when a state adds new grounds for divorce, its courts are not besieged by people seeking divorces who were not entitled to one under the previous laws. All that happens is that the same number of people get divorces but they regroup themselves into the new classifications.

Even where the "grounds" are actually present, they are

rarely the basic cause of the marital difficulty. Lawyers who hear enough clients' stories involving adultery are apt to find, for example, that the adultery, even where it exists without connivance or perjury, is usually a symptom of something else that is wrong about the marriage; the blonde seductress is not the cause of the broken marriage but its outcome. Often she comes into the picture because husband and wife have not been able to have genuinely satisfactory sexual intercourse and the husband needs reassurance as to his own virility. Likewise, the wife who makes her husband's life miserable by constant nagging may be reacting in an oblique way to an unresolved in-law problem. Yet the law looks only to the symptom, not the cause. If due "proof" is made that a ground for divorce exists, and no defense is offered, divorce must automatically follow, even though in point of fact the marriage might be salvageable if any effort were made to salvage it. Moreover, the fact that a husband and wife are unwilling or unable for ethical or financial reasons to go through the routine of proving a ground for divorce does not mean that their marriage is saved. If they can't or won't live together any more, they break up their homes anyway.

In 1947 an insurance company estimated that two million spouses were separated without benefit of divorce. Obviously the fact that these people could not get a divorce did not have the effect which the advocates of tough divorce laws promise, of inducing them to stick to their marriage vows and make the best of it. Instead, they in effect divorced themselves. Such a way out is often sought by members of lower income groups who cannot afford the court costs or attorneys' fees involved in starting a formal suit, proving guilt by two witnesses, etc., etc. The cost to society in terms of illegitimacy, unhappiness and family instability is, of course, enormous.

In 1948 a special Grand Jury was appointed in New York County (i.e., the Borough of Manhattan in the City of New York) to study matrimonial actions. It returned some indictments which resulted in the convictions of a number of professional witnesses and the disbarment of two attorneys. In addition to investigating specific cases, the Grand Jury conducted "further investigation into the broader aspects of the problem . . . with the assistance of the District Attorney." The conclusions they reached "confirmed what had long been suspected" by all students of matrimonial litigation:

> . . . widespread fraud, perjury, collusion and connivance pervade matrimonial actions of every type. In short, the Grand Jury is of the opinion that the present practices exude a stench and perpetuate a scandal involving the courts and the community. . . . The manner in which uncontested matrimonial actions are conducted encourages laxity and the other evils disclosed by this investigation. Cases go through on an assembly line basis, with no consideration of the family problems involved. Much more attention is given to meeting the formal requirements of the law than there is to the social desirability of preserving or of terminating the marriage.

These conclusions apply not only to New York, a "strict" divorce law state, but generally throughout the greater part of the country. As the New York County Grand Jury itself found: "A study of experience of other jurisdictions, with far more liberal divorce laws, indicates there, too, the presence of widespread fraud, perjury and collusion."

The typical procedure is simple. Once the parties have agreed to get a divorce and selected their "grounds," the spouse who they have decided should be the plaintiff (usually the wife) files a complaint containing all the proper allegations. Usually the defendant doesn't put in any answer to the complaint. In an undefended suit, judgment is ordinarily awarded to the plaintiff by default and the divorce is granted.

Many states have tried to circumvent this almost slot machine method of getting a divorce by ruling that no judgment in a divorce case must go by default unless the plaintiff has first proved his case to the court. In practice this has meant that the plaintiff goes through the formality of testifying or having a couple of friends testify that the defendant committed whatever offense is alleged. The plaintiff's lawyer tells him in advance exactly what questions will be asked and all that remains is for the plaintiff, his witnesses, his lawyer and the judge or referee each to read his lines on cue.

In some states, an attempt has been made to stop collusive divorce by appointing a proctor, district attorney or other public official whose duty it is to appear in any undefended divorce suit, to investigate whether there is any evidence of collusion and to put in a defense if the official thinks one exists. This has not worked successfully either. It is pretty difficult for a third party to uncover evidence of collusion or to prove that the defendant has a valid defense if the husband and wife involved do not want to co-operate with him.

The New York County Grand Jury's study indicated that: "the adoption of . . . [such] procedural provisions might help to reduce the evils prevalent under our existing system" but that none the less "the ideal solution is not to be found in converting undefended matrimonial actions into adversary proceedings." The Grand Jury also concluded "that the isolated prosecution of an occasional witness or attorney is not the remedy." Nor in view of the fact that the fraud and perjury exposed in New York is equally characteristic of other jurisdictions with liberal "grounds" for divorce, does the answer seem to lie in more "grounds" for divorce. The focus of debate has in recent years shifted away from all of these.

As the special New York Grand Jury put it: ". . . the fundamental defect in our system is that the present matrimonial statutes are concerned primarily with the rules of terminating, rather than preserving, a marriage. It is the considered opinion of this Jury that the best approach to the problem is one that has as its primary objective the cementing, rather than the disintegration of the family unit." As the prime means of implementing this approach, the Grand Jury recommended "the centralization of all matrimonial litigation and related family problems in one court."

Today, in New York and elsewhere, cases involving the family are scattered among a great many different courts. In New York City, for example, cases of assault and the like between husband and wife go to the Magistrate's Court; criminal charges arising out of failure to support to the Domestic Relations Court; children's offenses to the Children's Court; matters of inheritance to the Surrogate's Court; abortion to General Sessions Court; annulment and divorce to the Supreme Court, and so forth and so on, since these are only a few of the Courts concerned with marriage and family affairs in this one city alone.

If all litigation involving the family as such were put in one court, as has to a considerable extent been done in Judge Alexander's court in Toledo, Ohio, and a few courts elsewhere, a long step forward will have been taken in straightening out the present mess. Such a court, as the New York County Grand Jury pointed out, must "be equipped with probation officers, psychiatrists, and case workers. It should be prepared to render assistance to persons not financially able to retain private counsel. . . . Such a court, with power to investigate matrimonial matters, could make a complete study of each case with the primary objective of preserving the family unit. It would seek not merely to ascertain whether there is sufficient legal evidence to terminate a marriage but to discover and remove the factors which are contributing to its breakdown."

This suggestion that there be developed and specially equipped a unified family court is in essence the proposal put forward also by a Committee of the American Bar Association and the recently formed Interprofessional Commission on Marriage and Divorce Laws.

Some years ago the American Bar Association appointed a distinguished committee under the chairmanship of Judge

Alexander to investigate the divorce picture and to make recommendations for improvements in the law. The committee
in its initial report found the question of what should be the
grounds for divorce relatively unimportant. It directed its
attention to the problem of taking divorce suits out of the
category of adversary litigation and removing from them the
orthodox and meaningless inquiry: is the defendant guilty as
charged? Instead it, like the special New York Grand Jury,
proposed that jurisdiction over divorce cases be put in the
hands of a family court, modeled after some of the better
juvenile courts which now exist. Like them, the family court
would substitute diagnosis and therapy for guilt and punishment. Its criterion would not be "who is guilty of what?" but
"what is best for this particular family?" Either or both
spouses could file an application for help. There would be no
plaintiff and no defendant and no previously cut and dried
proof of adultery or cruelty or any other offense which the
law now holds is *ipso facto* reason for termininating a marriage. The case would not be called John Doe against Mary
Doe, but something like "In the Interest of the John Doe
Family." The court would utilize the services of its professional workers—social and psychiatric case workers, clinical
psychologists, psychiatrists, marriage counselors and such, in
order to try to help the Does to find the real root of their
marital trouble and to correct it, if possible. Only after there
had been a complete investigation and report could either
party file a petition for divorce. It is quite likely that in many
cases no such petition would be filed.

While in many states today the judge or some other official connected with the court is theoretically supposed to attempt to reconcile couples, a program offering genuine help is
a rarity. Where it has been offered, the percentage of reconciliations effected is encouraging indeed. A Los Angeles
court, for example, reported successful reconciliation in over
35 per cent of the cases handled by the court over a four year
period. The first report from Seattle, Washington, where a

new over-all plan for helping the family was just adopted in 1949, indicates 43 per cent of apparent reconciliations.

Even if the services of the family court did not succeed in mending the marriage, the family would still be benefited by the time spent in the preliminary investigation and effort. If a divorce suit were eventually brought, the court would be in a better position, knowing something of the family, to reach intelligent decisions regarding custody, support, and all the other questions which arise when a marriage is formally dissolved.

Judge Alexander's Bar Association Committee has branched out and he is now the chairman of an independently constituted Interprofessional Commission on Marriage and Divorce Laws, which is intensively studying the whole phenomenon of divorce in 20th Century United States. The type of family court approach to the problem which Judge Alexander's own court typifies is opposed by some proponents of strict divorce laws. Yet the family court procedure, which always attempts and often succeeds in effecting reconciliation, is far more likely to prevent divorce than divorce laws tough in the sense of the extremely limited grounds for divorce they enumerate.

The pre-hashed ten-minute hearing in an action for a divorce in New York on the ground of adultery is much more likely to end up in a divorce than the filing of a family court petition which opens the whole family situation to expert examination and assistance.

Notwithstanding the urgent and obvious need for a reorganization of our court setup with reference to matrimonial actions, and the support of official and unofficial expert groups for such a reorganization, there is a tough battle ahead. This is in large part due to the opposition of the Catholic Church and the inability of the groups favoring marriage and divorce law to organize themselves effectively. Bills have been introduced into the New York Legislature merely to "liberalize" the "grounds" for divorce in New York. Not only did such bills get nowhere; their sponsors were defeated for re-election. As a matter of fact, every legislative effort even to study the situation has been defeated.

The Grand Jury urged the enactment of a bill by the New York State Legislature "providing for the creation of a state commission to study and analyze the problems relating to marriage, divorce, separation and annulment of marriage." Such a bill, which commits no one to anything, has not only failed of passage; it has never even managed to get out of committee although investigatory commissions are very popular in New York and this subject matter is certainly as important at least to study as any other to which the legislators have directed their attention.

On the same day on which the New York Assembly Ways and Means Committee at the regular 1951 session of the State Legislature killed the proposal, sponsored by Assemblywoman Janet Hill Gordon, for a commission to investigate marriage and divorce laws, the Legislature appropriated $100,000 for a commission to study comic books. The fact that most of the press, the public, the experts in the field, and the clergy, with almost the sole exception of the Catholic Church, were solidly behind the Gordon Bill made no difference at all.

Until the groundswell for reformulating our divorce laws in terms of contemporary realities proves irresistible, those laws will continue to serve not the function of "punishment" which they were designed to serve in an era long past but as a cover-up for an anarchic system of divorce by mutual consent which fools no one, which thrives on collusion, perjury, and fraud, and which adds up to society's making no effort to cure its sick marriages or preserve its own basic unit, the family.

CHAPTER 20

The Effects of Divorce

A VARIETY of very practical problems arise in connection with the dissolution of the marriage. Unless the parties have previously gotten together on a separation agreement, financial arrangements must be made and enforced and provision must be made for the custody of the children of the marriage, if any. This chapter concerns what the courts are likely to do if the parties have failed to agree on these matters. Even if there is a separation agreement, the court, at least theoretically, has the duty to ascertain that its terms are not designed to reduce either the wife or the children to destitution or for that matter to prostitution. If the agreement does not stand up under the court's scrutiny, the situation may be the same as if no agreement had been made. Finally, aside from what the court does specifically in each case, there are general consequences of divorce in terms of ex-husbands' and ex-wives' rights in relation to each other, their ability to enter into a valid second marriage and so forth.

The word "alimony" is apt to evoke an image of an ex-chorus girl blithely collecting $500 a week for the rest of her life from the unfortunate man who had the dubious privilege of being her husband for six months. While such cases do exist, they are few and far between. Actually few people can live in luxury on alimony. The more usual case which confronts lawyers trying to draft separation agreements or judges trying to fix alimony in a divorce case involves people of modest incomes.

A man, his wife and two children may live quite comfortably together on an income of $100 a week. But if there is a divorce and this amount must be divided so as to support two households, one for the wife and the children and the other some kind of bachelor quarters for the husband, obviously the standard of living for all will drop substantially. If the husband marries again and acquires a new family to support, the economic bite is apt to become even worse. The reader has but to take pencil and paper and try to divide his own family income two or three ways in order to get a convincing demonstration that for most people, staying married costs a lot less than being divorced.

By alimony we mean the money awarded by a court for the support of the wife alone or the wife and children. All states have some provision for awarding a wife temporary alimony and a sum sufficient to pay her lawyer while she is bringing suit for divorce. In some states the husband is forced to make these contributions to his wife only if she can prove that she has no funds of her own. In other states the right of the wife to support from her husband is considered so important that the court will order him to continue to support her during the pendency of the suit even if his failure to do so would not actually leave her destitute. In some states the wife can be ordered to pay temporary alimony to the husband if he would otherwise be destitute while the case is pending. Often husband and wife wage a more bitter fight as to the amount of temporary alimony than one would think warranted in view of the fact that it is awarded only for the duration of the trial of the divorce suit, which even in a state with overcrowded court calendars like New York is not apt to take more than six months and will probably take less. The reason why the parties fight so vigorously about temporary alimony is that courts tend to fix permanent alimony at pretty much the same rate as that fixed for temporary support.

In Pennsylvania the courts can and do award temporary alimony while a divorce suit is pending but permanent alimony is only decreed for the support of an insane spouse. The Pennsylvania legislature has taken the position that the duty to support is an incident of marriage and that once the marriage is terminated—regardless of where the "fault" or "guilt" lies—there is no justification for the husband's being saddled with the burden of supporting his ex-wife. The only exception to this rule is, as indicated above, the comparatively rare case where one spouse is insane. This rule does not, of course, relieve either of the divorced spouses from their parental obligations to support the children of the marriage. Whatever the virtues of the Pennsylvania position, there is no doubt but that it represents a minority viewpoint in this country. For the most part the states have not viewed divorce as a complete abrogation of the financial obligation of the husband to the wife.

In terms of the economics of the problem, courts appear to have in mind three objectives in allocating property and fixing alimony: (1) to return to each party, as far as is possible, the property which originally belonged to him and which both have been using or holding during their marriage; (2) to divide between them property which has been accumulated during their marriage by the joint efforts of both; (3) to make certain that the wife and children will not be left destitute on the one hand or an impossible burden imposed on the husband, on the other. Over all, of course, the determining factor is the standard of living of the parties.

Clearly, even if a wife needs, say, fifty dollars a week to maintain herself and two children decently, the court will nonetheless not award her that amount if her husband earns only sixty dollars a week. And whatever may be the court's private opinion as to whether, when the finances are in this range, the couple can "afford" a divorce, courts in this country do not—and in our opinion should not—assert any right to compel couples to stay together for financial reasons.

They do the best they can in allocating what money is available. Somewhere along the line, however, economic realities have gotten confused with the guilt principles underlying our entire divorce structure and the amount of alimony awarded may be (and in some states, *must* be) influenced by the court's decision as to who is the "guilty" spouse and who the "innocent" one.

It is somewhat astonishing to find these questions of guilt and innocence popping up even in those states that have adopted as their guiding principle in all economic matters relating to the family the concept that property resulting from earnings accumulated during the marriage rightly belongs equally to both spouses. These are the so-called "community property" states. They recognize that while the wife, who takes care of the house and the children, may not be making a direct financial contribution to the family capital, she plays an important part in her husband's being able to earn and save money. Theoretically, when a couple living in such a state are divorced, what they have acquired through the efforts of one or both during their marriage should be divided equally between them. Yet the records are replete with cases where the courts in community property states have given the "innocent" spouse substantially more of the community property than the "guilty" one.

In states which do not have community property, the general rule is that each party is to get back property which he brought to the marriage, if that is possible, as well as property which he personally acquired or accumulated even though it may have been held in both the spouses' names or in the name of the other spouse during the marriage. If, for example, the wife inherited $5,000 which had been held in a joint bank account or invested in securities in the names of both, a court would ordinarily order that property restored to the wife. If the husband had made his wife the nominal owner of his business for some reason, a court, on a showing that the wife was only holding the property for him, would probably order it to be reconveyed to him. In some cases, however—again involving the guilt pinciple—the wife or the husband is occasionally awarded part of the other's separate property.

In Louisiana and Maine, for example, the husband may be given part of the wife's property if the divorce was granted for the wife's fault. In Nebraska, Michigan, and Vermont, the wife's property is subject to division only if she has been found guilty of adultery. In Massachusetts, the court can require part of the wife's property to be turned over to the husband only if she has been found guilty of adultery *and* the custody of the children has been awarded to the husband; this rule would appear to be primarily for the benefit of the children, rather than the husband, though its effect would be to relieve the husband of some of the burden of supporting the children.

In some states the division of the husband's property is likewise conditioned on the court's findings of guilt. In Arkansas, a plaintiff wife to whom a divorce is granted, is entitled to one third of all of the husband's personal property (this would include stocks, bank accounts, cars, jewelry, etc.) and a life interest in one third of his real property.

In other states such as Illinois, Indiana, Massachusetts, Michigan, Rhode Island, and West Virginia, the court can, in some situations, grant the "innocent" party the same rights in the other's real property as he or she would have had if the "guilty" spouse had died. In New Hampshire and South Dakota, property of both husband and wife may be divided regardless of fault.

Aside from the division of property, the court may in about half the states award a lump sum instead of requiring that regular, continuing payments be made for support. In Indiana, the court must award the wife a specific lump sum, but the husband may be permitted to pay it off in installments. In most cases in most states, however, provision for the wife's support is made in terms of regular payments rather than by a lump sum. Many litigants do not have sufficient capital to warrant awarding any lump sum, certainly not one large enough to maintain the wife indefinitely. Moreover, sometimes the court feels that a woman who has not been used to handling money should not in any event be entrusted with a large sum which is supposed to support her for the rest of her life unless she remarries.

The question of how much alimony will be ordered in any given case is difficult to answer. Some states have set maximum limits on the amount which the court can decree. In Minnesota, for example, a wife cannot be awarded more than half of her husband's future earnings. In Louisiana, the wife cannot get more than one third of the husband's income. In most states, however, the amount to be awarded is left entirely to the discretion of the court. Many factors may enter into the court's determination of the proper amount. The husband's income and the wife's, if any, what property each of them owns, their expectations as to inheriting property, the wife's potential earning capacity are all relevant. Whether or not there are children is also material, not only in making provision for the support of the children, but also because if the wife has custody, she may be less able to take a job. In most states, the fact that the wife can or does work does not necessarily relieve the husband of his responsibility to contribute to her support. The court will also consider the wife's background, education, professional training, working experience and future job prospects.

While the husband's obligation to support his wife is not vitiated by the fact that her parents are prosperous enough to support her, the financial status of the wife's parents can be relevant in fixing the amount of alimony. In one such case, the court pointed out that the wife had moved back to her parents' home with the child and that her parents seemed well able to keep their daughter and grandchild with them. This being the case, the court felt justified in awarding somewhat less alimony than would have been indicated if the wife had had to pay rent out of the payments from her husband.

In some states, including California, Illinois, Massachusetts, North Dakota, Ohio, Oklahoma, and Oregon, the court may order the wife to pay alimony to the husband. Actually such an order is rare but not unusual in two types of situations. The first is where the husband is incapacitated and unable to earn his own living and the wife has some means. If, for example, a wife is granted a divorce on the ground that her husband is insane, the court may not let her shift the burden of responsibility for the husband entirely on to the state. The second type of situation in which a husband may be given alimony arises where he has spent time or money on the wife's property or enhanced it with his labor.

Take, for example, the case of Joe, a plumber, who marries Helen, a farmer's daughter. Shortly after their marriage Helen's father dies, leaving her his farm. Joe gives up his plumbing business and devotes himself entirely to farming. Several years later the couple are divorced. At this point Joe is in an economic position more closely resembling that of the wife than the husband in the typical situation. He has given up his own work and has devoted himself to improving his wife's property. Unless the court makes some award to him, he has nothing to show for the years he spent in working the farm instead of advancing himself in his own trade. Nor does such an award involve any injustice to Helen who has had an unpaid worker for her property during all the years of their marriage.

Where the court has granted no alimony at all in the first instance, there is some authority to the effect that none can thereafter be awarded even if the circumstances of the parties have changed substantially. In most cases, however, that part of the divorce decree which relates to alimony does not have the same kind of finality which we usually associate with a judgment. The husband may apply for a decrease in alimony or the wife for an increase if changed circumstances make the original award unsuitable. The business failure of the husband or the remarriage of the wife would be examples of such changed circumstances. In many cases, alimony payments automatically stop when the wife remarries, either because a statute so provides or because the decree has a provision to this effect. In other cases, an application to the court may be necessary in order to relieve the husband of the necessity of making further payments. The remarriage of the husband, however, is not usually considered a change in circumstances warranting the modification of the decree; his obligation to his first wife is considered paramount.

Other circumstances which might warrant modification of alimony would be the fact that the wife had inherited or otherwise acquired substantial property of her own or now had an independent income; a substantial increase or decrease in the husband's income; illness of the wife necessitating a temporary or permanent increase in alimony to cover medical expenses; the temporary or permanent incapacitation of the husband grave enough to prevent his earning a living.

New Hampshire has an interesting rule which prohibits a court from granting to a wife more than three years alimony where there are no children of the marriage. At the end of the three year period, the husband may be ordered to pay for an additional three year period if there is good reason. Similar application may be made at the end of each successive three year period. Unless the wife is physically or mentally incapacitated, however, it is not likely that she will be awarded alimony for longer than the first period which gives her a chance to make whatever adjustments are necessary for her to make before she starts earning her own living.

Support for the children of a marriage is governed by somewhat different standards, except that again the economic level to which the parties are accustomed is the crucial factor. Since both parents are responsible for the support of their children, either or both can usually be required to contribute, regardless of whether custody has been awarded to either of them or to a third party. Provisions made for the support of children are generally unaffected by the remarriage of either parent. Thus, the court would not permit a father to decrease the amount of his contribution to his children's support merely on a showing that the mother had married a wealthy man who was capable of supporting the children of her first marriage. If, however, the second husband wished to adopt his wife's children and their father consented, the duty to support the children could then be shifted from the natural to the adopting parent just as in any adoption proceeding.

Other factors short of adoption could, however, be grounds for modifying the amount of money which the father is obliged to contribute for the child's support: for example, a showing that the child had finished school and was earning a living, diminution of the father's income because of business reverses, illness or the like, the marriage of a daughter to whose support the father was contributing. Conversely, the amount payable to the children might be increased if it were shown that the father's income or property had increased substantially and that the amount which he had been ordered to contribute to the children was now out of proportion to his means. The amount might also be increased to cover unusual medical expenses of the child or to enable him to go to college or technical school.

Frequently, the decree itself specifies at what age the child shall no longer be entitled to support from the father. Otherwise he must continue payment until the child reaches whatever age that particular state specifies as the limit of parents' responsibility in general to support their children.

The courts have reached varying results in deciding which of the divorced parents has the right to the child's earnings. Some have felt that the person having custody should have the primary right. Others have felt that where the father was contributing to the support of a child in his mother's custody, he was entitled to the earnings as a setoff against his duty to support.

Enforcing a decree which provides for periodic payments

presents greater difficulty than collecting a judgment for a specific amount. In the latter case, one single concentrated effort at collection will usually do the trick if there are funds. Where the husband has been ordered to make weekly or monthly payments, the wife may have to go to court several times a year or several times in a period of years if the husband does not pay. In the meantime, since in most cases the payments ordered are not large enough to enable much to be saved from one week to the next, the wife and children may be left entirely without funds. In most states a decree requiring the husband to support his wife and children can be enforced by imprisoning him for contempt of court if he falls behind in his payments. Wives do not ordinarily invoke such drastic measures nor will courts order them if the husband is trying in good faith to meet his obligation but is prevented by illness, unemployment or some other circumstance beyond his control. Aside from the fact that imprisonment for debt is alien to our legal system, it may in this situation be self-defeating. The husband's incarceration may solve the problem of where he gets his meals but it does not feed the wife or children.

If the husband owns property, the problem may be slightly simpler since his property can be attached if he fails to make payments. Many courts will insist on the husband's posting a bond or putting up security to guarantee support payments if he is financially able to do so. A so-called garnishee order against the husband's salary is a possible remedy. Under such an order, a court officer collects directly from the husband's employer and pays over the money so collected to the wife. Such a remedy is, however, not totally effective since it has to be repeated from scratch every time thereafter the husband is in default. In some cases, where the husband is a chronic defaulter, he may, by threat of imprisonment for nonpayment, be induced to consent to having his employer deduct the alimony payments from his wages and send them directly to the wife. In some states the husband is required to pay the indicated amount directly into court and a court officer makes the payments to the wife.

As is true of abandonment and failure to support where undivorced couples are concerned, the husband's leaving the state may enable him to evade his alimony obligations. Here again, if the wife can afford to follow the husband or to employ legal help in his new state, the judgment of the home state will ordinarily be recognized and enforced by the courts of the new state.

Except as stated in court orders or in the separation agreement between the parties relating to division of property, divorce terminates all rights and claims that husband and wife may normally have with reference to each other. It wipes out the right of each to inherit any part of the other's property on death. The parties no longer have any right to be appointed administrator of each other's estate. The wife is no longer entitled to use her husband's credit for any purpose. In some states, the court in granting the divorce will award the right to the marital homestead to one or the other spouse. In other states, the court is without power to act at all in this respect. All of the other rights of husband and wife as described in Chapters 4 and 5 are terminated by divorce.

Divorce cannot, however, terminate the fact that there are children of the marriage who must be cared for. In some cases where the husband does not wish or feels himself unable to care for the children, he makes no claim for their custody. Occasionally, too, one finds a woman, unwilling or incapable of assuming a mother's role, who really does not want the burden of her child or children and who is willing to give her husband full custody.

Often, however, the court is faced with the problem of two parents, both of whom want custody. The problem of deciding custody has sometimes been tied in with the omnipresent guilt element in the divorce. In Georgia, for example, the "innocent" party has the superior right to custody though the court may award custody to the other parent or to a third

party if it sees fit. In Louisiana, the spouse to whom the
divorce is granted is given custody unless there is very strong
reason for awarding custody to the other. In Massachusetts,
the statute provides that the claims of the parents shall be given
equal weight "in the absence of misconduct" but practically
all grounds for divorce recognized by the state involve misconduct. Oregon gives preference to the party "not at fault."
In Alabama, the custody of a child over seven must be
awarded to the husband if the wife has abandoned him.

Other states have provided by statute that the mother
should be given preference. Nevada gives preference to
the mother if the child is young. California also looks to the
mother if the child is young, but prefers the father if the child
is of an age to require preparation and education for "labor
or business." The Utah statute provides that a child under
ten shall be given to the mother unless she is proven unfit.
A child over ten in Utah may choose the parent with whom
he wishes to live, but the court may overrule the child's selec-
tion if it considers that parent unfit.

While other states have not fixed the preferences by
statute, but have merely instructed the courts to act in the
child's best interest, the Utah statute actually reflects the custom in most states. Young children are usually left with their
mother if she wants them unless it can be proved that she
has neglected them or that she is morally or mentally unfit to
rear them.

Where the child is past the infancy stage, courts sometimes feel that the custody of a boy should be awarded to
the father, but this is by no means a general rule. Older
children are often consulted by the court as to their preference, particularly where the court feels that either parent
would be a fit and proper person to raise the child, and the
child's interests would probably be equally well served no
matter who got custody.

The question of what renders a parent "unfit" is difficult
to answer categorically. There are cases where a mother has

been denied custody because of her adultery and others where she has been given custody despite the fact that she was proven guilty of both bigamy and adultery. Often the courts seem influenced by whether or not the unfitness which has been alleged is likely to enter into the child's day-to-day life. There is a practical distinction between a woman who is shown to have committed adultery on a single occasion without the child's being aware of it and a woman who makes a habit of bringing men into her home and having intercourse with them there. A similar distinction can be made in relation to the father's sexual activities if his fitness is in question.

The fact that the mother works outside the home ordinarily does not render her unfit, even if it can be shown that her working is not economically necessary. However, it might if it could be shown that she neglected the child or that she was in the habit of going out evenings and leaving the child alone or that she failed to feed, clothe, and care for the child properly. Obviously any parent who had treated a child cruelly would be found to be unfit; the distinction between "discipline" and cruelty would, of course, be drawn differently by different courts.

In some cases, a parent has been deemed unfit because it was proven that he was a Communist and would be likely to try to influence the child in the direction of communism. In other cases, courts have said they have no power to deny custody because of the political beliefs of the parent.

Like a support order, a court's decree awarding custody is not necessarily the last word on the subject for all time. The decree will stand unless and until the circumstances have changed sufficiently so as to convince the court that the child's current interests are no longer best served by leaving him in the custody of the parent to whom custody was originally awarded. The mere fact that one parent can offer the child more economic advantages than the other is not sufficient to warrant changing the custody of the child or for that matter to determine custody in the first place. If it can be shown, however, that the parent with whom the child has been living has neglected him or is raising him in manifestly unfit conditions, the court has the power to change its previous order and give custody to the other parent or to a grandparent or other relative or, in extreme cases, to have the child placed in a child care institution if there is no parent or close relative whom the court judges fit to have the child. Ordinarily the courts require that the reasons for changing a custody order be substantial ones since they recognize the disadvantages inherent in too often or too lightly changing a child's environment.

It is, happily, becoming rare for a court to divide permanent custody of a child; that is, to require him to make his home part of the time with one parent and part with the other. Courts, however, will usually grant liberal rights of visitation to the parent not having custody, as well as the right to have the child with him during vacation periods, over weekends and the like, so that parent and child will continue to maintain a relationship. The different kinds of visitation arrangements discussed in the chapter on separation agreements are frequently incorporated in divorce decrees by the courts. Sometimes a particularly determined parent manages to evade the court's order giving the other parent the right to see the children by removing them from the state. As in the alimony situation, a parent who can afford to follow the ex-spouse may be able to have the home state's decree enforced in the state where the spouse and offspring have taken up their residence. But the remedy is even less satisfactory here than in the support situation.

For example, Mary moves with her son from Massachusetts to Arizona in order to avoid having Bill, her ex-husband visit the child every Saturday as the Massachusetts court has ordered. If Bill follows her, the Arizona court may consider itself entitled to review the whole custody and visitation question afresh since the child is now considered the responsibility of the state of Arizona. Let us assume, however, that the

Arizona court affirms the judgment of the Massachusetts court and upholds Bill's right to see the child. Bill has a job in Boston and cannot stay in Arizona more than a week or two. Even if he should give up his job and move to Arizona so as to be near the child, he has no guarantee that Mary will not promptly move to California. It is in practical terms impossible for him to see the child as the court said he might unless the child is kept in Massachusetts. In order to avoid this kind of situation, some states (including Massachusetts) prohibit taking a child who is the subject of a custody order out of the state without the permission of the court.

If the parent who has been awarded custody dies, the other parent has a right to custody superior to that of anyone else, including usually even any other relative who was the deceased parent's choice. If the surviving parent is unfit, the child will of course be placed in other hands. Even if he is not unfit, there may be cases where the court will decide that the child's welfare demands leaving him with another person who has been closer to the child than the surviving parent. Generally, however, if the surviving parent has maintained his interest in the child and kept in close contact with him, he will be given custody.

In many states, the court in granting a divorce will, if the wife has so requested, grant her the right to resume her maiden name or the name of a former husband. In a few states, the right of the wife to resume the name she bore prior to the marriage is denied if there are children of the marriage. Even if no such change of name is requested of or granted by the divorce court, the wife can ordinarily take advantage of the common-law right of any person to change his name so long as he is not doing it for fraudulent reasons or to evade creditors. The resumption of the maiden name is, however, at the option of the wife. The husband has no right to demand that she cease using his name unless, of course, she is using it fraudulently, for example, pretending that she is still married to him for purposes of getting credit.

Divorce, in theory, is supposed to terminate a marriage so that both parties are left free to marry again. A number of states, however, have limited the right to remarry. They tend to utilize one of three different kinds of restrictions. Of these, the most common is the statute which prohibits either party from remarrying for a fixed period of time. In the following states neither can remarry for a period of one year after the divorce is granted: Arizona, California, Delaware, Iowa (court may shorten the period if it wishes), Wisconsin, and Wyoming. A waiting period of six months for both parties is required in Colorado, District of Columbia, Kansas, Massachusetts, Minnesota, Nebraska, Oklahoma, Oregon, Rhode Island, Utah and Washington. Alabama requires a waiting period of two months which may be waived by the court, and New Jersey has a mandatory three months wait. Texas prohibits both parties from remarrying for one year if the divorce is granted for cruelty; in other cases the state places no restriction on the right to remarry. Louisiana imposes the waiting period before the divorce; except in cases involving adultery or the conviction of crime, no divorce is granted until one year after a legal separation has been awarded. New York provides for a three month waiting period where the divorce is granted for the absence and presumed death of a spouse.

These waiting periods have been rationalized on two distinct grounds. In the first place, they are supposed to give the husband and wife a last chance for reconciliation before the marriage is completely terminated. Realistically, they are probably quite unsuccessful in achieving any such end. We are coming to realize that if there is to be any hope of reconciliation at all, the effort must be made *early*. Once a divorce suit has been started (and particularly where it has been contested), the parties tend to become embittered against each other by the wrangling over questions of guilt and innocence, property and custody, and the like. The present law so encourages accusations and vilifications in divorce litigation that even if any hope of reconciliation existed before, it would vanish with the institution and development of the divorce action.

The proposal of Judge Alexander's group, it will be remembered, involves concentrating the reconciliation effort in the period *before* either party is permitted to file a petition of divorce. By the time a divorce suit is actually over, in most cases the husband and wife are so furious with each other because of matters which have arisen during the proceedings that they not only tend to lose sight of the good parts of their marriage, but consider their incompatibility greater than they thought it was in the first place. One indignant wife of our acquaintance was probably typical in saying, "I never knew what a *skunk* Harry was until I started to divorce him."

The other ostensible purpose of the waiting period is to protect the parties from rushing headlong into ill-considered second marriages. There are undoubtedly cases where one or both parties do tend to marry on the rebound as a kind of sop to wounded vanity, a way of saying to the world in effect, "See, *someone* wants me." But this is not the pattern in most cases. Unless the divorce was impelled by the fact that one of the spouses wanted to marry someone else, divorcées tend to be cautious about rushing into marriage again. Having just gotten out of an unhappy situation, they are not anxious to plunge into misery again unless they are very sure about their second choice. Often they want a taste of freedom from the responsibility and ties which irked them during marriage. And, as a practical matter, unless there has been a prolonged separation before the divorce, they need to get back into circulation again as eligible, unattached men and women before they have the opportunity to remarry. Moreover, the effectiveness of the waiting period is diminished by the fact that people who wish to remarry immediately usually make it their business to bring the divorce suit in one of the many states which place no restrictions whatever on the right to remarry, or they may simply go to another state to get remarried hoping in this way to avoid the waiting period requirement.

There are cogent arguments against compulsory statutory waiting periods. For one thing, if a state relies on the divorce period for reconciliation, it is less likely to make any effort toward reconciliation at an earlier and possibly more effective time. Furthermore, some authorities feel that the knowledge that there will be a period after the divorce during which they will not be completely free tends to hurry people into the divorce courts so as to start the time running and get rid of the restrictions at the earliest possible time. Thirdly, since people frequently evade or attempt to evade the waiting period by going out of the state to remarry, it is more apt to lead to bigamy and illegitimacy problems and to create general chaos than to accomplish the reunion of a pair of spouses who have already been torn further apart by the abrasive effects of the divorce proceedings.

Whether or not the restriction on remarriage can be avoided by marrying outside the state depends somewhat on the form of the restriction. In some of the states the waiting period is imposed by the court's granting two decrees, an inter-locutory decree and a final one. This means that, having heard the case and decided that the plaintiff was entitled to a divorce, the court grants a first or interlocutory decree to that effect in, say, January. But the parties are not divorced by that decree. They are in effect merely promised that they will be divorced the following June when the final decree is handed down. If either attempts to remarry during the time that elapses between decrees, bigamy is the result, no matter where the remarriage takes place. The spouses are no freer to marry before the divorce is final than they are while the trial of the divorce action is going on. The device of the interlocutory decree is used by such states as California, Colorado, Delaware, Massachusetts, Nebraska, New Jersey, New York, Utah, Vermont, Washington, and Wisconsin.

In other states which have waiting periods, however,

THE EFFECTS OF DIVORCE

the court generally grants only one decree. The divorce is final but prohibits the parties from remarrying for a given period of time. The question of whether these prohibitions can be avoided by going out of the state to marry depends on a number of factors. Some states have taken the position that a person divorced within their borders, whose divorce decree prohibits remarriage, cannot contract a valid marriage by having the ceremony performed elsewhere. Others have taken the contrary position and held that prohibitions of this type are effective to prevent remarriage in the state granting the divorce but have no extraterritorial effect; consequently, if the second marriage was valid in the state in which it took place, it will be recognized by the state which granted the divorce.

In some cases the validity of the second marriage will depend on the particular facts relating to the residence of the parties. Many people try to evade the restrictions against remarriage by simply crossing a state line or two with the vague belief that once they have succeeded in finding a state which will marry them, they are safe. There are undoubtedly hundreds of couples who have done just that and have gotten away with it because no one happened to challenge the validity of the second marriage. The hazards, however, are obvious —a vindictive ex-spouse, the possibility of blackmail, prosecution for bigamy, the chance that the children of the second marriage will be illegitimate, or the risk of a fight on the validity of the second marriage after the death of one spouse in the hope of defeating the right of the second wife or husband or the children of the second marriage to inherit. It is advisable to have legal advice before undertaking a second marriage if there is a restriction on remarriage involved in the divorce decree.

In some states, the restriction against remarriage has a punitive undertone and runs only against the defendant. In Georgia, the court may, in its discretion, prohibit the defendant from remarrying for a certain period. In Massachusetts and Vermont the decree does not become final for six months, but the defendant cannot remarry for an additional period of two years unless the plaintiff dies in the meantime. In Mississippi, the court may prohibit the defendant in an adultery suit from remarrying for an indefinite period, but application for permission to remarry will be entertained after one year from the time of the decree. In New York, a defendant divorced for adultery cannot remarry during the lifetime of the ex-spouse, but the court may waive the restriction after the expiration of three years from the time of the decree. South Dakota likewise prohibits the remarriage of the defendant in an adultery suit during the lifetime of the ex-spouse. In Virginia, the court may prohibit the defendant from remarrying but an application for permission to remarry may be filed after six months. In West Virginia, the plaintiff cannot remarry for sixty days and the court may prohibit the defendant from remarrying for any time up to one year.

Some states which do not prohibit remarriage generally, do prohibit the defendant in an adultery suit from marrying the person with whom he was accused of having committed adultery. Louisiana, Pennsylvania, New Hampshire, and Tennessee have this type of restriction designed perhaps to punish adulterers and perhaps with the naive belief that people will not commit adultery with each other if by so doing they are foreclosing their chances of marrying in the future.

Statutes impinging on the remarriage of the defendant alone, in general or to his partner in adultery, do not call for interlocutory decrees. The validity of a second marriage outside the state depends, therefore, on the attitude of the states involved (the home state and the state granting the divorce) towards out-of-state marriages. Consultation with a lawyer familiar with the facts of the case and the law of all states involved is advisable before trying to evade a restriction against remarriage. In many cases, permission to remarry within the state may be obtained by application to the court, thus removing altogether the necessity for seeking another place to marry.

One other purely temporary restriction on the right to remarry must be noted. If the losing party files an appeal from the divorce decree, the divorce is not usually considered final until the appeal has been either decided or dismissed by the higher court.

There is on the whole less complaint by litigants, by lawyers, and by other professional workers in the field, and less to complain about, in the practical operation of the laws and decisions governing the period after divorce, than there is about those relating to the grounds and methods of obtaining divorce. Yet it is quite obvious that the kind of family court contemplated by Judge Alexander's group, discussed in the preceding chapter, would be in a far better position to handle questions of support, property, and above all custody than most of our courts are today.

The divorce court in most states is a court of general jurisdiction, which means that it handles divorce cases pretty much on the same basis as any other litigation coming before it. Unlike a family court such as Judge Alexander's or the few others that can be found in all of the United States, the usual divorce court does not have available to it trained social case workers to investigate and report what the family situation is, nor consulting experts like psychiatrists, psychologists, clergymen, and the like to help it decide what should be done. The best it can do, as in the case where Joe sues to get Tom to pay for a dozen barrels of apples which Tom says were rotten, is to try to sort the grains of truth out of the ton of abuse and accusation which the law practically requires husband and wife to hurl at each other. But from the standpoint of the community at large, what happens to Joe's children if he and his wife get divorced, is apt to be a lot more important than whether he gets paid for his apples.

It is unquestionably true that divorce, even where the alternative of a permanently disturbed home is worse, is hard on the children. In any event, some effort should be made to utilize all existing bodies of knowledge to help the parties work out a design for at least reasonably harmonious living short of divorce. If that is not possible, surely a special family court specially equipped and staffed should pass upon such vital questions as with whom the children shall live, how they and their mother should be supported, and the like. Under the present state of the law in most jurisdictions, this can be best done only if the parents succeed in keeping as much of their difficulties as possible *out* of court by means of a separation agreement or other private arrangement (also usually made without benefit of advice by experts). Less attention to the fixing of particular grounds for divorce and more concern with the human beings whose lives are drastically affected by the fact of divorce whatever the grounds, would almost surely lead to the adoption of the family court system.

CHAPTER 21

Migratory Divorce

𝓜 ANY HUSBANDS and wives, faced in their home states with superannuated laws requiring one or the other to be proven "guilty" of an offense which neither wishes to acknowledge (or of which neither may be guilty), seek their divorces instead in the so-called quick divorce states. And the results are a legal Department of Utter Confusion. A staid law journal recently printed an article on the validity of such migratory divorces, entitled "Is you is or is you ain't my ex-baby?" Two different judges in the same state, both with equal authority, decided a few weeks apart that a second wife can challenge the validity of her husband's divorce from his first wife and that she cannot. A baby who is legitimate in one state may become a bastard if wheeled across an invisible state line. A couple may be lawfully married in one state and guilty of adultery every time they copulate in another.

As the chart set forth in the back of the book shows, and as we have pointed out in Chapter 18, the various states have varying grounds for divorce, ranging from incompatibility as one of many grounds to adultery as the sole ground. In addition to grounds, however, it is necessary, in order for a person to get a divorce in a particular state, for him to have been a resident in that state for whatever period of time the statutes of that state specify as a condition precedent to bringing a divorce action.

Although the periods of residence required have always differed in the forty-eight states, a trend became especially clear in the early 1930's. Partly, no doubt, as a result of the depression, several states lowered their divorce residence requirements in order to attract out-of-state money. Many of these already had considerable latitude as far as grounds were concerned. In an apparent bid for the tourist trade in divorce, Nevada and Idaho call for a six weeks residence; Florida and Arkansas ninety days; Utah three months; North Carolina six months. As of the present writing, Wyoming is satisfied with sixty days. Alabama laws seem to waive residence if the Court has "jurisdiction" over both parties at the time the action is commenced. Many dissatisfied spouses from other states have been flying down there and picking up divorce decrees in the course of a long (but not lost) weekend. Recently the highest court of Alabama has cast considerable doubt on the validity of divorces thus obtained.

In some other states with short residence periods, it has become a custom for one spouse to arrive, take and pay for a hotel room for the requisite number of weeks, stay a day or two, return home and then come back when the time is up to claim a divorce decree. It is highly questionable whether these divorces would be recognized anywhere if the true facts came to light.

Most of the states, of course, continue to call for periods of residence ranging between one year and five—the latter being the necessary period in Massachusetts which is clearly not anxious to attract any migratory divorce business. The Virgin Islands, although not a state, is a United States territory, and it has become a mecca for divorce seekers since there, as in Nevada and Idaho, a six weeks' residence is sufficient.

When husband and wife both agree upon and participate in an out-of-state divorce which complies as to grounds and periods of residence with the law of the state selected, a later attack on the validity of the divorce by either of them is not likely, although it sometimes happens. Moreover, children of the dissolved marriage, relatives of one or both of the spouses, subsequent spouses or children, and the home state where the original spouses in fact resided, all may at some future time wish to have the divorce declared invalid. And where either the husband or the wife has obtained the out-of-state divorce without the other's consent, there is a good chance that the nonco-operating spouse will decide to challenge its validity.

When the validity of an out-of-state divorce is called into question, a vast array of conflicting precedents can almost always be marshalled on both sides. This confusion is, to a large extent, the result of the courts' efforts to reconcile the three often irreconcilable principles which are commonly involved in an out-of-state divorce situation: (1) the right of each state to fix the rules governing the marriage and divorce of its own residents; (2) the theory that a person who has gone out of his own state to seek or participate in a divorce proceeding should not thereafter be permitted to change his mind and attack it—the theory of estoppel; and (3) the "full faith and credit" clause of the federal Constitution which demands that each state accord to the acts and proceedings of all the other states the same finality and effect which it accords to its own.

It was clear to the men who drafted the American Constitution that if a true union were to be forged, the states could not be left free to act as independent sovereignties which is how, to a considerable extent, they did act during and after the Revolutionary War. Tariff barriers were set up at state borders. Each state printed its own currency and Connecticut coin was not readily accepted in New Jersey or vice versa. Men felt loyalty primarily not to the nation, but to their native states, and feelings often ran high between the residents of different states. As a result, political weakness and economic ruin threatened the new nation. One of the primary aims of the Constitutional Convention was to foster mutual respect and co-operation between the states. Towards this end, the full faith and credit clause was incorporated in the

Constitution. It meant, for example, that if a Rhode Island court tried and decided a case between X and Y, any other state in which either of the parties lived or had property would respect and enforce the judgment of the Rhode Island court and the case could not be retried in every state. The full faith and credit idea was not particularly revolutionary. Other nations had, prior to this time, extended what is called comity to each other on, however, a strictly voluntary basis, by recognizing the validity of rules made and statutes created under the laws of another nation.

For example, a couple who had been married in France would not, if they traveled to London, find themselves locked in an English jail on a morals charge. If the marriage was legal in France, England would also so regard it even though the couple had not complied with the same requirements which would have been necessary if they had been married in England. While the concept of full faith and credit was not new to the United States, it was something of an extension of the comity practiced by independent nations since it was compulsory and not voluntary in character.

The full faith and credit clause was not intended to overcome the equally fundamental principle that no state could act with reference to a person or a situation unless it had jurisdiction in the premises; that is, unless it had some direct connection with the subject matter or the people involved.

If Joe Jones and Richard Smith, both residents of Illinois, have a disagreement about the quality of a gross of paper boxes sold by Jones to Smith in Illinois, Smith cannot arbitrarily decide to sue Jones in a California court so as to make it tough and expensive for Jones to defend the suit. The California court would not, under Anglo-American doctrine as to the jurisdiction of courts, take cognizance of the case unless there was some factual basis for its doing so—as, for example, if the paper boxes were actually in California or Jones had moved there or had other assets there.

The law of each state governs the circumstances which

under the law of that state will be regarded as sufficient factual basis for that state to assume jurisdiction over a particular divorce action. The simplest case, of course, is where the couple has lived in the state as man and wife and are still there. A court may also have jurisdiction in a divorce suit because the defendant resides in the state and it is the logical place where he may be served, given an opportunity to defend the action and be compelled to live up to the decree rendered. Sometimes the courts of a state will take jurisdiction because the offense for which the divorce is sought was committed in the state. In the typical migratory divorce case, however, the court takes jurisdiction because that particular state is alleged to be the domicile or residence of the plaintiff. Ordinarily a married woman's domicile is presumed to follow that of her husband but today, under the laws of many states, the wife has a right to set up a separate domicile of her own if she so desires.

Legally speaking, domicile is a question both of where one is and where one intends to remain. The relevant Latin expression is *"animus manendi"*—the intention to remain in a place and regard it as one's permanent home. Questions as to domicile often arise in many other legal contexts besides divorce.

Take the case of Milton White, a man of means who owns a house in Connecticut and has an apartment in New York as well. He spends about half his time in each place. When he dies, the inquiry as to where his "domicile" was will determine where his estate should be administered, what state may tax it as a whole, and so forth. Mr. White's actions and statements as to where he considered himself domiciled during his lifetime will be decisive. If it can be shown that he consistently voted in Connecticut, that he did jury duty there, sent his children to school there and was in the habit of filing income tax returns as a Connecticut resident, the authorities of both states will probably agree that that's where he was domiciled.

Applying this kind of test to the alleged domicile in the

typical migratory divorce situation, it would seem at first glance that the plaintiff has no domicile in the state granting the divorce and hence that the courts of that state have no jurisdiction over the marriage. For in the usual migratory divorce case, the plaintiff has in fact gone to another state with the intention of remaining only as long as is necessary to get the divorce.

Thus, Ellen and George live in Portland, Maine, and have lived there for the ten years of their married life. They separate and agree to get a divorce. Since neither has grounds for divorce under Maine law and they don't wish to fake any, they agree that Ellen is to go to Reno and get a divorce there. Ellen packs her bags, leaves her children with her mother in Portland so that they will not miss school, and goes to Reno with her return ticket carefully stashed away in her purse. On arrival she registers at a hotel in Reno, stays there six weeks and at the end of that period applies for and is granted a divorce. George retains a Nevada attorney to appear for him in the divorce action, but he does not go there nor does the attorney contest Ellen's claim. The moment the decree is granted, Ellen repacks her bags, takes the train back to Portland and returns to her apartment with her children.

Obviously by the ordinary tests she had no domicile in Nevada because her actions at every step indicate that she had no intention whatever of making Nevada her home. The facts that she did not give up her apartment in Portland, took no furniture with her, left her children in Portland with her mother, and went back there the moment the divorce decree was granted, all make clear that Maine never ceased, in a realistic, factual sense, to be her domicile. However, this is where the full faith and credit clause comes in. For the question whether she was domiciled in Nevada is so far as the Nevada divorce decree is concerned, a question of Nevada law and under Nevada law, the six weeks' residence there is sufficient to give the Nevada court jurisdiction. Furthermore, the doctrine of estoppel may also come into operation, for even if by all ordinary common-sense standards, Ellen was clearly not domiciled in Nevada, the courts of Maine may well take the position, if she ever so claims, that she will not be heard to challenge the validity of the divorce which she herself obtained. What the decision will be if her divorce is ever called into question will depend on who questions it, for what purpose, in what state, and what the then last word of the United States Supreme Court on the subject is.

In the year 1942, that Court handed down a decision which had far-reaching effects on the whole subject of migratory divorce. The case involved a prosecution for bigamy against a man named O. B. Williams and his wife Lillie Hendrix Williams. Both had been previously married, both went to Nevada and got divorces there. In neither Nevada case did their first spouses appear; they remained in North Carolina and had nothing to do with the proceedings. After they got their divorces in Nevada, Williams and the "former" Mrs. Hendrix were married and returned to North Carolina to live. That state claimed that their marriage was bigamous and commenced a criminal prosecution for bigamy against them. Mr. and Mrs. Williams argued that North Carolina was obliged by the Federal Constitution to give full faith and credit to the decrees of the Nevada court because each of them had resided there for the six weeks required under Nevada law to give them divorces there. They claimed that it was irrelevant that North Carolina, where the parties and their former spouses were actually resident in the factual sense, would not have granted the divorces on the same grounds or under the same conditions. The Supreme Court agreed that the judgment of the Nevada court was entitled to be respected in North Carolina.

This did not, however, end the troubles of the luckless pair. Taking advantage of some rather unclear language in the decision, North Carolina proceeded again to attack the validity of their marriage on the ground that the couple had

not actually been residents of Nevada in the sense that
neither had any intention of staying there indefinitely. The case
again came to the Supreme Court and this time the Court
ruled in favor of North Carolina. The result of this decision
seemed to be that an out-of-state divorce decree was entitled
to full faith and credit unless the basis of the jurisdiction of
the court granting the divorce; that is, the domicile of the
plaintiff, could be shown to have been fictitious. This question
was apparently to be subject to independent examination in
the courts of the states other than the one where the divorce
was handed down, at least in cases where the defendant was
not present and did not participate in the action.

The *Williams* case, which contained strong dissents on
the part of some of the Supreme Court justices, was followed by
many state court decisions and articles in law reviews and
other legal periodicals attempting to see it in proper perspective. Many explanations and interpretations were advanced and
no one could be quite sure what any court would decide in
a case where the facts were not identical with the facts in the
Williams case. And since the chances of identical cases coming
up are never good, that meant that the *Williams* case had
done little to clarify what had been in any event a very
confused situation before they arose.

Some time later another case involving home state recognition of an out-of-state divorce came before the United
States Supreme Court. In this case Mrs. S. went from
Massachusetts to Florida with her children, telling her husband that she was going for a vacation. After she got to
Florida, she informed him that she had no intention of returning and filed suit for divorce against him there. The husband
engaged a Florida attorney and put in an answer to the complaint in which he denied all of the allegations of his wife's
complaint including her claim that she was a *bona fide*
resident of Florida. Mr. S. went to Florida himself.

What happened next has to be recreated from the dry
lines of the reported case. Mr. S. probably took the position

that his wife was welcome to a divorce if she wanted it provided he got the children. The husband and wife finally agreed that the children were to live with Mr. S. during the school year and with Mrs. S. during vacations. In view of the fact that Mrs. S. was apparently anxious to get the divorce so that she might remarry, it can safely be assumed that her consent to this kind of custody arrangement was predicated on her husband's promise that if she agreed he would not attempt to prevent her from getting the divorce. At any rate, whatever we may guess the background to have been, it appears on the record that on the day of the hearing, the wife put in evidence to prove her Florida domicile and the husband, who was actually present in court himself, made no effort to refute her evidence. His only participation in the actual trial was to have his lawyer present to the court the stipulation the parties had made regarding custody.

After the divorce was granted, the wife remarried and remained in Florida with her second husband until some months later when the illness of her father-in-law necessitated her return to Massachusetts with her new husband. Mr. S. promptly brought suit there against the second husband for alienation of his wife's affections and also commenced action against his wife alleging, among other things, that the Florida divorce was invalid. The United States Supreme Court ruled this time that Massachusetts was constitutionally obligated to recognize the Florida court's judgment on the question of the validity of Mrs. S.'s residence. The Court pointed out that Mr. S. had put in an answer denying that his wife was domiciled in Florida and that both he and his lawyer were present at the hearing and had full opportunity to disprove the claims made by Mrs. S. as to her residence. They had chosen not to do so, said the Court, and the decision as to the wife's domicile by the Florida court was entitled to recognition by all other states.

This decision being confined, as are all decisions, to the facts of the particular case decided, has not, unfortunately, had

the result of clarifying the migratory divorce picture sufficiently to predict with any certainty what factual combinations will result in a divorce entitled to full faith and credit
throughout the nation. Some states have taken the position
that the decisive factor in the case of Mr. and Mrs. S. was the
husband's presence in person at the Florida hearing. Others
have maintained that the court meant that any issue which
either was litigated or *could have been* litigated in Florida
could not be reviewed by the courts of another state. Under
this latter theory, the fact that the defendant in the S. case
had been personally served, had entered an appearance by
attorney and had put in an answer denying the plaintiff's
residence would be enough to make the Florida Court's judgment concerning the validity of the plaintiff's residence final
even if there had been no contest on this issue in court.

Additional decisions of the United States Supreme Court
have also given rise to further discussion and uncertainty.
This much seems fairly clear, however, even from the morass
of conflicting opinions as to how far the Supreme Court's
decisions circumscribe the right to challenge a migratory
divorce: If a spouse goes out of his home state to procure
a divorce and returns again immediately thereafter, the divorce is open to challenge by the other spouse unless she has
been personally served with process in the state where the
divorce was obtained or has participated in the divorce action
at least to the extent of hiring a lawyer to enter an appearance for him.

For example: Mr. and Mrs. A. live in New York. Mr. A.,
over his wife's protests or without her knowledge, goes to
Nevada and files suit for a divorce. Mrs. A. is duly given notice that the action is pending. On the advice of her New
York lawyer, however, she does absolutely nothing. She
neither goes to Nevada nor has a Nevada lawyer appear for
her. Mr. A. secures his divorce decree in Nevada by default
and returns to his home state. The validity of the divorce
can be successfully challenged either by Mrs. A. or by any

other person who has a legitimate interest in proving that the divorce was invalid. If such a challenge is made, the home state court may hear evidence pertaining to Mr. A.'s domicile in Nevada. If it finds that he had only a colorable domicile, the home state court can declare, consistently with the United States Supreme Court decisions, that the Nevada court lacked jurisdiction to try the case and that its decision is therefore void. It can do so because Mrs. A. was not served in Nevada, and did not participate in the Nevada suit so that the question of Mr. A.'s domicile was not litigated and could not, in view of the fact that Mrs. A. was no party to the action, have been litigated by the Nevada court.

In the example just given, Mrs. A., if she had so desired, could have fought the divorce suit since in fact she knew about it. On application to the Nevada court she might have secured an order forcing Mr. A. to pay the expenses of her going to Nevada to fight the case. This, however, would have involved her appearing in the Nevada action and had she done so, the chances are that whatever the Nevada court decided as to her husband's domicile would have been the last word on the subject. And Nevada courts are not prone to decide questions of domicile against those who invoke their jurisdiction, especially since their statute is fully complied with by the six weeks residence. She could, of course, also have defended the suit by denying the facts alleged in her husband's complaint as to cruelty or whatever other grounds the divorce was based on; she is not restricted to fighting on the domicile question alone. But to do any of these things she would have had to appear in the Nevada action.

Mrs. A.'s decision as to whether to defend the suit or wait until her husband returns home and then challenge the divorce will depend somewhat on her judgment as to whether or not he *will* return after getting the divorce. If Mr. A. has a business and property in the home state, Mrs. A. would be safe in doing nothing about the Nevada divorce and waiting until he returned home to have it declared invalid. If, on the other hand, Mr. A. has no ties in the home state and is likely to stay on in Nevada after getting the divorce, Mrs. A. may prefer to take part in the Nevada suit. If Mr. A. is apt to move on to a third state, its law would have to be examined to see which way its courts were likely to jump.

Now suppose Mrs. A. does not contest the Nevada suit and in fact on thinking it over decides to let bygones be bygones and accept the fact that Mr. A. no longer loves her and is the proud possessor of a nice red-ribboned Nevada divorce decree. Suppose, further, that on the basis of that decree, she decides to marry Mr. B., an old family friend who has stood by her in all her trouble. At this point, Mr. A. realizes he has made a terrible mistake, decides he wants his wife back and starts an action in the courts of their home state, New York, to have Mrs. A.'s second marriage declared void on the ground that the divorce which he himself got in Nevada is no good. Here, entirely apart from the full faith and credit clause, Mr. A. is stopped dead in his tracks by the doctrine of estoppel.

The doctrine of estoppel, as previously stated, means that one who has participated in an action loses his right to complain of it. Thus, Mr. A. who got the divorce in Nevada has no right to ask the New York court to declare invalid the Reno divorce which he himself obtained even though he is now prepared to admit that he was never really domiciled in Nevada. The law, for obvious reasons, will not let him make the admission. Moreover, if Mrs. A. had actually contested the Nevada suit or even just filed an appearance or an answer, she too would probably be, under the doctrine of estoppel, foreclosed from challenging the validity of the divorce. According to some courts, even if Mrs. A. does not participate in the divorce action, she forfeits her right to question the divorce if on the basis of it she subsequently remarries. In some states, a husband who takes no part in the actual divorce action but urges his wife to get the divorce or provides her with the money necessary to get it, is also estopped from challenging it.

When an out-of-state divorce is obtained pursuant to agreement between husband and wife (as many of them are) there's a good chance that neither of them will want to, or be in a legal position to, challenge it. However, others may be interested in doing so.

Consider the case of Mr. and Mrs. Arthur B. who were actually residents of New Jersey but who co-operated in obtaining a Florida divorce. Shortly thereafter Arthur married Sylvia. This marriage did not fare well either and after two years Sylvia brought suit for an annulment of the marriage on the ground that Arthur was still married to his first wife at the time he purported to marry Sylvia. She claimed that the divorce obtained by Arthur's first wife was invalid because she had never been domiciled in Florida but had in fact retained her residence in New Jersey and had returned there immediately after securing the divorce decree. Arthur had entered an appearance and an answer in the Florida divorce suit. The court denied the annulment, holding that neither the parties to the Florida suit nor anyone else could challenge the Florida judgment because Arthur's entering an appearance and answer in the suit meant that the issue *could* have been litigated in the Florida court. The court went on to point out that if a second wife (or husband) were permitted to challenge the validity of the spouse's prior divorce, many second marriages would, in view of the unsettled state of the law, be marriages "at will" subject to annulment any time the undivorced spouse (or both) tired of the union.

Within a few weeks of the decision in the Arthur B. case, another judge of the same court in the same state came to a directly opposite conclusion on a similar set of facts and held that the second wife was not necessarily precluded from challenging the divorce even though her husband too had entered an appearance in the Florida divorce court. The judge who heard Sylvia's case obviously interpreted the United States Supreme Court decisions to mean one thing and the other judge interpreted them quite differently. With such variations within a single state, it is hardly surprising to find that there is no uniformity among the various states as to the circumstances, if any, in which a second spouse can question the validity of an out-of-state divorce.

In addition to past, present, and future spouses, other persons may have an interest which the law will recognize in having an out-of-state (or for that matter a home state) divorce declared invalid. It goes without saying that one who seeks to upset a divorce must be able to show that he personally has a direct interest in having it invalidated. The situation is no different in a divorce action from what it is in any other kind of action: only those who have a direct interest and something concrete to gain will be heard. The state itself, of course, may concern itself with the validity of a divorce or marriage in an adultery or bigamy prosecution (as in the *Williams* case) but this is on the theory that the state as the custodian of general public morality has a direct concern.

Children are not ordinarily permitted to attack divorces obtained by their parents despite the obvious advantages that inure to them from an unbroken home and the company and guidance of both their parents. Perhaps this is in part because even if the divorce were thrown out, there is no way in which a court could or would restore the home in fact as well as law if the parties do not wish it restored. Nor will most courts permit a child to upset his parents' divorce on the ground that insufficient provision has been made for his support. Again, merely voiding the divorce would not necessarily assure that the child would be better provided for. Moreover, the law provides other direct means whereby a parent may be forced to provide properly for his offspring and which do not involve any such complicated questions of law as whether a divorce is valid or not. In any event, the parent must support the child.

A child has, however, in some states been permitted to challenge his parents' divorce where one of them has died without leaving a Will, and the child would, under the state's law governing intestate succession, be entitled to a greater share of his parent's estate if he could prove that his parents' second marriage was void.

For example: John and Mary Jones, parents of Tommy, procure an out-of-state divorce. John then marries Elaine and they have four children. John dies, leaving no Will. Under the laws of the state, Elaine, John's wife, is entitled to one third of John's estate and the rest must be divided among all his five children. If, however, Tommy can prove that his parents' divorce was invalid, John's second marriage is void and neither Elaine nor her four children are entitled to share in John's estate at all. It would, instead, be divided between Tommy, John's only legitimate child, and Mary, who would still be considered his wife. Whether or not Tommy will be permitted to challenge the validity of the divorce will depend on the usual variety of factors including the circumstances of the divorce (that is, whether the defendant was personally served or participated in it or whether it was completely unilateral) and on how the particular state in which the question is raised regards its obligations to recognize foreign divorces. Of course, had John had a properly drawn Will, the whole problem would not have arisen with reference to the children and Mary could not have challenged the validity of the divorce which she co-operated in obtaining.

We have seen that the law does not generally prohibit a parent from cutting off even a minor child or obligate him to give any set share of his estate to his children. The existence of an unambiguous Will removes from the children of a prior marriage such an opportunity as Tommy had to have his parents' divorce declared invalid.

Even where the courts have held that an out-of-state divorce cannot be challenged if the defendant appeared or participated in it, exception may, however, be made for a child whose legitimacy is at issue. In one such case, a New York couple had obtained a divorce in Arkansas. After the divorce there was a reconciliation and the couple started living together again in their home state without bothering to go through the formality of remarrying. Their child, Peter, was born three years after the divorce. He was permitted to show that the court which granted the divorce lacked jurisdiction in order to prove that his parents were still married at the time of his birth and that he was therefore legitimate. The court which heard the case indicated that the divorce might not have been subject to any challenge at all had not a child's legitimacy been at stake.

In a Pennsylvania case a child was permitted to impugn the divorce which his parents had obtained for the express purpose of depriving him of his rights. This case involved a trust fund set up by Casper. In his Will, he provided that a sum of money was to be held in trust and the income paid to Casper's married daughter, Rose, during her lifetime. At her death, the entire trust fund was to be turned over to her children. If, however, Rose's husband died or she divorced him, the trust fund was to be turned over to her at once. When the contents of her father's Will were made known, Rose was indignant that he had not left her the money outright. She and her husband, Charles, devised a scheme whereby they might get their hands on the entire trust fund at once. They agreed to get a divorce, have the fund turned over to Rose and then remarry. The court permitted the divorce so obtained to be challenged on behalf of the couple's two minor children because its sole purpose was to divest them of their rights.

Occasionally parents of divorcées or other relatives may stand to gain under inheritance laws, poorly drawn Will provisions or otherwise from the invalidity of a divorce. The outcome of cases where they have attempted to get a declaration of invalidity are about as varied and unpredictable as the facts which give rise to the cases. There are a startling number of permutations and combinations possible, each of which is likely to go off on its own peculiar facts. In general, it may be said that it is extremely difficult for anyone to challenge the validity of an out-of-state divorce in which both spouses participated. Conversely, it is in many states relatively simple to have thrown out an out-of-state divorce obtained by one party without the participation or even knowledge of the other. Hence, though the courts of Nevada and other states will grant divorces on the basis solely of the plaintiff's residence for the specified time, plus proof of "grounds," such a divorce will not be recognized in most states of the Union for most purposes. We say "for most purposes" because in the *Williams* and other cases, the United States Supreme Court seems to imply that a divorce may be valid in some contexts by reason of the operation of the full faith and credit clause and invalid in others. Since even the judges themselves are not in agreement as to what recent decisions mean, it is only the very desperate and the very foolhardy who will rely on a divorce granted by a state where only one spouse has actually resided and then only for the required period and the other spouse has not participated in the divorce proceedings.

Seven states have tried to set down definite standards for the recognition of out-of-state divorces which they hope will eventually be adopted by the rest of the states. This Uniform Divorce Recognition Act has been adopted by California, Nebraska, New Hampshire, South Carolina, Rhode Island, Washington, and Wisconsin. The California law, which is typical of the rest, provides that an out-of-state divorce will not be recognized if both spouses were domiciled in California at the time of the divorce. A person is presumed to be domiciled in California if he lived in that state within twelve months prior to the commencement of the suit and resumed residence there within eighteen months after his departure to get a divorce, or if he maintained a place of residence in California during his absence. These facts raise a presumption that the person's residence was in California throughout. The presumption can be refuted by evidence showing that the person had in fact a *bona fide* domicile in the state granting the divorce.

The constitutionality of the Uniform Divorce Recognition Acts has not yet been finally decided. Their sponsors take the position that the Supreme Court decisions only compel one state to recognize another state's judgment as to jurisdiction if the facts are exactly as they were in the case of Mr. and Mrs. S. previously discussed; in other words, where the defendant has merely appeared by attorney or answered the complaint they maintain that the decision of the divorce granting state as to domicile is not final and can be challenged elsewhere. It remains to be seen whether the Supreme Court will accept this limited interpretation of its decision.

Most of the out-of-state divorces which are the subject of judicial controversy in this country are divorces granted by the courts of the various states of the United States or, as in the case of the Virgin Islands, of American territories. Americans occasionally obtain divorces in other countries as well in their effort to escape the indecent exposure and/or the mumbo jumbo which is involved in so many American divorce proceedings. If the validity of a foreign divorce decree is drawn into question in an American court, the full faith and credit clause has, of course, no application; it attaches only to the judgments of courts of sister states. However, the principle of comity from which the full faith and credit clause derives, does come into operation. Where a divorce is procured by an American couple in another country on the basis of full compliance with its requirements as to grounds, residence, etc., the courts of the United States will ordinarily accord it recognition if the laws pursuant to which it was obtained do not offend the public policy of the state called upon to judge its validity. The courts may, of course, be less rigorous in their demands if both spouses involved are at the time of the divorce permanent residents of, or at least physically present in, the foreign jurisdiction than if the usual pattern of out-of-state divorces is followed and one spouse has gone abroad solely for the purpose of getting a divorce.

For some time Mexico has done a land office business in divorces. These range from decrees based on actual presence in Mexico, at least for a short period, of both parties, to mail-order judgments issued despite the fact that neither party ever went to Mexico at all. The mail-order divorces are uniformly held not to be worth the fancy paper on which they are set forth. They can be challenged by any one at any time. Many courts have gone so far as to hold with reference to mail-order divorces that the doctrine of estoppel does not apply at all—that the co-operating spouse and even the person who got the divorce may thereafter attack its validity. Somewhat greater effect has been given to Mexican divorces based on the actual physical presence in Mexico of one or both parties, but the cases in most states are not clear and at best a divorce secured in a foreign country in which neither party actually resides has a constant potential for future trouble.

To a large extent the migratory divorce is the refuge of moderately well-to-do people. In most cases the wife is the one who travels to get the divorce so that the husband need not lose time from his business and also because of the vague tradition of gallantry which permits the lady to do the divorcing. If the wife works, the cost of her taking time off from her job is one of the factors the spouses weigh in computing the expense of the divorce. In any event, the cost of the usual out-of-state divorce is high. Travel is expensive as is living in the most popular divorce centers such as Reno and Miami, although all of these have a wide range of accommodations available to the tourist trade. The Virgin

Islands proudly assert that they offer pleasant living at a relatively low cost; six dollars a day for a room in a guest house, complete with all meals, is typical. Transportation to the Virgin Islands is, however, higher than to many of the quick divorce states within the continental United States.

Legal fees vary greatly from place to place and in each place. In some of the states offering divorce bargains, the competition between lawyers for business is great and the person who waits to find a lawyer until she or he gets there sometimes can shop around and find one who is willing to take the case for rather less than the average fee. This procedure, of course, gives no guarantee as to the competence of the attorney who has to walk a legal tightrope if he hopes to attain for his client a divorce that will stand up elsewhere. In addition to the legal fees payable to the plaintiff's attorney who does the bulk of the "work" (that is, drafting a routine complaint and conducting a more or less perfunctory hearing when there is no contest), the defendant usually has a lawyer who must also be paid. At current prices, the overall minimum cost of a migratory divorce that involves anything but local travel is probably at least $1000.

Because the cost of procuring a divorce in one of the quick divorce states is so high, such a divorce is completely out of the question for the members of lower income groups in other states. Hence, the phenomenon of migratory divorce adds the further evil of special privilege to the perjury, fraud, and collusion which so many home-state divorces entail. There is a widespread feeling that strict divorce laws affect only people who can't afford to pay for the privilege of evading them.

In addition to disrespect for the law, migratory divorce breeds confusion and uncertainty as to marital status, legitimacy of children, and property rights. It has as a matter of fact little to recommend it except that it affords to a limited group of people with money a dignified way out of the impasse created by the divorce laws of their home states. So long as New York, for example, continues to take the position that no amount of drunkenness or cruelty, no degree of marital misery, however great, warrants a divorce in the absence of proof of sexual infidelity, many New Yorkers will prefer Reno for six weeks to the New York alternatives of either conceding or inventing adultery. Either way a crime must be committed if a New Yorker is to obtain a divorce: either adultery (itself a crime) or perjury as to adultery or residence.

The migratory divorce is an additional bit of evidence that a stringent law at odds with the mores of the society it purports to govern will be broken one way or another. As one New York reporter caustically summed up the situation: the rich go to Reno, the middle class arrange for trumped up divorce suits in New York and the poor just desert.

Migratory divorce reflects the failure of the individual states to do an effective job in promoting family welfare. Husbands and wives who find their marriage intolerable will get out of it somehow especially when the state offers them no help in trying to salvage it. It has been suggested that a federal divorce law may be the answer. But such a law would probably give rise to more problems than it would cure. In the first place, it would necessitate an amendment to the United States Constitution since under our federal system marriage and family welfare are the exclusive domain of the individual states. And perhaps for some time to come this is the way it should be. As Justice Oliver Wendell Holmes, Jr., pointed out there is a great advantage inherent in having forty-eight laboratories for social experimentation at least until a pattern emerges which would clearly serve the best interests of our vast and variegated population. Moreover, a law governing marriage and divorce which would have any chance of getting through our already burdened and highly political Congress is apt to be a kind of lowest common denominator law.

It is not without significance that the divorce law which

Congress maintains in effect for the District of Columbia, now under its jurisdiction, does not permit divorce for cruelty, unless there has been a legal separation for two years, or for neglect to provide or incurable insanity. A federal divorce law would almost surely be substantively inadequate, would no doubt give rise to the same type of abuse that characterizes the enforcement of the state divorce laws and would be harder to change. Until the states individually adopt the family court technique, and mold it in terms of their own special needs and problems, our divorce courts will remain rat mazes where divorce is granted to those sufficiently well coached by expensive legal talent in taking the proper turns.

Conclusion

*M*OST PEOPLE want to—and do—get married. The heavy artillery of all our legislation about sex induces to that end. We have seen how the law seems to make marriage a virtual necessity for all people by heavily penalizing almost every form of sexual gratification except intercourse between husband and wife. Even the tax laws conspire to this end by making the impact of the income tax less severe on the married than on the single. And even the laws of nature obligingly impel in the same direction for recent statistics prove that married men at least live longer than their brothers who never take the oath.

Yet, viewed in the light of society's interest in having people marry and stay married, the over-all picture of our laws affecting marriage and the family seems rather haphazard. The statute books and court reports are heavy with laws whose purpose and utility disappeared a hundred years ago. Vast gaps exist in some areas where legislation is badly needed as, for example, in connection with artificial insemination. In some respects, particularly with reference to sexual relationships and their aftermath, the law is so out of key with what the vast majority of people believe and do that most perfectly respectable people are technically sex criminals.

At the same time, the law has made distinct progress in some areas. The laws affecting illegitimate children and adoptions, for example, have shown steady improvement. This is perhaps in large measure due to the fact that social agencies working in these fields have made a concentrated effort to bring the problems here to the attention of the legislatures and the public. There has also been a healthy trend toward preventing hasty marriages, child marriages and unions of people physically or mentally unfit for marriage. In a few large cities the courts can and do offer constructive help to people having matrimonial difficulties. The recommendations of the committee of the American Bar Association and of the Interprofessional Commission on Marriage and Divorce for the formation of Family Courts may eventually lead in the direction of stabilizing marriages by offering help rather than punishment for families in trouble.

On a nonlegal front, there have likewise been encouraging developments. Every year more colleges and universities offer courses designed to educate their students for marriage. An increasing number of excellent books are making people aware of the emotional and psychological factors which make or break a marriage. More and more we are coming to realize that when a marriage is broken the split, like old age, tends to come on slowly and imperceptibly and not dramatically and suddenly at the moment when a husband discovers his wife in bed with another man or vice versa. The "grounds" set forth in a divorce petition thus become only a convenient label which the parties use in order to effect a formal dissolution of their marriage long after it has ceased to be a going concern.

The real problem in stabilizing marriage is to give help to the couple *before* their differences have become unreconcilable. A bad marriage is in many respects like a decaying tooth. If therapy is sought and found when the first danger signs appear, the tooth can often be saved. If dental care is not available at all or is not available until the tooth is throbbing unbearably, the tooth will probably have to be extracted. As we go into the second half of the twentieth century, the state which marshals all its forces in the direction of lifelong monogamy does not, except in rare instances, offer any real help to people having marital difficulties. The same states which fight tooth decay by putting fluorine in drinking water or maintaining public dental-health clinics rarely have anything whatever in the nature of a clinic for the prevention or cure of broken marriages. If their attitude toward marriage carried over to their attitude toward dentistry, they would try to prevent tooth decay by forbidding teeth to decay and making it as difficult as possible for anyone who had the temerity to get a toothache to obtain treatment.

Since the community as such offers scant help to people in marital trouble, they will turn, probably with increasing desperation, to whatever sources they think help may come from. Probably the most futile and at the same time the most likely thing which an unhappy husband or wife can do is to turn to friends or relatives for advice. If the people consulted have a genuine affection for one of the spouses, they are apt to take sides quickly and never see the real problem in perspective at all. Not infrequently, moreover, friends who appear to be solicitous of the couple's welfare are actually enjoying a sense of their own superiority because the troubles are not theirs. Subconsciously they may not really want the troubles confided in them to be resolved. Even if, however, the perfect confidante is available, there is an over-all objection to him as the ultimate source of help. A sick marriage is no more the place for amateur treatment than a sick body. It is easy for an amateur to make a glib diagnosis such as: "The Smiths' marriage is going on the rocks because Susan is such a nag." But it is apt to take an expert to ferret out the reason why Susan feels the need, at one and the same time, to cling to and drive her husband to distraction.

Doctors, lawyers, and ministers who have broad experience in matrimonial difficulties, and who are not personally involved with the couple can often help troubled spouses to understand and do something about their own problems. If the trouble with a particular marriage is deeply rooted in a psychological difficulty, they may recognize the symptoms and refer one or both parties to a psychiatrist or some other psychotherapist. Doctors, particularly, can often be of great help if the couple's real difficulty lies in sexual ignorance. Unfortunately the professional training of doctors, lawyers, and ministers rarely takes into account their future function as marriage counselors.

Law schools give short shrift even to the law of marriage and the family; it is usually an optional course for one semester and in any event does nothing at all to indicate, much less to teach, the many skills—psychological insight, counseling techniques, and so forth—needed by any one who is going to treat sick marriages. Similarly, medical and theological schools tend to confine the preparation of their students for their inevitable role as marriage counselors in terms of their own over-all curricula. Their graduates can be expected to know, respectively, the physiology of marriage and its philosophy, ethics, and metaphysics. By and large, however, the students in one discipline rarely have their attention directed to the need for a fusion of all the disciplines if we are to have a group of trained experts to deal with marital problems and to do something about an ailing marriage before it is too late. Here the counseling techniques of social work, the clinical tests and approach of the psychologist, the sociologists' frame of reference, and the like, are also needed. No one group, standing alone, can do the job.

Gradually, there has been a recognition of the fact that marriage counseling, to be effective, must embrace something of all these skills and disciplines plus something else—experience, and, perhaps most important, a mature and well integrated personality.

Within the past few years, we have seen glimmerings of a new profession—marriage counseling. It is a composite kind of profession which cuts across conventional professional lines and acknowledges a need and place for them all. The idea is for all the experts who come into contact with disturbed marriages to join their resources and experience for the purpose of making a concerted attack on family instability.

Typical of this new trend is, for example, the American Association of Marriage Counselors, Inc., a New York non-profit corporation, whose nation-wide membership includes doctors, lawyers, clergymen, social workers, sociologists, and psychologists. They meet to discuss and pool their experiences in the field of marriage counseling. It is their belief that together they may be able to tackle the growing threat to family life which no one profession alone has been able to handle. They have formulated minimum qualifications for marriage counselors on three levels: professional training, experience, and personality. As of the present writing, they are conducting a survey of existing marriage counseling services in the United States and developing a list of accredited counselors. It is hoped by many that eventually marriage counseling will become a postgraduate special field like, say, psychiatry in medicine, but with this difference, that it will be open to the members not of one profession but to graduates in the various fields enumerated above and perhaps others as well. In the meantime, leaders in each of the fields are seeking to embody in the preparation for that field some training in marriage counseling. Some of them hope that in addition there will eventually be a distinct profession of marriage counseling for which candidates can train directly, their subject matter the portion of each separate field relevant to marriage and family relationships. At least three schools today offer such a program.

What are in effect marriage-counseling clinics exist in connection with some courts in a few large cities. There are a few pilot independent marriage-consultation centers and there are individuals scattered throughout the country whose functioning suggests what can be done. As their services grow and are successfully utilized, public awareness of them will grow, causing a greater demand which will in turn call forth a greater supply. Eventually we may come to view marriage-preservation clinics in much the same manner as we today regard clinics for the preservation of physical

GROUNDS FOR DIVORCE

	ADULTERY	CRUELTY [5]	DESERTION	ALCOHOLISM	NON-SUPPORT	IMPOTENCE	DRUG ADDICTION	CONVICTION OF CRIME OR IMPRISONMENT	INSANITY	SEPARATION	ATTEMPT TO SECURE DIVORCE OUT OF STATE	VENEREAL DISEASE	GROSS NEGLECT OF DUTY	VAGRANCY OF SPOUSE	ABSENCE WITHOUT BEING HEARD FROM	OTHER GROUNDS
ALABAMA	✓	✓	✓	✓	✓	✓	✓	✓	✓	✓						Crime Against Nature ✓
ARIZONA	✓	✓	✓	✓	✓	✓		✓		✓						
ARKANSAS	✓	✓	✓	✓		✓		✓	✓	✓						
CALIFORNIA	✓	✓	✓	✓	✓	✓	✓	✓	✓							
COLORADO	✓	✓	✓	✓	✓			✓	✓							
CONNECTICUT	✓	✓	✓	✓				✓	✓							
DELAWARE	✓	[1]	✓	✓	✓	✓		✓	✓	✓						
DIST. OF COLUMBIA	✓	✓	✓	✓		✓		✓								
FLORIDA	✓	✓	✓	✓		✓		✓	✓	✓	✓					
GEORGIA	✓	✓	✓	✓	✓	✓		✓				✓				
IDAHO	✓	✓	✓	✓				✓	✓	✓						
ILLINOIS	✓	✓	✓	✓	✓	✓		✓								
INDIANA	✓	✓	✓	✓	✓	✓		✓	✓			✓				
IOWA	✓	✓	✓	✓				✓	✓				✓			
KANSAS	✓	✓	✓	✓	✓	✓	✓	✓	✓	✓						
KENTUCKY	✓	✓	✓	✓		✓	✓	✓	✓	✓						Fugitive from Justice ✓
LOUISIANA [2]	✓	✓	✓	✓		✓		✓		✓						
MAINE	✓	✓	✓	✓	✓	✓	✓	✓	✓			✓				
MARYLAND	✓	✓	✓	✓	✓	✓		✓		✓						
MASSACHUSETTS	✓	✓	✓	✓	✓	✓	✓	✓								
MICHIGAN	✓	✓	✓	✓	✓	✓	✓	✓ [3]			✓					
MINNESOTA	✓	✓	✓	✓		✓		✓	✓							
MISSISSIPPI	✓	✓	✓	✓		✓	✓	✓	✓							

STATE															
NEW HAMPSHIRE	✓	✓	✓	✓							✓				✓
NEW JERSEY	✓	✓	✓								✓				
NEW MEXICO	✓	✓	✓	✓				✓			✓				Incompatibility
NEW YORK	✓							✓							
NORTH CAROLINA	✓						✓	✓			✓				
NORTH DAKOTA	✓	✓	✓	✓				✓		✓	✓				
OHIO	✓	✓	✓	✓					✓	✓	✓				
OKLAHOMA	✓	✓	✓	✓						✓	✓				
OREGON	✓	✓	✓	✓				✓		✓	✓				
PENNSYLVANIA	✓	✓	✓	✓							✓				
RHODE ISLAND	✓	✓	✓	✓				✓			✓				Gross Misbehavior
SOUTH CAROLINA	✓	✓	✓												
SOUTH DAKOTA	✓	✓	✓	✓						✓	✓				
TENNESSEE	✓	✓	✓	✓						✓	✓				
TEXAS	✓	✓	✓	✓						✓	✓				
UTAH	✓	✓	✓	✓						✓	✓				
VERMONT	✓	✓	✓	✓				✓		✓	✓				Intolerable Severity
VIRGINIA	✓	✓	✓							✓	✓				
WASHINGTON	✓	✓	✓	✓						✓	✓				
WEST VIRGINIA	✓	✓	✓	✓			✓			✓	✓				
WISCONSIN	✓	✓	✓	✓						✓	✓				
WYOMING	✓	✓	✓	✓						✓	✓	✓			

[1] Cruelty is a ground for separation. A divorce may be obtained two years after the separation.

[2] No divorce will be granted in Louisiana. (except for ...) the grounds for divorce.

[3] A sentence ...

NOTE: This does not purport to be a complete chart of the grounds for divorce. In addition to the foregoing, many states also grant divorce for causes which are, strictly speaking, grounds for annulment such as bigamy, pregnancy at time of marriage, and so forth.

namely as an essential public service. It may well
 such clinics will, like the social-service agencies in
ption field, help to focus attention on the gaps and
nisms characteristic of the laws affecting marriage
 family. They may even constitute the nucleus of a
 group to make those laws consonant with contem-
conditions and mores and to point out how the law
n become a source of sustenance and strength for the
an family.